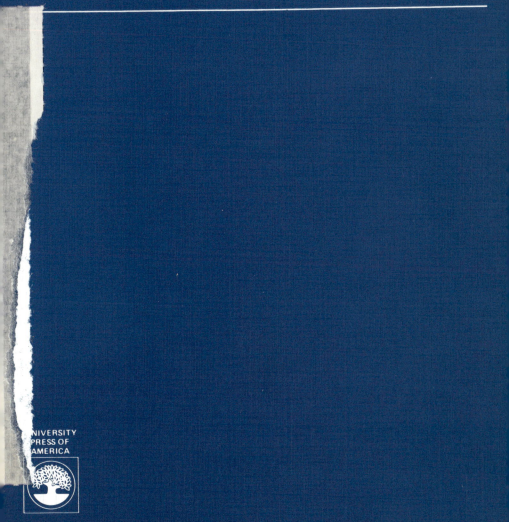

DEEDS
AND RULES
IN CHRISTIAN ETHICS

Paul Ramsey

UNIVERSITY
PRESS OF
AMERICA

Deeds and Rules in Christian Ethics

BOOKS BY PAUL RAMSEY

ETHICS AT THE EDGES OF LIFE: Medical and Legal Intersections
THE ETHICS OF FETAL RESEARCH
THE PATIENT AS PERSON: Explorations in Medical Ethics
FABRICATED MAN: The Ethics of Genetic Control
THE JUST WAR: Force and Political Responsibility
DEEDS AND RULES IN CHRISTIAN ETHICS
WHO SPEAKS FOR THE CHURCH? A Critique of the 1966 Geneva Conference on Church and Society
NINE MODERN MORALISTS
CHRISTIAN ETHICS AND THE SIT-IN
WAR AND THE CHRISTIAN CONSCIENCE: How Shall Modern War be Conducted Justly?
BASIC CHRISTIAN ETHICS

EDITED BY PAUL RAMSEY

ETHICAL WRITINGS (by Jonathan Edwards), forthcoming
DOING EVIL TO ACHIEVE GOOD: Moral Choice in Conflict Situations
  (with Richard A. McCormick, S.J.)
THE STUDY OF RELIGION IN COLLEGES AND UNIVERSITIES
  (with John F. Wilson)
NORM AND CONTEXT IN CHRISTIAN ETHICS
  (with Gene H. Outka)
RELIGION: Humanistic Scholarship in America
FREEDOM OF THE WILL (by Jonathan Edwards)
FAITH AND ETHICS: The Theology of H. Richard Niebuhr

DEEDS
AND RULES
IN CHRISTIAN ETHICS

Paul Ramsey

UNIVERSITY
PRESS OF
AMERICA

LANHAM • NEW YORK • LONDON

Library of Congress Cataloging in Publication Data

Ramsey, Paul.
    Deeds and rules in Christian ethics.

    Reprint. Originally published: New York : Scribner,
[1967]
    Includes bibliographical references and index.
    1. Christian ethics.   I. Title.
[BJ1251.R28   1983]   241   83-10257
ISBN 0-8191-3355-8 (pbk.)

Portions of this book appeared first in the following maga-
zines (some in slightly different form): *Ethics,* Vol. LXVI,
No. 3 (April 1966); *Religion in Life,* Vol. XXXV, No. 2
(Spring 1966); *Christianity and Crisis,* Vol. 23 (January 6,
1964); *Theology Today,* Vol. XXI, No. 4 (January
1965). Copyright © 1966 Paul Ramsey. Copyright ©
1964 Christianity and Crisis, Inc.

The quotations from *Ethics* in *A Christian Context* by
Paul Lehmann (Copyright 1963 by Paul Lehmann) scat-
tered throughout Chapter IV are used by the permission
of Harper & Row, Publishers, Inc.

DEDICATED
TO
MY DAUGHTER MARCIA'S
DAUGHTER
Lauren Elaine Wood
UPON HER SECOND
BIRTHDAY

Contents

viii

Deeds and Rules in Christian Ethics

I

Introduction

It is the fashion today to speak of certain dons or professors as men who "do" philosophy or "do" ethics. This manner of speaking is itself very revealing, since it suggests the separation of a thinker's being from his doing. It suggests the triumph, at the very heart of philosophy in the contemporary period, of technical reason or mental action over a philosopher's concern in his being for being itself and truth itself. Has there not occurred in our time a severe contraction of the range of reason, and a reduction of the life of the mind to the doing of propositional puzzles? To this, the definition of philosophy as the love of wisdom, and as not the doing of anything at all, seems infinitely to be preferred.

Nevertheless, I shall adopt this manner of speaking in this book on the method or methods of Christian ethics, and ask: How are we to *do* Christian ethics?

A leading thinker in the United States who engages in the doing of ethics is Professor William K. Frankena of the University of Michigan. He has modestly challenged Christian theologians to say more clearly what they mean to be doing when they are doing Christian ethics. Since evidently he reads us and has endeavored to come to clarity about the meaning of many of the contemporary treatises in this genre, he deserves an answer. Moreover, the formulation of his question to Christian ethicists

I

may serve to organize or reorganize the questions we think we are asking and answering about the nature of the Christian life. His formulation of the issue may also help to bring to some conclusion, or to an end, some of the confused and fruitless debates that are going on between the "old" and the "new" morality.

As with the question, How should we be *doing* Christian ethics? I shall adopt Frankena's terminology purely as a *heuristic* device in order to discover, if possible, the proper method or methods of Christian ethics. Perhaps there are better terms in which to proceed with this inquiry, or it may be that Frankena's terms should in the end be replaced by a better formulation. But first we ought to see how far they will take us.

Christian ethics proposes that the basic norm and the distinctive character of the Christian life is Christian love (*agapé*). If other ethics rest upon a concept of moral duty (*deontology*) or upon a goal to be achieved (*teleology*), Christian ethics finds its basis in *agapé*. The fundamental question concerning the Christian life is whether from *agapé* there comes any instruction concerning the moral life, or any formative influence productive of a Christian style of life. And the basic question concerning Christian ethics is whether agapism is a third type of normative theory beside the ethics of duty and the ethics of goal-seeking.

The strength of Frankena's book on *Ethics*[1] is that he gets beyond meta-ethics and the analysis of moral language and takes up the question of normative ethics; and it is an additional strength that the author does not promptly reduce Christian ethics either to deontology or to utilitarianism. Instead he seems open to the persuasion that Christian ethics offers a distinct type of normative theory. "It may be," he writes, "that we must regard pure agapism as a third kind of normative theory in addition to deontological and teleological ones." If not, it has already been covered by these types and Christian theologians may as well admit it, even if there may be some religious or emotional values still to be gained from continuing to use religious words for the very same norms which philosophers comprehend in other terms when they do ethics.

Then Professor Frankena points out that if Christian ethics

[1] Englewood Cliffs, N.J., 1963. The following quotations are from pp. 43–44.

is a possible theory of normative ethics it may or will or must take two forms, which he calls *act-agapism* and *rule-agapism*. These are the two possible views of how Christian love best exhibits itself in practice.

Act-agapism, says Frankena, holds that we are never to appeal to rules. Instead, "we are to tell what we should do in a particular situation simply by getting clear about the facts of that situation and then asking what is the loving or the most loving thing to do in it. In other words, we are to apply the law of love directly and separately in each case with which we are confronted."

Rule-agapism, by contrast, seeks "to determine what we ought to do, not by asking which *act* is the most loving, but by determining which *rules of action* are most love embodying."

In proposing that these are the two different forms which Christian ethics may take, Frankena uses terms drawn from the current debates among philosophical ethicists who have long been accustomed to speak of "act-utilitarianism" and "rule-utilitarianism." Theologians these days have a professional allergy against "rules"; and they will object to our using, even provisionally, Frankena's formulation in a discussion of the method or methods and types of Christian ethics. But surely it would be sheer emotionalism to object to the word "rule," simply because it is habitual to philosophers and strange, even offensive, to theologians. It should also be remembered that I am using the word only as a heuristic device to see how far it will take us toward discoveries ahead. If "rule" proves finally unusable for the purposes of Christian ethics, another word will have to be found—perhaps "principle," "middle axiom," "ideal," "directive," "guidance," "orders," "ordinances," the "structures" of *agapé* or of *koinonia* life, the "style" of the Christian life, or the "anatomy" or "pattern" of Christian responsibility.

Another objection will be directed against the coining of such a jargon-word as "agapism"; and, more important, against Frankena's seeming limitation of constructive Christian ethics to the *agapé* school of theologians. Here, however, we ought not to be distracted from the more important point Frankena addresses to Christian ethicists. The same two options remain in

Christian ethics, no matter what term is used to replace *agapé* in indicating the reality upon which the Christian life rests. The Christian life may still take two forms: it may be productive of *acts only* or of *rules also*.

For example, if Christian ethics is *koinonia-* (community-) ethics and if this can be demonstrated to be in any way different from *agapé*-ethics, then some Christian moralists in elaborating the ethics of the Christian community (the ethics of *koinonia*) will affirm that we are to tell what we should do in a particular situation simply by getting clear about the facts of that situation and then asking what is the fellowship-creating or the most fellowship-creating thing to do. Others will affirm that we are to determine what we ought to do by determining which *rules of action* are the most fellowship-creating or most aligned with the *koinonia* God is creating through his work with men. Thus there may be an act-*koinonia* ethics and a rule-*koinonia* ethics. The same decision must be made if any other term is believed to be the illuminating one to use in an analysis of the ethical reality beneath the Christian life.

Now, no philosopher who is an act-utilitarian would think of making his case by simply accusing the rule-utilitarian of having abandoned the principle of utility. He would not charge, at the beginning of the argument and to avoid any contest, that the rule-utilitarian is not applying the test of utility in his ethics, or that utility is any less the sovereign and the sole sovereign over right conduct, or that the lordship of utility has been weakened and divided where there are any utility-embodying rules. Nor would a rule-utilitarian stoop to conquer the act-utilitarian by calling him a "relativist" or a "subjectivist." It remained for theologians to invent these un-logics, in the debate (which as a consequence never ensues) between act-agapism or act-*koinonia* ethics and rule-agapism or rule-*koinonia* ethics.

The real issue is whether there are any *agapé*- or *koinonia*-embodying rules; and, if there are, what these rules may be. Theologians today are simply deceiving themselves and playing tricks with their readers when they pit the freedom and ultimacy of *agapé* (or covenant-obedience, or *koinonia*, or community, or any other primary theological or ethical concept) against rules, without asking whether *agapé* can and may or must work through rules and embody itself in certain principles which are regulative, or the guides of practice.

I seriously suggest that Frankena's analysis fits the issues now very much in debate among theological ethicists; and that to employ his clarifying terminology will remove some of the acrimony from these debates and help us get on with the doing of Christian ethics—or, if you prefer, it may help us better to clarify the church's proclamation in its relation to moral problems. For one thing, a rule-agapist should no longer accuse the act-agapist of being a materialist, a relativist, or subjectivist, or a compromiser, when he is only an act-agapist. And the proponent of Christian situational-ethics should no longer accuse the proponent of rule-agapism of being a legalist lacking in compassion when he only believes that Christian compassion can and may and must embody itself in certain rules of action.

Once this is understood to be the issue at stake, I also contend that it can be shown that a proper understanding of the moral life will be one in which Christians determine what we ought to do in very great measure by determining which rules of action are most love-embodying, but that there are also always situations in which we are to tell what we should do by getting clear about the facts of that situation and then asking what is the loving or the most loving thing to do in it. The latter may even be at work in every case of the creative casuistry of in-principled love going into action. But it will be an instance of thoughtlessness or sentimentality if any Christian in the conduct of his life or any theologian in the doing of Christian ethics seeks to overleap or avoid his responsibility for determining whether there are any love-embodying rules of action, and what these rules may be.

TO THE AMERICAN EDITION

This volume was originally published as an Occasional Paper of the *Scottish Journal of Theology*, No. 11, by Oliver and

Boyd, Edinburgh, 1965. Charles Scribner's Sons, Publishers, have suggested that I write a brief introduction to this American edition.

A few remarks are appropriate in regard to the three chapters that have been added in order to round out my present treatment of the methods of Christian ethics.

The first of these additions is Chapter VI, entitled "Two Concepts of General Rules in Christian Ethics." Originally presented as the 1965 Presidential Address at the annual meeting of the American Theological Society, this chapter repeats some of the themes contained in the Occasional Paper, *Deeds and Rules.* I have not sought to remove the repetition, since this may, indeed, serve the reader well as a summary and restatement of the main components of an admittedly concise analysis.

At the same time, this address takes a significant step in advance over *Deeds and Rules* as originally published. This was wryly referred to on the occasion of its presentation as "Ramsey's final step back from normlessness."[2] This is the reason it is included in the present volume: to amplify my examination of necessary ingredients in the Christian life and in ethical reflection upon this life of ours in all its dimensions of response and responsibility.

The final step is the introduction of a second concept of "general rules": *rules of practices.* This was not without anticipation in the first version of *Deeds and Rules.* In discussing the Quaker Report on sex morality, I remarked, "Taking Christian ethics with utmost seriousness requires that we consider the importance of the *ethos,* the social habits, the customs and laws of any society—whether this be church or civil society. . . . We must ask whether there are any *societal* rules that embody the highest general responsibility and which are the most fellowship-producing rules *for society as a whole,* or whether this is a matter of 'situational' acts only. . . . No social morality ever was founded, or ever will be founded, upon a situational ethics" (pp. 19–20 below). And Bishop Robinson's statement that the more a Christian "loves his neighbor, the more he will be concerned for the whole *ethos* of his society" (p. 27 below) con-

[2] But see p. 122, n. 41 below.

tained in germ the whole idea of societal rules, rules of practices; and it had only to be shown how the justification of such rules differs from the justification of acts. We must ask not only what love requires in relation to this or that person, but also what love requires *as a practice.*

From asking what love requires in relation to this or that person, it was argued in the original book, may come unique acts only, or action in accordance with rules as "guides" only, or action unexceptionally in accord with general rules (provided only that we do not programatically deny that *agapé* or reason or a charitable reason has knowledge into essential humanity and into the good in human relations). This was my first concept of general rules in Christian ethics. I was not wrong in contrasting this with Frankena's concept of "pure rule agapism" which seeks to determine what we ought to do by asking *which rules* of action are most love-embodying, with the stated implication that "we may and sometimes must obey a rule in a particular situation even though the action it calls for is seen not to be what love itself would directly require." I was not mistaken in saying that a Christian does not live in a world *primarily* peopled by rules of action, from among which he chooses. Therefore I sought for a first concept of general rules or general principles of behavior that are founded instead upon an apprehension of the nature of the person, his needs and fulfillment.

Still I was mistaken in supposing that what Frankena understands by a general rule can be no part of Christian ethics nor among the totality of Christian moral concerns. I mistakenly rejected his view (pp. 110–113 below) in the course of establishing that there is sufficient ground for at least some general principles in love for persons as such.

This has to be corrected, or supplemented, by taking up again the question of *rules of practices*; and by asking, as a second approach to general rules, whether there is not also a proper Christian concern for what love requires to be *practiced*, as it were, *as a practice*, or as a *societal* rule. The covenant of marriage may be a general rule that receives its justification from asking *both* questions: What does a caring love for this human being require? *and*, What does love require *as a practice*? One

7

may ask: What ought *I* to do generally? and he may ask: What ought generally to be done in a community? submitting both questions to the test of what most embodies the most love. In any case, these are two different questions, and two different concepts of rules of conduct that may possibly be general in application.

Joseph Fletcher, for example, affirmed in his *Morals and Medicine*[3] a general moral rule governing medical practice where there is respect for "The Patient's Right to Know the Truth" (Chap. 2). If a doctor has proper understanding of and regard for the freedom of the dying person he is attending in death, he will never permit himself to make a situational decision that the truth (the *patient's* truth) should perhaps be withheld from him. There is also in this chapter abundant secondary argument for this rule *as a practice*. (That the patient should not be told the truth if he does not want to hear it would be no exception to this rule.) This, then, is a general rule in both senses: it arises from the fullest sensitivity in loving care for the dying man who is the *subject* of his own dying, and it is the *practice* that would be most love-embodying *as a practice*. This judgment, which the author has not withdrawn and does not now reject, is, of course, quite inconsistent with the *exclusive* act-agapism set forth in his *Situation Ethics*.[4]

Thus the first of the three chapters added here is an integral part of an examination of the role of deeds and rules in the Christian life. In particular, there can be no Christian *social ethics* (but only social pragmatics) unless there are some *rules of practices* required by *agapé*. I therefore regard an inquiry into the *meaning of practices* as of the utmost importance for the whole of Christian ethics. This has to be said while acknowledging that today it may be church society and not the environing, secular society in which these practices may find expression. Still there will be practices if there is any society or any social *ethics*. The reader is therefore invited to attend to the *logic of practices* as a necessary part of serious reflection upon the questions of any sort of normative ethics. He should note that the justification of a prac-

---

[3] Princeton, N.J. 1954.
[4] Philadelphia, Pa., 1966.

tice is not the same as the justification of an action falling under it. Nor does the justification of a practice (if there is any) then permit direct appeals to the ultimate norm[s] to justify exceptional acts.

This brings us to the second and longest chapter added to this edition, Chapter VII. It is necessary to make something of theoretical importance out of *Situation Ethics*, and this I have undertaken to do. I venture to believe, also, that in my mainly methodological examination of "The Case of Joseph Fletcher," I have commented upon every one of "Joseph Fletcher's Cases" that are supposed to show the illuminating power of this novel approach to problems in the Christian moral life. The one kind of case to which I have not given sufficient consideration is the case of "justifiable adultery" to secure release from a Nazi concentration camp, and the practice of abortion to avoid the immediate murder of pregnant women in those camps. Such cases cannot be solved, they cannot even be properly analyzed, if we do not make very clear, in whatever moral verdict we come to, that "the *guilt* may often lie rather with the community than with the individual."[5] There is a distinction to be made between ethical justification and moral excusability; and it also ought not to be forgotten that a chief part of the business of ethics is to lay out the grounds for the criticism and condemnation of systems and institutions. That is surely as important as making individuals culprits, or exculpating them. In any case, the practitioners of Protestant ethics need to overcome their excessive individualism; and we should not pant after individual *excusability* more than did ever any priest in the confessional! This can only lead to the confusion of good reasoning in ethics. To demonstrate this, however, would have required an entire chapter in itself.

The final chapter included in this edition of *Deeds and Rules*, entitled "A Letter to John of Patmos from a Proponent of 'the New Morality,' " is, from the title, obviously relevant to all that has gone before. This chapter does not deny that there is a moment in the Christian life when (or that there is an answer to some of the questions of Christian ethics by which) we are to tell what we should do in some situations by simply get-

[5] Dietrich Bonhoeffer, *Ethics* (New York, 1955), p. 131 (italics added).

ting the facts clear and then asking what is the loving or the most loving thing to do. Still the concentration of every moral consideration into this method and the attempted reduction of the whole of Christian ethics today to act-agapism requires extrinsic explanation. This view is not apt to commend itself in a cool hour to a reasonable consciousness, except under rather strange, if contemporary, circumstances to which that mind has yielded. Chapter VIII is, therefore, an imaginative representation of some of those circumstances and compulsions that have today invaded the mind of the church. Perhaps this chapter also has the virtue of treating the "new morality" with the humor it, as a *theory of ethics,* so richly deserves.

PAUL RAMSEY

Princeton University
Princeton, New Jersey
November 16, 1966

II

On Taking Sexual Responsibility Seriously Enough

The "essay by a group of Friends" entitled *Towards a Quaker View of Sex*[1] reached profoundly into the question whether there are any rules of action embodying Christian responsibility in sexual behavior, or whether there are only acts that embody such responsibility. But then it flinched and drew back from the conclusion to which the argument itself was about to lead—indeed, to which it had led. This document provides, therefore, a significant case study in how we should understand the meaning of *Christian* responsibility, or the *Christian* meaning of responsibility. From an examination of this pamphlet we may learn how to do and how not to do Christian ethics.

When is it right for intercourse to take place? asked the Quakers.

> It should *not* happen until the partners come to know each other so well that the sexual contact becomes a consummation, a deeply meaningful total expression of a friendship in which each has accepted the other's reality and shared the other's interests.[2]

[1] Friends Home Service Committee, Friends House, Euston Road, London, 1963; Friends Book Store, 302 Arch St., Philadelphia, Penn.

[2] p. 45.

If that is when *not,* when *should* it?

In the Friends' answer to this question, *responsibility embodied in the act* reached the border where it had to become *responsibility embodied in a general rule.* Let us shorten these terms, and say that a crucial choice in Christian ethics is between act-responsibility and rule-responsibility. We can also say that the Friends reached the border where *Christian love embodied in an act* had to become *Christian love embodied in a general rule,* or where act-agapism, fully explored, was about to be replaced by rule-agapism:

> Could we say also that at least in spirit each should be committed to the other—should be open to the other in heart and mind? This would mean that each cared deeply about what might happen to the other and would do everything possible to meet the other's needs and lessen any suffering that had to be faced. It would mean a willingness to accept responsibility. . . .
>
> Should not there also be a commitment to a shared view of the nature and purpose of life?[3]

Why not affirm all this, reminiscent as these words are of the marriage vow? Precisely because they are. Precisely because that would be a rule or a pattern embodying responsibility. Therefore, these Friends say:

> At once we are aware that this is to ask for nothing less than the full commitment of marriage, indeed most marriages begin with a much less adequate basis.[4]

Thus the question of the meaning of responsibility in sexual ethics was simply begged in behalf of act-agapism or act-responsibility. Some such words might still be used as a "challenge" to sexual acts within marriage and to sexual acts outside of marriage, but we cannot "legislate" or "draw clear lines between good and evil," not even when an ethics of responsibility was probed to the point, and beyond the point, of drawing them.

Clearly, one cannot explore the meaning of Christian responsibility very profoundly without suddenly finding himself

[3] p. 45.
[4] p. 45.

discussing, in this connection, the moral meaning of *marriage* itself. He will therefore find himself discussing *marital* relations, and not *pre*marital relations. In making a judgment upon all this, a Christian has first to remind himself in no uncertain terms that the Christian view of sex and of marriage never was a theology of the marriage *ceremony*. Ours is not the task of defending bourgeois respectability or legal paper or church ceremonies and registers. None of these things has anything to do with defining a premarital or a conjugal relation. The man and the woman marry each other in fact when their consents are the response to and the responsibility for each other's reality which the Friends describe. Sexual consummation is then the consummation of an existing marriage, whether or not they have ever been—as we err in saying—"married."

This is acknowledged both in the sphere of the state and in the sphere of the church. In most state jurisdictions in the United States, one can get married according to all the regulations of the twenty-odd volumes of the state's marriage law or he can get married without them. This is provided by the last paragraph on the last page of Vol. 20, which usually states: "None of the foregoing is intended to abolish the common law," i.e. the unwritten law that lets people alone to make their marriages simply out of their will to be responsible to and for one another. (The rules of evidence that can later establish that they did this need not be brought into the question.) If it is judged desirable to legislate the omnicompetence of *legal* marriage, it is necessary for the legislature to enact a written law abolishing a "law" that was never written.

And in the sacrament of marriage in the Roman church, the parties are the priests administering the sacrament to one another (if only they are baptized and if their consents are as responsible as their words say). When the Council of Trent wanted to prohibit "clandestine marriages" (which were not "secret" but ordinary Christian sacramental marriages brought into being without a priest), it touched the sacrament co-donated by the two only by requiring a priest as witness. For one hundred and fifty years after Trent "surprise marriages" were valid and not infrequent in France. A man and a woman simply accosted a priest on the street and quickly said in his presence words expressive of their consenting to take one another responsibly. Thereafter, the priest could not deny that a marriage had taken place in his presence.

It is a matter of indifference that the summary words "wife" and "husband" or other words have to be used to prove common law marriage or to perform the sacrament of marriage, rather than the more extended statement of responsibility written by the Friends.

After seeing clearly what makes a marriage and the only morally important distinction between pre- and post-marital intercourse, if then anyone still wants to defend the need of a civil or religious ceremony he will have to do this for practical reasons that are ethically rather insignificant, if indeed they are not entirely non-moral. He will have somehow to link an ethic of responsibility in love with the need for practical, public tests of this. He will have to say with Peter Bertocci—who *connects* but does not *confuse* legal marriage with the moral meaning of the responsible love that makes marriage—

> In marrying they are saying that they wish others, both those who love them and all others on whom their activities impinge, to hold them responsible for a certain level of conduct. . . . The very fact that marriage does involve problems which lovers are not sure they can yet accept means that more is involved and more is to be demanded than the values of sexual love. . . . A love which is too narrow to accept the legal responsibility for the other person, and a love which blinds two persons to the community's need for the *kind of love* which will accept the fullest responsibility for the lives of others, is not all that love can be.[5]

They may, of course, need some such external test simply to know whether what they are talking about as lovers is the question of *pre*marital relations and not actually, in the ethical sense, a question only of their marital relations, or the consummation of their marriage. However important legalities and ceremonies may be, they are only external checks which exhibit to others

[5] "Towards a Christian View of Sex Education," in Simon Doniger, *Sex and Religion Today* (New York, 1953), pp. 178-9.

the fact that the lovers are married, and which may help the lovers themselves to be steadfast in the responsible resolve which alone made them married.

But these Friends drew back when they saw that to ask what they were driven to ask from within the interior of an ethics of responsibility was "to ask nothing less than the full commitment of marriage." They chose act-responsibility when a rule of action embodying responsibility appeared on the horizon and was obviously required by their own analysis.

For the Friends to return to acts only, required a lessening or weakening of their ethics of responsibility. It required less than the fullest response for them to reopen the question of genuinely premarital relations after that question had been closed by the emergence of full commitment to the other person's reality in what amounted to marriage. This is an interesting demonstration of the fact that act-responsibility can be established only by arbitrarily rejecting rule-responsibility once the rule of action embodying responsibility has been seen to flow from within sensitive reflection upon the moral life itself.

So the authors of the Quaker essay draw back from clarity about sexual responsibility. They choose rather a twilight zone where (according to their own description of human experience in this zone) not all is responsibility or full response. "A deliberate intention to avoid responsibility" is, of course, ruled out. (Even that is some sort of rule-morality!) But for irresponsibility to be absent, responsibility need not be present. Only in this twilight does act-responsibility again become possible for Christian conscience. The words now justifying the act are "openness," and a "seed" or "measure" of what was before under consideration.

> Where there is genuine tenderness, an openness to responsibility, and the seed of commitment, God is surely not shut out. Can we not say that God can enter any relationship in which there is a measure of selfless love?[6]

I suppose that no Christian since Augustine has denied that God is there where there is any measure or beauty or order or seed or any being at all!

At another place in the pamphlet, the authors reach down

6 Friends, p. 45.

to something even less a measure or seed of responsibility, and far more wayward, in order to exclude as "unrealistic" a rule of behavior embodying *agapé*-responsibility that was proposed by Sherwin Bailey.[7]

> He [Bailey] holds that to say "I love you" means nothing less than this: "I want you, just as you are, to share the whole of my life, and I ask you to take me, just as I am, to share the whole of your life." He further says that it ought never to be said unless marriage is possible, right, and at the time of speaking intended. That such a statement is unrealistic is at the root of our work.[8]

One would have thought that whether a rule of right conduct is realistic is not the first or the main point to be proven. Even so, what the Quakers refer to in order to refute Bailey is not acts that are governed by a measure or seed of responsibility but instead the conviction, drawn from "the actual experiences of people," that

> love cannot be confined to a pattern. The waywardness of love is part of its nature and this is both its glory and its tragedy. If love did not tend to leap every barrier, if it could be tamed, it would not be the tremendous creative power we know it to be and want it to be.[9]

There are, therefore, two steps by which these Friends withdraw from an analysis of the entire meaning of responsibility. First, they withdraw from full to only a measured responsibility (and this is correlated with flinching from rule-responsibility and an acceptance of act-responsibility in their underlying moral theory). Secondly, they bring into prominence love's asserted tendency to go further down the slope or up into the heights; and they substitute for even a measure or seed of responsibility in action love's own waywardness, its untameability, and the glory and tragedy of wanting to leap every barrier and escape every pattern.

If sincere Christian people, including theological ethicists, can be found simply refusing to take responsibility seriously

---

[7] *Common Sense about Sexual Ethics* (London, 1962), p. 116.
[8] Friends, p. 39.
[9] p. 39.

enough when rules of action, and not acts alone, threaten to emerge from this, is it to be expected that adolescent boys and girls will take any measure of sexual act-responsibility seriously? Was the editorial comment upon this Quaker document by the Jesuit weekly *America* (April 20, 1963) altogether wrong?

> In plain English, they mean that it is right for two kids to commit fornication if they *really* love each other. . . . If the sex act is only an act of love and not, in the intention of God and nature, an act of generation, there is no reason why people should not make it a gesture comparable to a kiss.

I do not mean that the only way to avoid this conclusion is to affirm, with Roman Catholics, that an act of sexual love is always also a *life*-giving act. But if we Protestants take the view that sexual love is primarily an act of unition between the man and the woman, then this viewpoint may still take two forms: sexual communication in the act, or communication within the rule or covenant of marriage.

Nor do I assert that an ethics of act-unition is at once to be accused of being "a purely subjective evaluation of the rightness and wrongness of sexual relationship" (as *America* said of the Quaker statement). Nevertheless, it may be that rules of action are to be found in an ethics of sexual love *qua* unitative; and this ought not *prima facie* to be excluded, as so often happens today among those who pride themselves on knowing all about the sexual revolution and who want to be compassionate or who only contemplate the "situation."

An act-personalism, or an act-responsibilism, or an act-agapism, or act-*koinonia* (community) ethics, or an act-unitive sex ethic is not a subjective vagary. It is simply wrong. Marriage as a rule of action embodying everything that Christian responsibility means in sexual life may be defined as the mutual and exclusive exchange of the right to acts that of themselves tend to establish and to nourish unity of life between the partners. The fact that Christian ethics knows this to be the truth about sexual responsibility ought not to be withheld from young people, no matter how much sexual behavior may be in revolution.

Somewhat contradicting the complete waywardness of human sexual love, the Friends report

> from the intimate experience of several of us, that it is possible to give substance to the traditional code, to live within its requirements, enriched by an experience of love at its most generous and tender, and conscious of our debt. to Christ in showing us what love implies.[10]

If Christ shows us what love implies, and if this comes not only from an experience of love at its most generous and tender, it may be asked, why we are not obliged to affirm that the (so-called) traditional code contains rules of action that simply embody Christian responsibility when the latter is full and strong?

The reason given for *not* affirming this is "the awareness that the traditional code, in itself, does not come from the heart." Yet the experience of living within its requirements did come from the heart, and from these Friends' debt to Christ in showing them what love implies. Actually, underneath their rejection of "the traditional code, in itself," is the human heart in the modern, post-Christian age. Undoubtedly it is the case that "for the great majority of men and women it has no roots in feeling or true conviction" today.

Christian ethics must certainly be able to do more than to take note of this fact, else there is no hope of restoring any sort of Christian *ethos* to the churches in the modern age, let alone the world at large. It can certainly be demonstrated that, historically speaking, the traditional code, in itself, came from the human heart as men were taught by Christ what love implied. The theologian is blinded and in error if he imagines that from Ephesians 5 came only an act-agapism and not the rule-agapism which established in the mind of Christendom its laws of marriage—elevating, for example, Roman contractual marriage into the full measure of the requirements of steadfast covenant. And he is a poor constructive ethicist who, without much argumentation, rules out the possibility that rules of action may still be fashioned by hearts instructed by Christ to know what love itself implies.

That was a profoundly penetrating remark of Professor Tom

[10] p. 41.

F. Driver, who launched the discussion of this Quaker statement among American Protestants,[11] upon the quandary of the ministry in regard to the hearts of modern men:

> . . . When traditional religious authority is not felt by a man to be binding upon his conscience, then it is not possible to preach to him the Law and the Gospel at the same time. Well aware of the disasters created by preaching the Law only, ministers tend to say more about the Gospel. But in the long run this has the effect of undermining the Law itself, at least in so far as the Law must be spelled out as a specific rule of conduct.

Why not, for once, try the preaching of "the Gospel contained in this Law," the law of marriage as a rule embodying Christian responsible action?

The fact that this is not done, and today can scarcely be done, requires explanation. It is due to the erosion of Christian substance from our churches, from the ministry, from theological ethics itself. This, in turn, explains the question-begging prejudice in favor of act-agapism, or act-responsibility ethics; or else the prejudice in favor of a merely situational ethics explains the erosion of Christian ethical substance. Which, it is difficult to tell.

One final and exceedingly important point must be mentioned in this discussion of the Quaker pamphlet as a case study in how to do and how not to do Christian ethics. Taking Christian ethics with utmost seriousness requires that we consider the importance of the *ethos*, the social habits, the customs and laws of any society—whether this be church or civil society. In the foregoing, we have asked whether individual responsibility is embodied in acts only or also in general rules of conduct. Now, we must ask whether there are any *societal* rules that embody the highest general responsibility and which are the most fellowship-producing rules for society as a whole, or whether this is a matter of "situational" acts only.

The Quaker essay notes that

> *there must be a morality of some sort to govern sexual relationships.* An experience so profound in its effect upon

11 "Taking Sex Seriously," *Christianity and Crisis*, October 14, 1963.

people and upon the community cannot be left wholly to private judgment. It will never be right for two people to say to each other "We'll do what we want, and what happens between us is nobody else's business." However private an act it is never without its impact on society, and we must never behave as though society—which includes our other friends—did not exist.[12]

How can Christians nourish the seeds of a wider social responsibility while seeming to praise only acts and never rules that embody personal responsibility between the two parties to sexual relations? Plainly, the waywardness of the human heart works against any *ethos*, customs, or laws that are generally good for all, and not only against "the traditional code." Protestant Christian ethics is often too profoundly personal to be ethically relevant, if in this is included even a minimum of concern for the social habits and customs of a people. Ordinarily, we do not take Christian ethics with enough seriousness to illumine the path men, women, and *society* should follow today. This suggests that only some form of rule-agapism, and not act-agapism, can be consistent with the elaboration of a Christian's social responsibilities. No social morality ever was founded, or ever will be founded, upon a situational ethic.[13]

[12] Friends, p. 40.

[13] When the foregoing was first published in *Christianity and Crisis*, January 6, 1964, the most intelligent letter the Editor received understood my quarrel with the Quakers to be "an example of the permanent quarrel between the legalistic and the compassionate approach to problems of human conduct," though the writer did go on to remark upon "the fruitfulness of this permanent quarrel when both sides are maintained with a good courage" (*C. & C.*, February 17, 1964). What did that writer take *agapé*, or Christian compassion, to mean? In this sentimental age when disciplined reflection seems not to be wanted even in the doing of Christian ethics, it is all but impossible to persuade anyone of this very simple point: supposing the Christian life to be founded on compassion alone, this may still take two forms: it may be productive of acts only, or of rules also. One has to *prove* in Christian ethical theory that we are to tell what we should do in a particular situation simply by getting clear about the facts of that situation and then asking what is the compassionate or the most compassionate thing to do, no less than one has to prove in Christian ethical theory that we are to determine what we ought to do by determining which rules of action are most compassion-embodying. Calling the rule-agapist by the name of "legalist" or the act-agapist by such names as "relativist" or "subjectivist" gets us nowhere, no matter how edifying it feels to fling around the word "compassion."

III

The Honest to God in for Christ's Sake Debate

In Great Britain theological professors and "professors" of the faith seem to take one another seriously; and, moreover, they do theological work on the unusual premise that a theological position may have practical import for the life of the church and of the individual Christian. As a consequence, a spate of articles, pamphlets, and volumes came out in response to Bishop John A. T. Robinson's *Honest to God* and to the essays in *Soundings*, edited by A. R. Vidler.[1] It was to be expected that theological issues should receive first attention, and that only afterward was a rumbling of drums called forth by the smoke signals sent up about "the new morality."

If I may be permitted to intervene in this discussion it would be to say that there needs to be imposed upon it some order and conceptual clarity; and that until this is done, by

[1] J. A. T. Robinson, *Honest to God* (London, 1963); A. R. Vidler, ed., *Soundings* (Cambridge, Eng., 1962) ; A. R. Vidler, ed., *Objections to Christian Belief* (Philadelphia and New York, 1964); Michael Ramsey, *Image Old and New*, (London, 1963); Eric Mascall, *Up and Down in Adria* (London, 1963); Alan Richardson, ed., *Four Anchors from the Stern* (London, 1963). [The last two titles are taken from Acts 27:27–29.] A more conservative response to Bishop Robinson was *For Christ's Sake* by O. Fielding Clarke (2nd ed., New York, 1963) . From the title of this work, and from Robinson's title, I have composed the title of the present chapter. It will require, however, an innately orthodox mind to appreciate the juxtaposition of the two prepositions.

protagonist and antagonist alike, only "dialogue" and word-play, or word-weapons, can result, and never a conclusion from the whole debate or from proponents of either side, who do not seem fully to grasp what is being proposed or opposed. What Bishop Robinson has written on theology, liturgy, and prayer seems to me far more significant and worthy of attention than what he has written on Christian ethics. Perhaps this impression is due to the fact that he knows more about those subjects than I do. In any case, he does not seem yet to have said clearly what he means to say about Christian morality. Without a firmer, analytical grasp on the position he means to expound, Robinson will not be able to be grasped, and rightly grappled with.

On first reading Robinson, one's attention will be drawn to the contentions into which he packs the most intellectual passion, and to passages where he verges on sensational illustrations of Christian freedom. From this one might suppose that Robinson is only an act-agapist (or call it what you will). He is certainly not a subjectivist, or a relativist, or a giver-in to the current moral laxity, or an apostate from the ethical insights once delivered to the saints. Yet he is an ambiguous proponent of act-agapism. He does not always say that the Christian is to tell what he should do simply by getting the facts clear and asking which *actions* best embody love. This is, of course, his central theme; but this is not all he means to say concerning the Christian life.

Robinson's voice is the voice of pure act-agapism, but his hands are the hands of rule-agapism (cf. Genesis 27:22). We shall have to ask what is the relation between his voice and the skins of the kids and the goats upon his hands and upon the smooth of his neck; and where in fact he got those skins and the goodly garments of Rebekah's elder son (cf. Genesis 27:15). We shall have to ask for an account of the rule-agapism which holds pride of second place in his system; and what coherence there is between this and the utterances of a seemingly pure act-agapism. Then and only then will we properly grasp Robinson's writings on Christian morality, and be able to prove their insufficiency, or their incoherence, as a constructive statement of Christian ethics. This will be my second illustration of the illuminating and heuristic power of Frankena's setting of the terms for Christian theories of normative ethics.

The act-agapism is plain to see. According to Robinson, the ultimate norm requires us "to open oneself to another *unconditionally* in love," or to meet "the unconditional in the conditioned in unconditional personal relationship."[2] Jesus' proclamation of the Kingdom of God announced not the Year nor even the Day, but the Moment of the Lord. His parables and teachings were "illustrations of what love may *at any moment* require of anyone."[3] We are to be men for others as Jesus Christ was "the man for others." This means "having no absolutes but his love, being totally uncommitted in every other respect but totally committed in this." It means "accepting as the basis of moral judgments the actual concrete relationship in all its particularity."[4] Love alone is the standard because love has "a built-in moral compass" enabling it to "home" intuitively upon the need of the other (note well!) in the singleness of the moment of encounter with him. This is "an ethic of radical responsiveness";[5] in short, an ethic of pure act-*agapé*. "Love's casuistry" is summed up in Joseph Fletcher's rephrasing of St. Augustine's *dilige et quod vis fac*: "love and *then* what you will, do."[6]

There is nothing wrong with any of these statements except their two silent, unexamined assumptions: (1) that Christian love has in itself no *breadth* to match its personal depth and therefore no rule-implying power, and (2) that love "homes in" only upon *the moment* in the neighbor's reality, for which it cares. This may explain why, when writing in this vein, Robinson finds it impossible to conceive that there may be a *moral bond* between persons (e.g. marriage) and not only an act-response or responsibility renewed every moment. The church's teachings on marriage seem to him either to bespeak the external commands of

[2] *Honest to God*, pp. 99, 105.
[3] p. 114.
[4] pp. 110–11 (italics added).
[5] p. 115.
[6] p. 119. Also, Joseph Fletcher, "The New Look in Christian Ethics," *Harvard Divinity Bulletin*, October 1959, p. 10. In my *Basic Christian Ethics* (New York, 1950), I expressed this as: "Love, and do as you *then* please." However, we shall see that doing everything that love requires, everything without a single exception, may include more than single acts.

a God "up" or "out there"; or to furnish the world with meta-physical or quasi-physical "occult realities."[7] Perhaps the Bishop of Woolwich should learn from St. Augustine what St. Augustine learned from the Platonists, namely, how to *conceive*, how even to *think*, of spiritual substance or a spiritual bond that may be all the more real because it is not a "quasi-physical," or "occult," *thing*.

Pure act-agapism continues to be expressed in Bishop Robinson's recent book, *Christian Morals Today*,[8] where however this is interspersed with much else. In fact, there is so much rule-agapism, or some other source of principles and directives, set forth in this volume that one must demand that the author say where he got these goodly garments and skins in which to clothe personal encounter, or whence he thinks the Christian derives them. Still the asserted momentary *freedom of agape* (which often seems to mean love's *inability* to bind itself in any way other than in acts that are the response of depth to depth) is never withdrawn.

This, of course, cannot be demonstrated by statements which only assert the sole *primacy* of love (which rule-agapism would also affirm). It cannot be demonstrated by Robinson's "treating persons as persons with unconditional seriousness";[9] nor by his statement that "the most searching demands of pure personal relationship" is "the basis of *all* moral judgments"[10] (since moral judgments may include judgments also concerning rules of action and need not concern acts only); nor even by his "persons matter more, imponderably more, than any principles"[11] (since the question at issue is whether there are principles that embody love for persons or only acts of radical responsiveness to them).

Yet, pure act-agapism seems still to be Robinson's point of view. This becomes clear, first, in the description of the "inductive approach" to moral questions: "The ends are not prescribed, the answers are not settled beforehand. But this is only to say that a real *decision* is involved in any responsible moral choice."[12]

---

[7] pp. 107, 108.
[8] (London, and Philadelphia, 1964).
[9] pp. 36–37.
[10] p. 8.
[11] p. 42.
[12] p. 41. I would find proof of pure act-agapism in Robinson's statement,

Pure act-agapism seems evident, secondly, in that rather a-gnostic discussion of "the morality of involvement and discovery . . . searching out a satisfactory moral basis for personal life and for society."[13] Here the premium is placed on a searching that never arrives at any answers, or at only quite provisional ones governing still questing acts of involvement. Here stress is emphatically placed on the seeming hypocrisy of Christians who join humanists, who are deeply impressed by the impenetrable mystery of moral existence, and go on a moral slumming expedition with them but in the belief that Christians know in advance that certain things are always wrong. The Christian should go in search of a presence, not a proposition. "The Christian *goes in* trusting that God is always *in the situation before him* and that if and as he genuinely gives himself in love he will find God— for God is Love; and if he serves people, with no thought for them but as persons, he will discover himself ministering to Christ."[14]

It might be remarked that this is a good deal to know when setting out on pilgrimage; and that (to turn Robinson's argument on himself) the Christian who knows this might as well wait at the end of the road for his humanist brother to arrive there. Still, the theory of Christian normative ethics implied in this is pure act-agapism: the Christian life leads from love to love, and there are only situational acts in between.

Pure act-agapism seems evident, thirdly, from the remarks concerning sexual morality on the next to last page. I am inclined to treat this as something of a lapse after the amount and degree of better moral reasoning this book contains, and which we have yet to consider under the heading of rule-agapism and the questions to be raised about this. Still there it is, pretty clearly expressed. Robinson wants the present generation of youth

---

concerning his own children, that he "would much rather give them the built-in moral values to use the freedom creatively . . ." (p. 44), except for the fact that the expression "moral values" leaves it uncertain whether this means only *instant agapé* with its built-in moral compass zeroing in upon a personal encounter or whether this may mean other values implied in, the fruit of, *agapé*, or values derived from some other source.

[13] p. 39, quoting James Hemming, "Moral Education in Chaos," in *New Society*, September 1963.

[14] pp. 38–39 (italics added).

to be "genuinely free—to decide responsibly for themselves what love at its deepest really requires *of them.*" The author knows full well that a young girl may simply be "the victim of emotional blackmail"—a susceptibility to which, indeed, our contemporary culture imposes on all young people because of its emphasis on romantic love as the sole determiner of meaningful acts. However subtle the dangers of mutual exploitation and the mutual violation of the humanity of the partners, Robinson at this point offers only an internal, attitudinal corrective. He joins with young people in a desire, which he may have first attributed to them, for "a basis for morality that makes sense in terms of personal relationships." "They want *honesty* in sex," he writes, "as in everything else. . . . [Chastity] is honesty in sex; having physical relationships that *truthfully express* the degree of personal commitment that is there underneath."[15]

To which it has to be said, very simply, that if the supreme criterion in Christian sexual morality is honesty and the truthful expression of personal commitment, such an ethic may still take either of two forms: act-honesty and act-truthfulness, or rule-honesty and rule-truthfulness. These are merely shorthand expressions for saying that, on one view, a Christian tells what he should do by asking only which act (or acts) best embodies personal honesty and truthfulness in sexual relations; while, in another view which assigns equal primacy to honesty in love as the sole norm, a Christian tells what he should do by asking whether there are any rules of conduct which best embody love, and if so what these rules may be.

So far the voice of Jacob.

Now let us direct attention to the goodly garments. To do so is to take up again the point at which we had arrived in discussing the Quaker document. It is to ask: What interpretation does Bishop Robinson give of societal rules of behavior, customs, and laws? What, indeed, is his view of the relation between the

[15] p. 45. This is reminiscent of the passage in *Honest to God* (p. 119) which suggests that a man ask himself, *"How much* do you love her?" and then "accept *for himself* the decision that, if he doesn't, or doesn't very deeply, then his action is immoral, or if he does, then he will respect her far too much to use her or take liberties with her." If there is only an inner, attitudinal question and an inner, attitudinal answer, then this *does* suggest that, if he does love and does love very deeply, then no matter what actions follow he does not use her or take liberties with her.

agapé-norm and those habitual excellencies of personal conduct (commonly called *virtues*) which make a man a dependable char· acter in any social group, and without which he is good for nothing in love to God or neighbor?

There was already in the chapter on "the new morality" in *Honest to God* a logical place for societal rules of action, whether these are to be understood to be among the utterances of love itself (rule-agapism), or to have been "stolen from Esau" and quite without uniquely Christian justification. Love's responses, Robinson wrote, "may, and should, be hedged about by the laws and conventions of society, for these are the dykes of love in a wayward and loveless world."[16] A Christian "cannot but rely, in deep humility, upon guiding rules, upon the cumulative experience of one's own and other people's obedience. It is this bank of experience which gives us our working rules of 'right' and 'wrong,' and without them we could not but flounder."[17]

This requirement of a Christian social ethic is even more stressed by Robinson in his more recent *Christian Morals Today.*

> No person, no society, can continue or cohere for any length of time without an accepted ethic, just as ordered life becomes impossible without a recognised legal system or a stable economy. And the Christian least of all can be disinterested in these fields. The more he loves his neighbour, the more he will be concerned that the whole *ethos* of his society—cultural, moral, legal, political and economic —is a good one, preserving personality rather than destroying it.[18]

> A moral net there must be in any society. Christians must be to the fore in every age helping to construct it, criticise it, and keep it in repair.[19]

> The deeper one's concern for persons, the more effectively one wants to see love buttressed by law.[20]

The foregoing quotations use not a few expressions, whether denotative or connotative, for what I call "rules of action." Con-

[16] *Honest to God*, p. 118.
[17] pp. 119–20.
[18] *Christian Morals Today*, p. 12.
[19] p. 18.
[20] p. 26.

cerning "rules of action" the important question is not whether among them there are any that are generally and universally valid. That depressing question, or at least the paramount position assigned it, is more a product of the fear of certitude in a relativistic age than it is of anything else. There are really important questions to be clarified and settled before we modern men could give open-minded consideration to the possibility that there may be general rules of right conduct. It is significant that Rob inson does not flinch as much as does the Quaker document from drawing a generally valid conclusion, and this will be pointed out in the sequel, along with the question how this comports either with his act-agapism or with his insistence upon having only "working" rules when he is discussing rules at all. Still the fundamental question is whence come these rules and the ethical justification of them, whether they be generally or less than generally valid.

Are there rules of behavior that are simply corollaries of the idea of covenant, or of Christian love? Does *agapé* itself require elaboration in terms of those dispositional or character traits cataloged by St. Paul as the works or fruits of the Spirit? Does the love of Christ for his church in-principle itself in terms of a very definite understanding of the conjugal love of man and wife and of the moral bond established by *agapé* between them? That would be rule-agapism.

Do the needed rules of action, the dykes and buttresses of love, simply arise in the mind's eye when Christians gaze steadily at the conditional—the particular situation in all its concreteness—in which they should display unconditional love for persons? Do Christians simply make up the rules out of the lumber of the facts as a carpenter builds a table to serve some human need? Do the experiences they bank contain in themselves no moral meaning except as these are assumed into *agapé* and are shaped by it into patterns of action that vary indefinitely in the course of time and cultural change? That, too, would be a form of rule-agapism.

Do any of the rules of action with which *agapé* directs us to care for persons arise, not from the breadth and immanent wisdom of *agapé* itself, or from the mere facts "edified" so that they serve to buttress love in a loveless and wayward world, but from some other ethical justification than love itself alone supplies? Are the good garments, are the net and the dyke, and the laws of society and its conventions in any measure made of moral material that is not to be reduced to or found implied in Christian love? In addition to the standard that is distinctive and also primary in Christian ethics, are there any principles, or sources of moral wisdom, that while secondary and not distinctive are nevertheless necessary in a complete Christian theory of ethics? That would be agapism *mixed* with some other theory of normative ethics.[21] A *Christian* natural law theory would be an illustration of this possibility in Christian social ethics. But the category of mixed agapism ought not to be restricted to this example. *Any* notion of "the orders" belongs to this classification. Presumably the three median types of Christian social outlook which H. Richard Niebuhr discusses[22]—"Christ above Culture" (the Catholic synthesis), "Christ and Culture in Paradox" (e.g. Lutheranism), and "Christ Transforming Culture" (e.g. St. Augustine, Calvinism, F. D. Maurice)—all find in the culture-pole some inherent, if subordinate, directives beyond the fact that, on these views, the love of Christ demands *that* the Christian assume an indeterminate responsibility for the culture and the social institutions in which men dwell.

I shall now undertake to collect, in some reasonable order, the various suggestions Bishop Robinson has made in answer to the questions that have just been raised. In doing so, I do not mean to imply that the different ways he seems to proceed from the *agapé*-center in Christian ethics to an elaboration of additional directives are incompatible with one another. It seems, however, that these themes in his writings do require a drastic modification of the pure act-agapism to which he continues to give voice; and it *may* be that a choice will also have to be made between some of his different proposals concerning how a Christian proceeds to the business of "edifying" or borrowing rules of action.

21 "Mixed agapism" will be explained more fully in Chapter V.
22 *Christ and Culture* (New York, 1951).

1. *Polarity between rules and acts*

A first possibility is presented by the announced intention of the lectures on the "old" and the "new morality," published in *Christian Morals Today*. These terms refer to "two starting-points," to a "perennial polarity" in Christian ethics. They are "not antithetical but complementary." Between these perennially necessary poles there is a "genuine dialectic," each is a "corrective" of the other; "one cannot be true at the expense of the other."[23] An individual or a whole generation or a culture may start at one end rather than at the other; but both are right and necessary. Each needs the emphasis that the other cherishes. These "complementary rather than contradictory attempts to do justice to the great polarities which lie at the heart of the Christian ethic" ought never to become a "sterile antagonism."[24] There are only "differences of 'way in' to certain abiding realities in Christian ethics which *all* Christians have an equal interest in holding in their proper, creative tension. . . . Neither side wishes to destroy that tension."[25]

Since it is quite clear which "way in," which pole, Bishop Robinson himself espouses, and which he believes to be the right or most illuminating way to do Christian ethics, or at least the right "way in" to be taken in this generation, there may be some slight question about whether these statements are to be taken with utmost seriousness. Is this one of Kierkegaard's pseudonyms speaking?

Still this is the announced perennial method of Christian ethics; and concerning it the following basic questions have to be asked: Whence come the goodly garments of the other pole? Are they taken from Rebekah with no questions asked? Are the accepted moral judgments simply "there," among the social facts like pieces of lumber to be used by Christian love in constructing a proper human dwelling place? That would be rule-agapism of the "social engineering" type. Or is law and a socially accepted ethic the product of a multitude of past acts of obedience among

23 *Christian Morals Today*, p. 10.
24 p. 20.
25 p. 34.

the children of God (rule-agapism), and in this sense to be received from our elder brother into dialogue with contemporary Christian conscience? This would mean that the Christian life in all ages consists of an unceasing dialogue and tension between rule-agapism and act-agapism. Or is a conventionally accepted ethic—the net which love needs—the product of an even older brother, the *jus gentium,* in which are contained principles of perhaps general validity, perhaps less than general validity? That would be a form of mixed agapism in which elements of the other "way in" are obtained from an Esau whose goods and prowess do not themselves belong to or originate with the people of God. Robinson addresses himself to none of these questions, except that we may suppose he would suspect that the last possibility must be based on a belief in "occult" realities.

This is the place to append the fundamental objection to be brought against this author's Christian ethical analysis, and it is an objection that is even more telling against the unexamined assumptions of other Christian situationalists today. These lectures discuss three of the polarities in Christian ethics under the headings, "Fixity and Freedom," "Law and Love," and "Authority and Experience." Bishop Robinson asserts that these are "really . . . the *same* polarity under three *aspects.*"[26] This has to be questioned and rejected at the beginning of any discussion of Christian ethics today. This asserts that "fixity," "law," and "authority" are but aspects of or alternative ways of expressing one "way in"; while "freedom," "love," and "experience" belong together in forming the other pole. Robinson has his conclusion from the start and begs the most essential question when he identifies the antinomy of Law and Gospel (Love) with those other antinomies. This leads him metaphorically to identify Law with "the rocks" and the Gospel (Love) with "the rapids."[27] It is, of course, the method of act-agapism that is enshrined in the view that these chapter titles do but state the same polarity under slightly differing aspects; and we have seen that Bishop Robinson is not consistently concerned with rapidly changing acts of love. I had heard that the Gospel was rather a Rock, and in no case

26 p. 11 (italics added).
27 pp. 18, 20.

should one thoughtlessly presume that Love may not lead to constancy (rule-agapism).[28] It is a common and basic error of Christian situationalism to begin with the premise that *agapé* in its freedom cannot bind itself unreservedly and change not.

2. *Working rules*

Taking Bishop Robinson's "way in" upon moral and social questions, there may be two sorts of rules which are the product of love as it shapes itself for action. These will be discussed in this and the next numbered section. The first is that there are provisional, "working" rules, of less than general validity in which love finds expression, but which love in its sovereign freedom remains ready to change at any moment by adopting another rule, or by making an exception in a particular situation while leaving the rule still standing as ordinarily wise and required by love.

Out there, there is only "a world of relativities" into which a Christian enters with his single absolute (*agapé*). With these relativities he makes contact and in their midst he serves his neighbor "through a casuistry obedient to love."[29] So far, this is act-agapism working over or through the pieces of lumber of which experience consists. So far, love does not itself have the breadth or substance to be productive of rules, habits, styles, "working" or otherwise; nor does love itself seem to be the agent that substantially builds up "the bank of experience" or edifies the materials of experience into some more acceptable order. There is in *Honest to God* mainly the assertion *that* a social order will be needed and confidence that it will be *there*. If the Christian shores this up or keeps it in repair, it will be not from prin-

---

[28] For this reason, I am pleased to observe that the quotations Bishop Robinson takes from my *Basic Christian Ethics* (New York, 1950) are all used in his chapter on "Law and Love," none when he is dealing with "Fixity and Freedom" or with "Authority and Experience." From my youth up I have known that the dialectic of Law and Gospel is by no means the same dialectic as that which goes on between fixity and freedom and between authority and experience. Does not Love teach with an authority that neither results from experience nor relies upon it, or upon an "inductive method"? And does not Love exhibit itself in constancies that a less worthy freedom sometimes falsely calls fixities?

[29] *Honest to God*, p. 116. Also, Joseph Fletcher, *op. cit.*, p. 10.

ciples of his own (which lead rather to *agapé*-acts that come from and penetrate to the person); it will be simply because some social fabric is necessary. Thus, the *agapé*-situationalism that is mainly characteristic of the chapter on ethics in *Honest to God* is *ethically* quite unqualified.

The possibility of securing the minimum moral foundations of a social ethics (if these do not devolve from love itself) by recognizing some God-given structures amid the relationships into which we are called is likewise passed over. This can be seen in what is said about the prismatic case (of response to the needs and claims of more than one neighbor) in which the inner logic must be discovered by which there evolves a Christian social ethic out of the teachings of Jesus. Jesus does not adjudicate conflicting claims. Nevertheless the disciple of Christ will have to ask himself who is going to maintain the widow after she has pledged her total means of support or the children of the man who has given everything to a beggar. Of course, love must consider these and a multitude of other different needs and claims; and it will consider them all "equally unreservedly." One may ask, Does love not *devolve* or *discern* amid these relationships some ethically important differences between near and distant neighbors, or any reason to approve the special care of one's own children? To such questions, Robinson gives no definitive answer, but only a situational decision in the presence, it would seem, of equal, myriad, chaotic claims. ". . . If we have the heart of the matter in us, if our eye is single, then love will find the way, its own particular way in every individual situation."[30] This seems to reject rule-agapism, since it implies that love is *productive* of acts only and never also of rules for the ordering of human reality; and it also rejects agapism mixed with some other source of the guidance of action, since it implies that love *finds* only decisions to be made and acts to be done, never any order—or at least no moral order—*in* the world of surrounding personal claims.

Robinson's viewpoint is different, or more fully expounded, in *Christian Morals Today*. Here the two alternatives each go beyond pure situationalism: there are working rules of less than

[30] p. 112.

general validity, or there are rules of general validity which embody love. Either or both of these views may be the implication of the basic normative proposition of agapism, that *"nothing else makes a thing right or wrong."*[31]

There is not much to be said about the first type of rules—working rules of less than general validity—except to say that from age to age love is the architect of them. The "church of the old covenant helped to provide a series of [moral nets] for the societies in which it lived, *refining it successively . . . ."* So also there are "blocs of ethical material" in the New Testament which are a fabric for the upbuilding of the person and the community. But what comes to us of unconditional importance through the teachings of the church "also *judges* that net, and enables us to recognize that what may be the embodiment of the divine command in one generation can be its distortion in the next."[32] Christians are bound to construct a net, to repair the net, but also to criticize[33] and transform it in the direction that love requires. "The plea for the priority of love fully recognizes the obligation upon Christians in each generation to help fashion and frame the moral net which will best preserve the body and soul of their *society*."[34] This is one form of rule-agapism.

3. General rules

However, there are also generally valid rules of action that love itself implies. Bishop Robinson states the thesis of pure rule-agapism when he writes, "In Christian ethics the only pure statement is the command to love: every other injunction depends on it and is an explication or application of it." For there *are* other injunctions, e.g. the proscription of cruelty to children, and of rape. These derivative rules are sufficient to show that "there are some things of which one can say that it is so inconceivable that they could ever be an expression of love . . . that they are

---

[31] p. 119. It is a rather hopeless task, however, to convince Christian people that the religious reiteration of this premise is no substitute for ethical reflection; or to convince Christian ethicists today that this premise of general ethics does not of itself lead to one conclusion only: act-agapism.

[32] *Christian Morals Today*, p. 17 (italics added).

[33] p. 18.

[34] p. 31.

for Christians always wrong."[35] Such moral injunctions are simple corollaries or implications of covenant-love. They are as unconditionally wrong as love is unconditionally right.

This statement that there are some things that are "always wrong" seems to contradict the statement in Robinson's earlier book that "nothing can of itself always be labelled as 'wrong.' "[36] He therefore explains that "they are so persistently wrong *for that reason*," i.e. for the reason that it is inconceivable that they could ever be an expression of love.[37] Let us try to imagine a set of conditions that might be said to justify an exception to one of these rules. Suppose that the only survivors of a nuclear holocaust are the Bishop of Woolwich and a sex-frustrated female missionary of child-bearing age. Would rape be justified in order to replenish the earth? This would be as certainly wrong in an ethic such as Robinson holds which prohibits the use of a person as a mere, unwilling means for any ulterior purpose, as it would be judged wrong in an ethic that derives its Christian substance from the supernatural end of man and refuses to allow this to be replaced by the supreme good of the continuation of persons like us upon this planet. Therefore, it is quite clear that Robinson should not have immediately translated (as he seems to do) the notation "always wrong" into *"working rules* which for *practical purposes* one can lay down as guides to Christian conduct." An extrinsic explanation would have to be given for this strange reluctance to let *agapé* reach certitude.

Robinson immediately rises again to the procedure of pure rule-agapism when he writes that "these various commandments are comprehended under the one command of love and based on it. Apart from this there are no unbreakable rules." If one wanted to express the whole task of Christian ethical reflection, that last statement should read: in and from love, there *are*, or there may be, unbreakable rules, and the question to be relentlessly pressed is what these rules are.

The fact that there are some things that are "always wrong

---

[35] p. 16.

[36] *Honest to God*, p. 118.

[37] *Christian Morals Today*, p. 16. The quotations that follow are from this same page.

for the reason that it is inconceivable that they could ever be an expression of love" does not remove the fact that these things are *inherently* wrong, wrong in themselves, even though this is because of the lovelessness that is always in them. To say otherwise would be rather like a rule-utilitarian who felt bound always to be singing the praises of the principle of utility, and who as a consequence refuses ever to talk about rules of action except to explain that anything that is wrong is wrong for the reason that it is inconceivable that under any circumstances it could be an expression of utility. Such a man would simply not be getting on with the business of doing utilitarian ethics.

It is always necessary to begin somewhere—even if it is with rape or promiscuity or prostitution—in order to discover whether there are any rules of conduct embodying love, or acts only. But there is more extensive elaboration of rule-agapism in Robinson's book on ethics. He began his first lecture by saying that he might not have delivered any of these lectures but for "a strong sense that *keeping promises* is a rather important part of Christian ethics."[38] Moreover, in answer to the accusation that the chapter on "the new morality" in *Honest to God* could be used to give warrant to Mr. Profumo's *act* of lying to the House of Commons in order to save his family from public disgrace, Bishop Robinson writes finely of "the searching claims of Christian love. Such love demands that we lay ourselves open. . . . To 'save' a person one loves from the opportunities of making this response could not be described in Christian terms as 'necessary for the sake of love.'" This seems to introduce the requirement of *truth-telling*; and, indeed, so far is Robinson's understanding of Christian love from being a mere sentiment that it would be surprising if the searching claims of Christian love were productive of anything short of these and other rules of conduct. And later on he writes, "I would, of course, be the first to agree that there are a whole class of actions—like stealing, lying, killing, committing adultery—which are so fundamentally destructive of human relationships that no differences of century or society can change their character."[39] These are all promising suggestions for

[38] pp. 7–8 (italics added).
[39] p. 16, from which subsequent quotations are also taken.

an exploration that has in view answering the question whether *agapé* is productive of rules also or of acts only.

However, Robinson promptly drew back again from his own best thoughts. "But this does not, of course, mean," he wrote, "that stealing and lying can in certain circumstances never be right." To support this he said something that is entirely mistaken: "All Christians would admit that they could be." Never have Christians—at least not those Christians whose vocation it is to reflect as ethicists upon the nature of the Christian life— admitted any such thing. Instead they have asked: What is the meaning of the forbidden theft, what is the meaning of truth-telling, what is the forbidden murder? They have explored, or deepened, or restricted the moral meaning of these categories or rules of conduct. There was once a man who was asked to define the difference between adultery and fornication, and who, hesitating a moment, replied: "Well, I've tried them both, and to me there wasn't any difference." To which the proper reply is that the question did not ask him to take the "inductive approach"; and his answer makes it clear that he is greatly in need of clarifying his categories. The work of Christian ethics in clarifying the categories—truth-telling, promise-keeping, theft, lying, murder— is not ordinarily a matter of love allowing an exception to a fixed definition of these terms but a matter of love illuminating the meaning of them. What looks like a right to deviate from the rule is really love's duty to do so because of the love-full meaning of the "natural justice" summarized in these classes of actions, or because of an expansion, or deepening, of the meaning of these rules of conduct. This is the way love sensitizes and instructs conscience.

An illustration of this is the traditional treatment of "justified" theft. This was an "exception" only when externally, or statistically, viewed. The moral reasoning on which this piece of casuistry was based was a love-informed determination of the created destination of property right to the common good, or common use. This was "love's casuistry"; and then, with the principles governing property in mind, love proceeded to the ordering of human reality generally and to particular cases of application. It was the bourgeois period with its notions of absolute property right that made the prohibition of theft not only a fixed rule but a fixed rule with a certain and a non-Christian moral meaning so that thereafter theft could only be a (forbidden) exception.

Robinson's ethic of the exceptional case is a product of the control bourgeois ethics still has over his ethical categories. We shall see that to great degree a bourgeois understanding of "the marriage line," or a Victorian stress on social respectability and legality, is also determinative of "the old morality" he wishes to overcome. This leads him in the direction of a possibly responsible exception to *this* rule, rather than always to deeper reflection about the Christian meaning of marriage. Robinson's ethic of the exception was more unqualified in *Honest to God*, where he was trying to show that "nothing can of itself always be labelled as 'wrong' "; and where he illustrated this mathematically by saying that sex relations before marriage and divorce may be wrong "in 99 cases or even 100 cases out of 100, but they are not intrinsically so, for the only intrinsic evil is lack of love."[40]

In the next chapter we will be dealing with a Christian ethicist—Paul Lehmann—who, in contrast to Robinson's most extreme statements of act-agapism, has set himself the task of expounding a situational ethic that specializes in the exception— or, if that be possible, makes a general principle of it.

We have seen now the extensive development of rule-agapism in Robinson's recent book. There is more. There where he is stressing the fact that the *content* of Christian morals seems to change from age to age, he points out that an unconditional, unvarying love in a multitude of responses "produces in Christians, however different or diversely placed, a direction, a cast, a style of life, which is recognizably and gloriously the same."[41] Before coming to *"what* precisely" Christians must do, the "direction," "cast," and "style of life" which is recognizably and gloriously the same would seem to be worth attention and further explication. This explication might have to be in quasi-aesthetic terms, or in imagery more than in concepts. Still that would be an im-

---

[40] *Honest to God*, p. 118. Here again the author's doing of "special ethics" is inhibited because he simply keeps on reiterating his "general ethics," or his systematic justification of any rules or acts.

[41] *Christian Morals Today*, p. 13.

portant part of the way to do Christian ethics. It would be in some measure an explication of "love's casuistry." Of course, the Holy Spirit doubtless is credited with putting into the mouth of a radical Christian responsiveness the determination of what that direction, or cast, or style shall be, if after the fact these acts turn out to be *recognizably* and gloriously the same. But if there is any work for Christian ethics to do, if there is any virtue in systematic reflection upon the nature of the Christian life, then that style of life will be its subject matter. In any case, a Christian ethics which contains this one statement alone—*that* Christian responses have a recognizably common style—no longer belongs to the class of act-agapism; and it ought no longer to demand unconditional surrender of the view that there are qualities that have general validity in Christian ethics which arise from love itself, and not acts only.

Finally, we need to take up the question of what Bishop Robinson deliberately calls "the *limits* of pre-marital sex for engaged couples."[42] That possibility was mathematically instanced in *Honest to God*; and we have already surrounded the exception the author means to talk about by ruling out prostitution, promiscuity, and adultery as always wrong because it is so inconceivable that these things could ever be an expression of love.[43] The question now to be raised is whether in trying to surround the exception more closely and thus get a grip on it (under the heading of "the *limits* of pre-marital sex for engaged couples"), it has not disappeared altogether. If this is so, then the question is whether *honesty* in sexual *ethics* does not require the Christian moralist to say so, and to state the rule that *truthfully expresses* the personal commitment he knows to be required in sexually responsible relations.

These are the issues which arise in connection with what

[42] p. 32, from which page subsequent quotations are also taken.

[43] These rules of conduct are much clearer in the Bishop's writings than they are in the moral revolution he is so anxious to take for granted in the doing of Christian ethics. That ancient profession has today been brought to ruin and disrepute by amateur competition. The age of chivalry is not dead in that its code and traveling minstrels can praise adultery no less than sex-before-marriage as a precious expression of freedom-in-love. And while promiscuity is not ruled in, it is also not ruled out by the new morality, except that persons in love should not concentrate on it, and except for the law of nature which makes it quite impossible for a man to have sexual relations with two women at the same time.

might be called the problem of "justified fornication"—if the reader will know that I am able to discuss cases and classes of things calmly and intend no prejudice by using this expression. To speak of "the limits of premarital sex for engaged couples" already marks off a class of things within the genus of things formerly called fornication (which itself is clearly distinguishable from both adultery and promiscuity); and it raises the question about the possible justification of this more restricted class of actions. The really remarkable thing is that when Bishop Robinson directs his Christian reflection to the limits of premarital sex for engaged couples, he can actually find no responsible case of it within these limits, and that what he says in general allows for none. This will be my final example from his writings of the edification to be found in the thought that there may be rules of action that best embody love.

Having introduced this question, Robinson says at once: "I believe the nexus between bed and board, between sex and the sharing of life at every level, must be pressed as strongly as ever by those who really care for persons as persons." This goes quite a long way on the basis of his "way in" upon moral problems. This is called, however, a "working rule." From the context at this point it is not clear whether by "working rule" he means a rule that is somewhat less than generally valid and to which there still may be an exception (yet one now very narrowly surrounded in view of the pattern of responsibility this rule affords); or whether this expression only means a *derivative* rule, a rule that depends on, but definitely follows from, "what a deep concern for persons as whole persons, in their entire social context, really requires."[44] If the latter is the case, then we may have discovered another class of things that are always wrong because it is so inconceivable that they could ever be an expression of love when love is strong and true and wholly honest.

This conclusion becomes clear on another page, to which Bishop Robinson is driven by his sense that *agapé* is the most "searching and demanding criterion of ethical judgement."[45] Persons deeply in love who are asking themselves about the limits of their premarital sexual relations should ask "what deep Chris-

[44] p. 33.
[45] p. 42.

40

tian love for the other person as a whole person (as opposed to exploitation and enjoyment, even if it is mutual) really demands —and that within the total social context." Unfortunately the answer that is suggested to this question is confused by what I have called a bourgeois conception of "the marriage line"; and the Bishop's quite correct judgment that acts within *this* line (of legal marriage) may not be based on a loving and caring and responsible relationship, and that acts outside *this* line need not be not so. But he writes boldly and without qualification: "Outside marriage sex is *bound* to be the expression of less than an unreserved sharing and commitment of one person to another."[46] Now, unless I fail to grasp some mysterious difference between a "bound" and a "line," Robinson has drawn a correct boundary, beneath—and replacing in principle—the merely legal line he began with, but a boundary nonetheless. This rule is said to be general, and unexceptional. It is in fact what Christianity has always meant by marriage, or the responsible consent to one another that alone makes marriage. In this sense there is nothing premarital about what Robinson is talking about. Beginning by asking about the limits upon premarital sexual relations between engaged couples, it turns out that marriage covers the whole ground of the action sought to be justified; and there remain only legal, or practical, considerations about whether public acknowledgment can or should be secured for the fact that a mutual acknowledgment of marital responsibility and the marriage relation itself has been assumed by the partners.

Enough has been said, I suppose, for the reader to be able to frame a reply to Robinson's rhetorical question: "Do we really want the furtiveness taken out of pre-marital sex?"[47] However, it is in order to remark upon the ethics of non-furtiveness (since the purpose here is to delineate rule-agapism as among the possible methods and systems of Christian ethics, and not to give a complete account of Christian sex and marriage ethics). The remark is simply this: a rule proscribing furtiveness as undesirable, and describing honesty as desirable, says a great deal about the

---

[46] p. 42 (italics added).

[47] p. 44. The answer, in part: any society, I suppose, needs to leave room for *secret* marriages, and perhaps for common law marriage, subsequently placing the enforcement of the law behind a responsibility that was entailed.

Christian style of life; and if only this were known to be what love requires, anyone who had any concern with strengthening the *ethos* and the accepted ethic in this regard could not then avoid the consequence that the better society might become the more furtiveness would have to be practiced furtively and lack of truthfulness dissimulated.

I draw a line here in order not to associate together the views of Robinson and H. A. Williams, who is a rather clear if un-developed proponent of act-agapism in Christian ethical analysis. Eric Mascall's chapter on "Pumping out the Bilge"[48] is a clever and correct answer to Williams' essay in *Soundings*; but I rather think his error needs to be more carefully identified. Also, it is Williams and not Robinson who deserves the attribution by the Archbishop of Canterbury of the belief that "fornication may be right if it is thought to produce good."[49]

Williams begins with an unexceptional statement of Chris-tian normative ethics: "generous self-giving love is the ultimate moral value."[50] This leads him at once to an ethics of the excep-tion from those classes of things, such as theft, once described as wicked in themselves and on which we have already commented sufficiently in the foregoing. Then we come to sexual ethics. On this subject there has been "an enormous amount of double-think," which Williams replaces by a similar degree of single-case thinking. He takes up the now famous case of the prostitute in the Greek film *Never on Sunday*. She picks up a young sailor, who, however, is in deep distress over his capacity to perform an act of sexual intercourse. "The prostitute gives herself to him in such a way that he acquires confidence and self-respect. He goes away a deeper fuller person than he came in." This, Williams writes, is "an act of charity which proclaims the glory of God. The man is now equipped as he was not before."[51] And upon the not unlike case in the English film, *The Mark*, of a man who was unable to desire sexually a mature woman of his own age, Williams' comment is: "Will he be able to summon up the nec-

---

[48] *Up and Down in Adria*, Chap. 2. See also *Four Anchors from the Stern*, pp. 32–34.

[49] Michael Ramsey, *Image Old and New* (London, 1963), p. 13.

[50] *Soundings*, ed. by A. R. Vidler, p. 80.

[51] p. 81.

essary courage or not? When he does, and they sleep together, he has been made whole. And where there is healing, there is Christ, whatever the Church may say about fornication. And the appropriate response is—Glory to God in the Highest."[52]

Now, I suppose that a radically monotheistic faith such as that of Christianity will find a way of interpreting *theologically* all that is and all the actions there are in the world; and that it will refuse to place anything outside of God's world in a dualistic realm of wickedness. Under the first article of the creed, we say that where there is any being, or measure, or order, or beauty, there God is. He enables the power of the murderer with his knife. And under the second article of the creed, if we take this with the seriousness of a Karl Barth, we know that covenant is the inner basis of the whole creation and that all the prostitutes and bankers who ever lived now have their beings and the reality of their lives in Him. We should, therefore, not be surprised to find more or less dim, or more or less clear, traces of agapistic attitudes and actions to be characteristic of this our common humanity (just as a less Christocentric anthropology would find among all men a potentiality, e.g., for natural justice).

A Christian, therefore, might not find this an altogether incredible portrait of a prostitute, where another sort of man who takes an inductive approach might note that she was a fictional character, and that prostitutes are really not like that in real life. Even a resolutely Christocentric interpretation of the being and nature of acts of prostitution will find it possible to give greater credence to the evidence that a prostitute who plies her trade while genuinely giving herself in sexual love to one man must not allow herself to be self-giving in sexual relations with all the others. One might find in this a clearer trace of the fact that covenant is the inner reality and the goal of sexual creation and of man-womanhood in all its breadth and depth; and conclude from this that man-womanhood was not made for such casual acts even if it may happen that healing takes place and that one comes away a deeper, fuller person than he went in. He might, of course, exclaim: Glory to the God of all covenants! He might return thanks for the fact that he had encountered *in act* more of a woman-person than he was a man-person. But it would still

[52] p. 82.

be the case that another person bore him in covenant and took his injury upon herself more than he bore her flesh or cared for her in the covenant of life with life. He should know this; or if he does not there is a deeper fault in him than any anxiety about his sexual powers and one less easily taken away. If he does know this, he might then *begin* to do Christian ethics.

More important it is to call attention to the fact—for which, of course, Williams is not responsible—that in our meager times the literary portrait of the saintly prostitute has become a matter of act-saintliness (and we can't even be sure of that, since it is the *effects*, the works, and not the *being* of sainthood that is in evidence). In Dostoievsky's Christ-figure, Sonia, it is her suffering and not her self-giving which her prostitution symbolizes, while her healing love is embodied in her relations with the miserable little family she sustains by her earnings, in the inner integrity of her whole personal style of life, and in relation to Raskolnikov's forgiveness and his possible resurrection from the dead. It is also a profound insight of Dostoievsky's that, when a woman is sought out of great (or weak) sexual need on the part of a man who wants only to use her, his sexual desire itself collapses if, she consenting, he catches a glimpse of the mystery of her personal freedom that his penetration is not going to touch or succeed in violating and that she does not bestow in thus physically yielding. This indicates more than a trace of the fact that human sexuality is *creation toward covenant* (to use Barth's phrase): by comparison with Williams' illustrations drawn from contemporary literature, we can see how far from Christian ground the present age has proceeded in its concern for the *individual psyche*.

This should enable us now to locate the formative idea and the essential clue to an understanding of act-agapism in its present vogue. The language of it is still Christian. Much is made of spiritual freedom, of love, and of freedom-in-love. But for all that, the basic philosophy of act-agapism is drawn from no Christian source. It is drawn rather from the atomistic individualism of secular thought in the modern period. This continues to be the acid that eats away at moral relations, and at the very idea that there are moral bonds between man and man, or between one moment and another.

The model for this freedom-in-love and an ethic of atomistic acts in Christian clothing is actually Jean Jacques Rousseau (making allowance for a liberal addition of Freudianism). For Rousseau there can be no bond (but only bargains) between two contracting individuals because there can and should be no bond established between one atomistic moment of willing, or consenting, and the next, and the next after that, which does not too much bind the latter and derogate upon the freedom of these later moments of willing. The sovereign individual may indeed say, "I now will actually what this other person wills, or at least what he says he wills." Is not this the basic premise of modern "contract" marriage which has invaded even the mind of the church today? But the sovereign individual cannot say without loss of freedom-in-act: "What he wills tomorrow [or what, e.g., marriage requires tomorrow], I too shall will."[53] The biblical covenant view of marriage, which lies behind our marriage law, affirms the will's competence to bind itself from one moment to another throughout all change, and therefore its competence to bind itself to another person and thus to exhibit a fuller freedom.

It is of the very greatest importance that we understand the connection between the presence or absence of bonds or structures between man and man, and the presence or absence of bonds or structures relating one moment to another. If act-agapism fails to discover any moral bonds between man and man, this is because it can find no sustaining moral bond between the present moment of action and a later moment of action. If rule-agapism devolves or discerns such bonds, this will be because on its view love connects one moment of action with another (pure rule-agapism), or finds that they are in fact already morally joined together (mixed rule-agapism).

I must add that for Mr. Williams' view of Christ's healing presence it would seem that the name of that film should not have been *Never on Sunday* but *Always on Sunday*, since that is the day the sacrament is enacted. The prostitute gave that man an outward and visible and moreover an effective sign of an inner and invisible work of the grace that seems most important for act-agapism (individual wholeness, or even just act-wholeness). This was at least a sacramental, or a signal instance—not of

[53] *The Social Contract*, Bk. II, chap. 1.

course of an ordinance but of an action—in which freedom-in-love came to concentration in material things.

For this same reason it may be observed that in some quarters divorce would seem to be a more appropriate sacrament than marriage. Marriage, traditionally and rightly understood, is something to which two people belong, in which they belong to one another, and which belongs to neither of the parties. It is a rule of life and a moral bond. It is a cause between them and greater than they are or than any of the acts of love in marriage. Of course, according to pure act-agapism, there is such a thing as marriage and perhaps it is deserving of that name. But marriage in this view consists of its renewal every moment in which the parties say, "I now will what this person wills as from the depths of personhood we meet one another with a love that remains as free as before."

If this marriage comes to an end, it may be felt to be as tragic as when a rule-bound marriage breaks: obviously the partners would not have set out along the conventional route society provides if they had such an ending in mind. Still the freedom of divorce is a material moment that exhibits in outward and visible signs the freedom-in-loving-acts of which the marriage all along consisted. It is the clearest prismatic way to make manifest the whole meaning of marriage. Thus, divorce that manifests freedom would seem a more appropriate sacrament than a marriage formed by acts and words that say, "What this person wills tomorrow or what our marriage requires tomorrow I too shall will, and her [or him] I will cherish through all change."

The moment of freedom in divorce as the sacrament would seem to be the logical conclusion in an age that gives paramount position to Rousseau's un-binding love, which today is even powerfully affecting our understanding of Christian freedom. Such is definitely not the conclusion to be drawn whenever and wherever the freedom of God's love in binding Himself to the world is taken as the model for all the covenants among men.[54]

I read recently an article on American family law that can

---

[54] The above does not necessarily establish the conclusion that marriage is quite indissoluble, but only that today most proponents and very many Christian proponents of its dissolubility base this on a theology of the individual that is entirely non-Christian even when this sounds highly Christian in its stress on the person and on "freedom."

serve as a test case, or "thought-experiment," that may help to determine whether it is individualistic freedom-in-love or the requirements of a responsible love that is at work in contemporary culture. This may also serve to make clear on which side of this line are to be located the operative principles of those of us doing Christian ethics today. For a comparatively short time, Anglo-American law has experimented with the freedom of divorce, this having been introduced into the centuries-old tradition of western morals less than a hundred years ago. It would not be surprising if there are vested rights and real needs of some of the parties involved in a divorce decree that our modern laws of marriage and divorce have not yet learned how to protect in the situation created by remarriage following divorce. Has the law done all it should have done to protect the rights of the ten million children of the total of four million American marriages that ended in divorce from 1944–54?

The legal article[55] to which I refer affirms that "the basic assumption (and fundamental contradiction) of family law in America has been that a father can give substantially equal opportunities to the children of his first marriage while simultaneously extending equal benefits to the offspring of his second (or third) marriage. To state the assumption is to reveal the basic problems it conceals." Granted that the writ of the law cannot insure all of the personal values that are theirs to the children of broken marriages, should we continue to allow their support, future education, etc., to be made a matter over which their parents *bargain*? "The results of giving to ex-husbands the privilege of having two sets of children have become alarmingly clear. The allocations of public money for aid to dependent children rise each year." Therefore, this author concludes, "some more legally satisfactory way must be devised and adopted by which society can act in a responsible and just manner towards the millions of American children whose rights to economic security and equality cannot be said to be treated with elementary due process in the ordinary divorce proceedings."

In addition to a humorous reference to a system of "divorce-

---

[55] Robert F. Drinan, S.J.: *The Rights of Children Whose Parents Are Divorced*. University of Illinois *Law Forum*, Family Law, Vol. 1962, Winter, pp. 618–32.

insurance," this author seriously proposes that a separate lawyer be appointed to represent the children in divorce proceedings and afterward for the years of their nonage. Thus would society stand *in loco parentis* for the parents who failed them in order to insure that the minimum rights of the children are not infringed by any subsequent remarriage with its new quiverful of children. This would mean that there might be divorce decrees specifically stipulating that the divorced parents cannot remarry where this would clearly make it impossible for them to fulfill their responsibilities toward already existing children. In any case, divorced parents would have to assume the burden of proving that they can adequately support two sets of children before they would be legally permitted to remarry.

Now, I am at the moment not interested in considering all of the arguments for or against this proposal for the reform of family law. It may be that its total effects would be to cause worse to befall. Still I think that this affords us an interesting test case for determining in thought whether freedom-in-love or a responsible love is the basic premise in our thinking about moral problems. According as our initial reactions to this suggestion vary, the secrets of many a heart will be revealed, and perhaps we can see from this whether we are primarily interested in an ethics of venereal freedom or an ethics of venereal responsibilities. I do not say that this proves the case for rule-agapism as against act-agapism. But I do say that this experiment in thought discloses what in many instances act-agapism comes down to. It is the boundless freedom of atomistic individualism that hides behind the terminology of Christian ethics as this is often used today. By this disclosure, the possibility of act-agapism has not been ruled out. However, the meaning of *agapé* should be kept quite clear. *Agapé* means, as Bishop Robinson said, "the overriding, unconditional claim of God's utterly gracious yet utterly demanding rule of righteous love."[56] While such an ethical standard may still allow room for act-agapism, we nevertheless have seen how it contains an inward pressure toward rule-agapism as also necessary in any adequate elaboration of Christian ethics.

[56] *Christian Morals Today*, p. 12.

IV

The Contextualism of Paul Lehmann

We have a more formidable position to place under scrutiny in the ethics that is being done by Professor Paul Lehmann of Union Theological Seminary in New York. Unlike John A. T. Robinson, Paul Lehmann makes the exception the rule. It will be seen that he is a thoroughgoing proponent of act-agapism, in the broad sense in which I am using this term of Frankena's. I would call his an act-*koinonia* ethics. At the same time, Lehmann gives extended exposition of the asserted *theological* basis for a Christian situationalism in ethics. This will enable us to abandon for the moment Frankena's classification of possible normative Christian ethical theories, in order to take up the problem of methods in Christian ethics from the point of view of its foundation in Christian theology. What does Christian theology imply for the doing of Christian ethics, for the methods of ethics and the meaning of the Christian life?

Paul Lehmann's book[1] is about *the context*—the theological and ecclesiological context—of Christian ethics. Despite the title, it is only quite subordinately a book about the meaning of ethics in this context. A second volume is promised that, pre-

[1] *Ethics in a Christian Context* (New York and Evanston, 1963). Henceforth in this chapter I shall refer to Professor Lehmann's book by its initials in parentheses (ECC), with the appropriate page number; and, in order to simplify references, I shall insert the citations directly into the text.

49

sumably, will elaborate the author's views on substantive ethics. This should also undertake to demonstrate "the contextual character of Christian ethics," to which only one chapter is devoted in the present volume. To that chapter the present essay will direct the reader's attention in the end. For here must be found the practical demonstrations that contextual Christian ethics succeeds (as Lehmann asserts it does) in overcoming the gap between the ethical claim and the ethical act; whether, if so, it then succeeds in avoiding on the one hand the supposed irrelevance and impotence of a preceptual understanding of Christian norms and on the other the capriciousness of ethical relativism; and finally whether it is a virtue in ethical reflection to have done all this.

The author knows, and it is to be hoped that the readers of the present book will know, that the highest respect to be paid a book which is the result of years of serious study and reflection is to wrestle with it all night long even at the risk of getting oneself wounded in the thigh. Besides, someone needs to challenge the easy assumption that is formative of church pronouncements precisely today when a Christian context has ceased to be formative of human life—to the effect that "the ethic which gives point and direction to the witness of the church to its risen Lord is eschatological . . . trinitarian . . . contextual."[2] The sudden introduction of that final, non-biblical, non-theological word should be disturbing to anyone concerned with Christian ethics. It forms no ethical trinity with the other two biblical categories; yet it is used today as if it did.

After three centuries in which every revival of Protestant Christianity has revived less of it, and after the recent decades of an increasingly Christ-less religiousness in the churches, it was predictable that celebrated theologians would begin their futile search for a religion-less Christianity to proclaim in a secular world that is supposed to have "come of age." Lehmann may yield too much to this Bonhoefferish mood. Yet the announced intention of this book is to show that "there are insights and conceptions rooted in the faith and ethics of the Reformation

[2] *Relations between Church and State in the United States of America,* adopted by the 175th General Assembly of the United Presbyterian Church in the United States of America, May 1963. Office of the General Assembly, Witherspoon Building, Philadelphia, Pa.

which are possessed of *formative power* for ethical theory and practice today" (ECC 13, italics added). The question is whether, in order for Christian insights to be formative of human life, we do not have to know more about what God is doing in the world than what we read in the Bible and in the papers (ECC 74). In any case, we may be able to learn from Lehmann whether a full-bodied understanding of the Christian life can be recovered, or even articulated, simply by dwelling upon the immediate encounter of today's world with the *theological ultimates* ingredient to the Christian context, without a significant Christian *ethical analysis* and guidance fully elaborated in between.

A. THE CONTEXT OF CHRISTIAN ETHICS

The author says many things about the context of Christian ethics that are both true and important. Moreover, he knows that primacy must be given to this context in all Christian action and reflection about morality. "This is why," he correctly says, "it makes all the difference in the world . . . in what context your ethical insights and practices are nourished" (ECC 65). Still the soil is not the same as the tree, nor are its roots the branches; nor, even, the composition of the nourishment the same as the fruit expected.

Christian behavior roots in God's action as this has been and is made known to us. Several statements can, therefore, be made partly about ethics in a Christian context but chiefly and correctly about the context of Christian ethics. Each of these propositions points to some ingredient in the soil that nourishes the Christian life, and which Christian ethics must take as its point of departure. These are, broadly speaking, *theological* statements which summarize Lehmann's understanding of the basis and the environs of Christian ethics: (1) Christian ethics is the ethics of the *koinonia*. (2) It calls for obedience to what God is doing in the world. (3) It means response to what God is doing to keep human life *human*. (4) It is Christological, or the ethics of messianism.[3]

---

[3] These four summary statements could be preceded by another in the first place, making five propositions in all. I would formulate this affirmatively as: "Christian ethics is theological ethics," with a view to embracing in this state-

We shall first examine what Lehmann says under each of these summary theological, ecclesiological, and Christological statements. In every case Lehmann must be criticized for having an inadequate understanding of the basis and the environs of the Christian life; and it will be pointed out that this leads him to a prejudice in favor of what he calls a contextual Christian ethics and what I call act-*koinonia* ethics. Then we will be prepared to take up his version of contextual ethics directly, and what he says about the particular moral problems he chooses to discuss. In the end, there is need for drastic revision of both Lehmann's theological statements and his constructive statements about Christian ethics; and the one weakness is a function of the other.

1. *Koinonia ethics*

Christian behavior roots in the *koinonia*. Christian ethics is *koinonia* ethics. It is "reflection upon the question, and its an-

---

ment the fanfare about *hermeneutics* with which the book opens. Although Lehmann says that Christian ethics is a "theological discipline," he most often expresses this negatively: Christian ethics is *not* biblical or New Testament ethics. Or else he expresses the same point in an as yet empty statement *that* there is a hermeneutical problem. The fact is that, just as epistemology (or man's ways of knowing) is by itself an empty science, one that can be best pursued in connection with ontology or in the course of debate about the modes of being, so the principles of hermeneutics (or the science of interpretation) can best be exhibited in the course of actually interpreting Scripture and in debates about its theological meaning. This is indeed the way Lehmann proceeds to use Scripture on many, many pages of this volume. Despite his opening gambit about there being a hermeneutical problem, and about Christian ethics as a theological discipline which is not the same as biblical ethics, he nowhere tells us what are his hermeneutical principles or argues for them, unless he does this by using them throughout the whole of the volume in the actual interpretations of Scripture he proposes. This seems to me to be an altogether correct procedure, and the only fruitful one. But then he ought not to have reduced to a footnote (pp. 26–27) two rather good books in the field of Christian ethics that likewise proceed at once to the interpretation of Scripture (without, however, an initial and purely ceremonial bow in the direction of hermeneutical principles that are empty until Scripture is interpreted). My own earlier work on Christian ethics does not subordinate the systematic to the genetic approach in Christian ethical analysis or beg the basic question about ethics as a theological discipline, any more than Lehmann does when he begins to do Christian ethics by introducing the very concept of situational ethics from an interpretation of the Corinthian Letters (p. 32), or by introducing the terms *koinonia* and "mature manhood" from an extended discussion of Ephesians 3–5 (pp. 48f.). By affirming that it does, Lehmann only avoids fundamental discussion of the basic theological categories in Christian ethics. Thus he avoids instructing me, and possibly receiving instruction.

swer: What am I, as a believer in Jesus Christ and a member of His church, to do?" (ECC 25). Lehmann believes (without sufficient proof) that Christian ethics is somehow uprooted if it consists in reflection upon the question: what *ought* or *should* I do, or what am I *required* to do, or what is *good* for me to do, as a believer in Jesus Christ and a member of His church? Thus, he *verbally* begins with the conclusion he seeks to establish, namely, that there is no gap between ethical claim and ethical act in the Christian life.

But, of course, there is no such thing as Christian ethics if God's action in laying His gracious claim upon human life and effectuating it in and through the *koinonia* is the same as all the ethical decisions and acts that take place in the church. The Divine claim and the human ethical act cannot be telescoped; nor can "What shall or should I do?" be telescoped into "What am I to do?" The ways of God and the ways of man must be juxtaposed "inconfusedly" even if "inseparably" in the church no less than in parabolic images (ECC 90). Therefore a "gap" which any ethics must acknowledge comes to expression, in Lehmann, in the relation between the ethical and the empirical reality of the church. (ECC 68f.). The actual church is only (but definitely) "a *laboratory* of the living word," "a *bridgehead* of maturity" (ECC 131, italics added). The *ecclesia*, as Brunner says, is only *as real as* its faith and love and hope, and *as real as* its fellowship of concern for one another (ECC 50 n.). There is a tension "between the hiddenness and the visibility of the *koinonia* in the world" (ECC 53n.). The *koinonia* that is really real is "God's fellowship-creating *mystery*" (ECC 58, italics added). It is not there simply to be indicated by sight to sight. Lehmann rightly avoids any dualism between the hidden and the visible character of the church; but he does this by saying that these two realities of the church are "dynamically and dialectically related in and through God's action in Christ, whose headship of the church makes the church at once the context and the custodian of the secret of the maturity of humanity" (ECC 72).

Perhaps the mystery of a "dynamic," "dialectical" relation between the hidden reality of the church and its inconfusedly but inseparably related empirical reality is sufficient for there to be Christian ethical reflection and action. Doubtless the ques-

tion: What *am* I to do? contains such a dynamic, dialectical relation between the "shall" or "ought" aspect of its meaning and
the determination of the human will in the *koinonia* by what
God is doing in the world. This seems clearly to be Lehmann's
meaning in what he says about the "sign" character and the "indicative" character of Christian moral action. In the *koinonia*,
ethics is "always fundamentally in an *indicative* rather than in
an *imperative* situation" (ECC 131); but this means "*indicative*
[I take it, in the sense of pointing] rather than *verifiable*" (ECC
112).

"There is," Lehmann writes, "also an imperative pressure
exerted by an indicative situation. The 'ought' factor cannot be
ignored in ethical theory"; only the "ought" factor is not primary in the context of Christian ethics (ECC 131). The hidden
reality of the *koinonia* lays a claim, an imperative, upon its
empirical reality; it judges the actual lives of its members. Why,
then, is not precisely this relationship between the "ought" factor and the actual life of the church better indicated by posing
the question; What *ought* I to do as a disciple of Christ and a
member of His *koinonia*? Or, What *should* I do as witness to
"the signs which point to and point up what God is doing in
the world"? (ECC 112). Or, What *shall* I do to signify that what
God is still doing in the world and in the churches was decisively
done in Jesus Christ? Certainly there has been no Christian ethics
that has used the more ordinary preceptual, normative terminology of ethics that has failed to say that the fundamental meaning
of the "right" and the "good" comes from the participation of
our moral reasoning itself in the grace and truth God has done
and is doing in the world. All that Lehmann avoids is the notion
that the chief cornerstone of Christian ethics is laid in the "weak,
dull and lifeless wouldings" of human beings toward the attainment of their own airy "shouldings."[4] The price paid for this
accomplishment is, I suggest, that he greatly foreshortens the
Christian *ethical* analysis into which otherwise he would have
been imperatively drawn.

Lehmann seems obsessed with removing from Christian
ethics any suggestion that its proper business is "trying to pre-

---

[4] Jonathan Edwards, *Treatise on the Religious Affections.*

scribe how Christians ought to behave." He is correct, of course, in some bad senses of that expression. Still the ethicist is engaged in a "reflective analysis" in which he endeavors "to rethink what the Christian faith implies, as regards their [Christians'] behavior" (ECC 23). But the unqualified statement that in the Christian context "ethics [can] now be a *descriptive* discipline" (ECC 14) is not only contradicted by the vast difference and dialectical relation between the hidden and the empirical reality of the *koinonia*; it is also well calculated to stifle the elaborations of those implications for behavior.

Perhaps this is the place to indicate that there is a good deal of cheap *koinonia* ethics abroad in the land for which Professor Lehmann, of course, is not entirely responsible, and to which his book gives little encouragement. It is too frequently said (in order to cut short the analysis of *Christian* ethical *concepts*) that Karl Barth changed the title of his *Christian Dogmatics* to *Church Dogmatics* very early in the writing of it; and some people (who have not read him enough or pondered him deeply enough) do not know that, in substance, Karl Barth could readily have changed the title back again. For Christ is the Head of the body. As Barth says, "The being of the community is a predicate of His being";[5] He is not a predicate of the being of the community, of the church, or the *koinonia*. "Our fellowship is with the Father and with His Son Jesus Christ";[6] our fellowship is not with the fellowship or with the *koinonia* or primarily with one another in it. Instead the *koinonia* is a group of joint-shareholders defined by the nature of what they share, not by their sharing, their fellowship, their "openness," *et cetera*.[7]

In this sense, Paul Lehmann knows that Christian ethics is *Christ-ian* ethics and not *koinonia* ethics. The church is grounded in "the inaugural act of God"; it "comes upon the historical scene as the answer of the disciples to that which God during the earthly life of Jesus had done in and through him" (ECC 46). The *koinonia* is a predicate of Him; not He a predicate of the community. Because the "new fellowship-reality" is first and

[5] *Church Dogmatics,* (Naperville, Ill., 1932–62), IV/2, p. 655.
[6] I John 1:3.
[7] Cf. C. H. Dodd, *The Johannine Epistles* (New York, 1946), p. 7.

basically "between Jesus Christ and the believers" Lehmann in fact introduces the term *koinonia* for the first time in the main body of the text with the apparent tentativeness it deserves: "We might, therefore, say that Christian ethics is *koinonia ethics . . .* (ECC 47). And when he sticks close to Scripture he defines the *koinonia* as *"the fellowship-creating reality* of Christ's presence in the world" (ECC 49). He stresses that the *"head of the body"* and "the *center* of the fellowship" are interchangeable figures; and proves this interchangeability by reference to the "I am" passage in the Fourth Gospel where Christ speaks of the love, than which there is none greater, by which He lays down His life.[8] Christ is the spirit whose flesh is the church. "Where Jesus Christ is, there is the *koinonia,*" Lehmann writes. One has lost his sense for the ethical reality of the *koinonia* in the world if and when he reverses this and says, "Where the church is, there is Jesus Christ" (ECC 53).

If it is held clearly and firmly in mind that Jesus Christ defines the Christian meaning of *koinonia,* then the proponent of *koinonia* ethics will have to assume the burden of proving that this category is somehow different from and more fruitful of Christian ethical understanding than *agapé.* For the ethics of Christian love likewise affirms that love is a predicate of Christ, not He a predicate of love in interpersonal relations. It is notable that Karl Barth, who yields to no one in the length and depth to which he explores the Christian life that is realized by the "upbuilding" of the "community," does not neglect to expound in this same context the concept and reality of *agapé* as the upbuilding in the individual of the mind of Christ;[9] and he exhaustively elucidates and articulates the meaning of the two-fold love-commandment.[10] The criticism of Lehmann implied at this point is not that he seems without argument to set *koinonia* ethics against *agapé* ethics. The criticism is not that Lehmann refuses to enter into collaboration or dialogue with *agapé* ethics in order that our common knowledge of the meaning of the Christian life may be advanced. It is rather that he foreshortens the elaboration of *koinonia* ethics (and consequently of the *agapé*

---

[8] John 15:13–14; and Lehmann, p. 52.
[9] *Church Dogmatics,* IV/2, §§67, 68.
[10] I/2, §18.

meaning of this) to such an extent that it may be prized for not being an ethic at all, i.e. for containing little clarification of the Christian moral requirement and only indications of the Christian context of ethics.

It seems to be one thing for Karl Barth to treat "Dogmatics as Ethics";[11] another thing for Paul Lehmann to write about "Ethics as Dogmatics." In Barth there is no less ethics than dogmatics; no less elaboration of the ethical claim than there is articulation of the context. Therefore he says more about the "actions and abstentions" that dogmatic ethics implies. Had Lehmann more fully elucidated ethics in the Christian context he would have fallen into saying more about what the Christian "may and can and must" do. The last word in that Barthian refrain is an imperative word! It (or other words indicating the divine claim) is just as necessary in a Christian ethics rooted in dogmatics as are words indicating that human freedom is rooted in God's permission (the basis of what the Christian "may" do) or in the reality and power of His action (the basis of what the Christian "can" do). But to say so much about the divine command would have seemed to Lehmann too preceptual! Instead, then, of continuing to press on earnestly in disciplined reflection upon what Christ teaches us *agapé* or *koinonia* implies, Lehmann turns rather to secular expressions to illuminate the meaning of *koinonia*. It is when the *agapé* meaning of the *koinonia* is kept clear that Lehmann is most able to avoid going to other sources in search of its meaning, e.g. there where the meaning of "maturity" as *self-acceptance through self-giving* is sharply contrasted with the psychological understanding of maturity as *self-realization through self-acceptance* (ECC 16).

2. *What God is doing*

A second statement that can be made ostensibly about ethics in a Christian context but actually and correctly about the context of Christian ethics is to say that this means obedience to what God is doing in the world (ECC Chap. 3). In the biblical and classical sense of the word, what God is doing in the world is "politics." He is governing and shaping human reality accord-

11 I/2, §22, 3.

ing to His will. It is appropriate to Lehmann's meaning, but not an apt denotation of the full truth, to say that God is a "politician" (ECC 83)—for Lehmann's God is something of an opportunist, more than He is a statesman. There can be no "preceptual apprehension of the will of God," he writes, not because of the complexity of the human situations in which our apprehensions take place but because of "the complexity of the will of God itself." The point is made simply by iteration and reiteration: "The will of God cannot be generalized" (ECC 77). A being of whom such a statement can be made scarcely deserves even the name of "politician," since a politician more often shapes human life by precepts, by having a will from which the community he governs can take normative direction.

Now, any such assertion pretends to know a lot about the will of God: Lehmann means it to be absolutely true for every situation that is God's doing and for every act of the will of God. He may be correct. If so, however, it is not because of a proper notion of the freedom of God. If God's transcendence is His freedom which cannot be prevented from making His will and acts immanent (and immanent in particular occasions), this same freedom cannot be supposed to have placed upon it the limitation that God cannot act generally or characteristically. If God can bind Himself in steadfast faithfulness to the particular, He can bind Himself in steadfast faithfulness in a general way. That would seem, indeed, to be part of the meaning of steadfastness, and of God's fidelity to His creatures through His statesmanship, or His rulership. Lehmann derogates upon the freedom of God to bind the world to Himself in a general way, or in one or some ways rather than others, and thereby to claim certain— and not a variety of—responses from disciples of Christ and members of His *koinonia*. It is, therefore, footless theological argument (and it is one more of Lehmann's iterations) for him to dismiss all edification from the Reformer's doctrine of the "threefold office of the law," on the ground that they were "led by this route back to a preceptual reading of the law." And there is a circular argument (i.e. no argument at all) disguised in the assertion that here the Reformers fell "below the level" of their best insights (ECC 78n.).

58

As for Lehmann's own view, he draws from Aristotle the *definition* that "politics is activity, and reflection upon activity, which aims at and analyzes what it takes to make and to keep human life *human* in the world." He adds to this what he calls a *description*, which the Bible supplies, to the effect that "what it takes to make and keep human life human in the world is 'the unsearchable riches of Christ'" (ECC 85). But why does not Lehmann say more about the meaning of the word "human"? Particularly if he were to derive the meaning of this word from what is entailed in "the unsearchable riches of Christ" in a fashion that does not just wrap an enigma in a mystery but undertakes to say fully what this means, then he would give us a *definition*, and likely a normative one implying imperatives and precepts. We would have been told something more about God's characteristic way of dealing with men than that he—habitually and generally!—plays peek-a-boo from behind the trees in the forest along the road of human history.

This, perhaps crude, metaphor is surely not greatly different from Lehmann's description of *koinonia* ethics as "a concrete, relational ethic in which the possibilities and the actualities of the human situation are continually breaking down and continually running out into what God is doing to put them together again. . . . But if one does believe and live by the fact that God is picking up the pieces, it is incumbent upon one to be clear about where and what the pieces are." How far is this from the second of Lehmann's "dismal alternatives"—an "absolutistic ethic" or a "thoroughgoing ethical capriciousness or relativism" (ECC 143)? In this account of the ethics we know in Christian revelation, has not Christ become a predicate of the pieces? It is left for Lehmann to dare to call this *character*istic of God: "in the light of God's *characteristic* behavior there is never any one way as against all others for dealing with any human situation"; and to glory in the fact that "God is not really so devoid of imagination as that" (ECC 141). Since God's "characteristic" behavior means that He can be, and likely is, behind two or three trees at once, there is never any one way for Christians to do what He is doing.

Barth can take ethics more seriously than Lehmann precisely because his theology is more adequate. While for Barth God is free (as Lehmann constantly stresses and hence is concerned with the exceptional all the time), He has also made Himself known quite historically in Jesus Christ. Jesus Christ becomes the datum for the moral life of a Christian in Barth in a way that He does not for Lehmann. In Him is all we know about the humanity of God (theology) and the humanity of man (anthropology). This is also all we are given to know about the freedom of God, i.e. His freedom to bind Himself to the world and the world to Himself. By contrast, God's freedom in Lehmann's thought is simply an autonomous theological speculation drawn from this world of rapid change. While there remains the possibility in Barth of entirely novel, free acts of God, there is a shape to the gospel of God and a shape to His action that enables us to reflect upon it for our knowledge into God and for our knowledge into the shape of Christian moral action.

3. *Keeping human life human (mature)*

The third statement to be made partly about ethics in a Christian context but still chiefly and correctly about the context of Christian ethics is that it is response to what God is doing in the world to keep human life *human*. "To keep life *human*" says not much more than "what God is doing in the world" until we are told what it means. The crucial ethical qualification of what Lehmann means by "human" is given by the New Testament meaning of "maturity" and of the "new humanity." "The fruit of this divine activity is human maturity, the wholeness of every man and of all men in the new humanity inaugurated and being fulfilled by Jesus Christ in the world" (ECC 124). The question to be raised later on is whether "wholeness" controls the meaning of "maturity" and of the human; or whether "maturity" in its New Testament sense controls the meaning of "wholeness." The latter is the intention if not the achievement of the author.

In any case, we must keep clear that "making human life *human*," "maturity" and the "new man" are Lehmann's three synonymous ethical terms. If one may say so, the "mature manhood," or "growing up," spoken of in Ephesians 4:13–16 is the norm; and to this, in turn, "the measure of the stature of the fulness of Christ" gives normative definition. The Christian moral norm is in the given; the gift is the norm. The imperative and the indicative co-inhere in Christ.

Yet for some strange reason Lehmann insists that "Christian ethics is oriented toward revelation rather than toward morality. . . . [It] *aims, not at morality but at maturity.* The mature life is the fruit of Christian faith. Morality is a by-product of maturity" (ECC 54). Either he makes here a merely *verbal* distinction between "ethics" and "morality"; or else he does not quite believe, with Barth, that Dogmatics is Ethics and for this reason he allows revelation and morality (or ethics) to fall apart. The first of these alternative interpretations seems to me to be closer to the author's intention, since everywhere *the ethical* or *the ethical reality* means *the mature,* the new in Christ, *the human.* The second of these interpretations, however, sums up the disaster that befalls Lehmann's ethics.

At issue here is not the ordinary and more than verbal distinction between morals or morality (social and individual behavior) and ethics (the "science" or knowledge of right conduct). Rather, the "ethical" is somehow quite non-normative, non-preceptual, and un-principled, and it allows for no use of the value-terminology (the "right" or the "good") which is to be found in all ethics other than Christian ethics in Lehmann's understanding of it, and with which "morality" abounds. "Christian ethics is primarily concerned not with the good but with the will of God; it aims at maturity, not at morality" (ECC 121).

Emil Brunner's definition, "The good is what God wills," and his statement that "the Good has its basis and its existence solely in the will of God,"[12] have already started down the slippery slope toward preceptual theological ethics because of his use of the word "good." The same is true of Karl Barth's use of the word "good," which Lehmann wishes to revise in this significant respect. He begins by appealing to Barth's statement that another word—the word "ethics"—has no meaning in itself to which an author must be bound in his use of it: "No concept possesses *as such* an absolutely general and intrinsically binding meaning, including the term, Ethics." Lehmann then proceeds

[12] *The Divine Imperative* (Philadelphia, 1947), p. 53.

to affirm the same thing of Barth's use of value-terminology in his Christian ethics, e.g. in the question Barth raises: "What is the *Good* in and above all alleged goodness of human behavior?" (ECC 272–73). Since the word "good" has no binding meaning, no one is bound to use it in his ethics. So Barth uses it, and Lehmann does not. But then it should be noticed that Lehmann thinks *not* using this word entails something of substantive importance in Christian ethics. This turns out to be more than a verbal matter. The problem of the *Good* is "extrinsic to the proper concern of a Christian ethic." Moreover, Lehmann is enough of a disciple of Barth for him to want to loosen the usage of the word "good" from Barth's own discussion of ethics. He calls this usage "a residual influence" upon him "of the classical and critical tradition in ethics" (ECC 273n.).

One need not enter upon a merely verbal dispute—so long as it is merely verbal. If, however, anything of substantive import is entailed in Lehmann's decision not to use the word "good" and Barth's decision to use it, then this must be called a residual influence of *the ethical problem* upon Barth's discussion—or better, it is a product of the extraordinary earnestness with which he pursues his reflection upon the ethical implications of Christian dogmatics. Concerning the statement in the Gospels that "there is none good but one, that is God," Karl Barth remarks that "to receive this truth is not to reject and abandon the question of *the goodness of human action. It is only with this truth that we take it up.*[13] It is true that under the doctrine of God—where Lehmann says Barth "located" ethics, neglecting the rest (ECC 271)—Karl Barth gives extended analysis simply of the proposition that "there is no good which is not obedience to God's command."[14] This is the source and the extent of Lehmann's ethics of "freedom in obedience." However, Karl Barth's undertaking for the entirety of Christian ethics requires another statement: *"there must be seen and demonstrated the fact and extent of the existence of good human action* under the lordship and efficacy of the divine command."[15]

Lehmann does not give, or seek to fulfill, such a description

---

[13] *Church Dogmatics*, II/2, p. 574 (italics added).
[14] II/2, p. 541.
[15] III/4, p. 6 (italics added).

of the task of Christian ethics. Instead, he separates *the ethical* from the good, revelation from morality. The reason given for this refusal to deal with morality, and for not exploring fully what this may mean even as a "byproduct" of orientation upon *the ethical*, upon maturity, is the fact that "the actuality of the new humanity in Christ" is the "immediate" and "direct" theological presupposition of what can only be called an *instant* Christian ethics. All one needs is to dwell in and say forth the context, and discern God's politics in the world, though even from this point of view it is not at all apparent why any and all statements about "humanity in general" must be taken to mean "humanity apart from Christ" and opposed to *particularistic* indications of "the new humanity in Christ" (ECC 121). Therefore, Lehmann concludes, "Christian thinking about ethics finds it beside the point to take up the question of the nature of an act and of the relation between the nature of an act and the nature of the good" (ECC 121–22). Thus, he again gives himself the conclusion that Christian ethics overcomes the fault of all other ethics, in that no gap appears between the nature of action and the nature of the good; this is one of the advantages of beginning and remaining with the given. Such a Christian ethics is, indeed, dynamically "on the move" and "more informal" according to the root meaning of that last word—unconstructed (ECC 122 and n.), that is, more unstructured—and reflection about the moral life is more undisciplined, than any analysis of the moral claims upon human behavior "in terms of a progressive movement from the partial to the perfect" (ECC 122). That last word opens up gaps and is incipiently preceptual.

It is true, of course, that "Be ye therefore mature" may be a better translation of Matt. 5:48 than "Be ye therefore perfect." But the term "maturity" in its New Testament meaning also opens up a gap between the nature of human acts and the nature of mature human conduct, unless a way can be found to avoid going into that subject. I suggest that Paul Lehmann succeeds in leaving his Christian ethics "unconstructed" by shifting contexts. This is accomplished by yet another translation of Matt. 5:48, with but one word inserted in a parenthesis: "men will be mature (whole) as their Father in heaven is" (ECC 123).

Instead of articulating more fully the meaning of maturity

for the actions and abstentions implied in and for Christian discipleship, Professor Lehmann turns from the Christian to a secular context for the illumination of the meaning of this category and for a demonstration of the way it comprehends the very texture of human existence; this texture tends to become the substantive of which Christ is predicate. His *language* indicates the emergence of other controlling thought-forms than are quite warranted by the "temple," "body," and "vine" imagery or metaphors in the New Testament, which ought always to be understood in terms of *agapé* covenant-relationships (and not *vice versa*): "A pattern of integrity in and through interrelatedness" (ECC 54). "For maturity *is* integrity in and through interrelatedness which makes it possible for each individual member of an organic whole to be himself in togetherness, and in togetherness each to be himself. This is maturity" (ECC 55). "The thrust of the *koinonia* into the world means that all ordinary conduct is *socialized* rather than *universalized*" (ECC 56). "The societal character of Christian faith and life" (ECC 61).

After saying that the *koinonia* is "a fellowship of maturity in love" (ECC 61), Lehmann readily puts "whole" for "Head," or "Lord," in the explanation of the meaning of this: "a fellowship in which each individual functions properly himself in relation to the whole, and the whole functions properly in so far as each individual is related to it" (ECC 62). He explains Luther's "through love being changed into each other" and Calvin's "let us be whatever we are for each other" by "organic interrelational differentiation" (ECC 66).

Of course, in the midst of "part-whole," "part-part," and " 'one' confronts the 'other' " language, a more adequate Christian contextual language often succeeds in reemerging: a "society in which all the parts properly function insofar as all the parts, one way or another, minister Christ to all the other parts" (ECC 68). But why be so hesitant in saying what "ministering Christ" may mean in ethical theory and moral actions or abstentions? Until an ethics in a Christian context is articulated more reflectively, the language of secular contextualism will tend to fill the vacuum left by—indeed exhibited by—repeated inarticulate reference to what God is doing in the world to keep human life human. Doubtless, the church is "the *context* and the *custodian* of the secret of the maturity of humanity" and "the *starting point* for the Christian life and for our thinking about Christian ethics" (ECC 72, italics added). But spinning on the spot is not the only alternative to imagining vainly that the Christian can make another beginning or that Christian ethics could ever reflect itself away from this ground in which it is nourished.

One need not, and I am not competent to, quarrel with Lehmann's translation of 1 Cor. 10:16–17 in which he finds the phrases "fellowship of belonging" and "we are what we are in belonging" (ECC 100n.). Nor need we forget all his passages in which the biblical meaning of human maturity is expounded. Still, one can wish that Lehmann had continued along the line of his own requirement for an "ethics of depth," i.e. "an *ethical analysis which tries to spell out what is involved in* human maturity as the final fruit of being 'firmly fixed in love . . . able to grasp . . . how wide and deep and long and high is the love of Christ.' "[16] Then would there have been more contact with the entire tradition of Christian ethical reflection. Then, I suspect, we might have heard something about *the law of Christ,* or some reasonable facsimile thereof; more about what a Christian can and may and must do; and more about the actions and abstentions implied for Christian discipleship. Instead we are told —and I venture to believe that such passages will prove especially meaningful to contemporary readers in and out of the churches—that "maturity is the full development in a human being of the power to be truly and fully himself in being fully related to others who also have the power to be truly and fully themselves" (ECC 101). In what direction would *you* look for an explication of ethics in *that* context? Moreover, it is ethics developed within this context that is apt to be productive of an indefinitely variable, dynamic, *instant* ethics so long as there are no imperative formulations brought against the concrete context and no preceptual claims made upon the texture of relationships. Ethics in a Christian context (or, for that matter, any ethics) is required and able to be far richer in ethical implications. It will be productive of knowledge *into* God, knowledge *into* human

[16] Eph. 3:18–21 and Lehmann p. 101 (italics added).

existence and knowledge *into ethics*—if these are not too authentically Barthian statements for Lehmann to accept. Even "wholeness" and "interrelatedness," when taken with utmost philosophical seriousness as the standard and definition of goodness, have produced a great tradition in the rational analysis of moral action and many great systems of ethics; but then no one pretends to have abolished the tension between the ethical claim and the ethical act, or that ethics, as such, has any business other than articulating exactly that.

The truth is that in Lehmann's ethics the development of a normative ethics of wholeness is inhibited by the degree to which Christian categories prevail, and the development of a Christian ethics is frustrated by his readiness to turn elsewhere for the meaning of maturity. In order to see quite clearly, however, that Lehmann's minimum notion of wholeness is drawn from the philosophy of self-realization developed in the modern era, with a liberal dosage of Freudianism, one need only ask: Why is it more "mature" for a person to develop organically in interpersonal relationships than for his maturity to be determined by wholly other claims, commands, obligations, imperatives, and by what's right? This is not a question to be begged, or one to be answered in Christian ethics by imparting the assumptions of the present age.

The business of Christian ethics is to exhibit and formulate the implications of "mature manhood" in the New Testament understanding of it as these may bear on all the concrete "wholes" in the world in which men are called to discipleship. Lehmann definitely tends to interpret "mature manhood" in the light of secular "wholeness" rather than interpreting the wholeness into which we must grow up as maturity measured by the stature of the fullness of Christ. The evidence for this is sufficient to call gravely into question his claim that "the contexual character of Christian ethics is not derived from an application to the Christian *koinonia* of a general theory of contextualism" (ECC 15).

To see this one has only to place what Lehmann means by "human" alongside of what Karl Barth means by that word. When Barth takes up specific ethical questions, such as "the humanity of human work," the question he asks is whether and to what extent it is human in the special sense of "fellow human,"[17] and this term in turn takes its entire meaning from a doctrine of creation and of the nature of man as a being created by Jesus Christ and toward Jesus Christ. An image of this is to be found in the creation of man and woman toward one another; and this has to be spelled out in Christian ethics. For Barth, Christology is not the same as anthropology; and even Christocentric anthropology is not the same as Christology. For Lehmann, "dogmatics as ethics" is largely restricted to Christology or theology; and this gives him no protection against unacknowledged anthropological insights drawn from non-Christian sources, to wit, secular contextualism. Thus, for example, trust, belonging, openness, and wholeness provide in large measure the meaning of humanity in the relations between the sexes in Lehmann's views, while Barth elaborates the Christocentric meaning of man-womanhood as our creation in and for "fellow humanity," which gives meaning to the belonging and the fidelity required by our creator.

The primacy of a general theory of contextualism begins to assert itself even in Lehmann's discussion of the theological and ecclesiological context of Christian ethics, and of the methodology for developing the ethics required or made possible by this context. It becomes even more plainly evident when we come to questions of application and to what is said in this volume concerning "the contextual character of Christian ethics." We shall have to take the author at his word in reporting a recent "discovery" of "the extent to which my own approach to ethics has been affected by the intellectual climate so formatively shaped, if not inaugurated, by [William] James" (ECC 192n.; cf. 195n.); and this raises the crucial question about just how formative the Christian biblical context or the faith and ethics of the Reformation have been for Lehmann's ethical theory.

4. Christocentric ethics

Christian ethics is *ex animo* an ethics of messianism (ECC 104). This means it is Christological. Granting that the Messiah "is unintelligible apart from the covenant community, the corpo-

---

[17] *Church Dogmatics*, III/4, p. 535.

rate structure of God's activity in the world" (ECC 58), Lehmann devotes an entire chapter to the proposition that the *koinonia* is unintelligible apart from the Messiah, and that He is no predicate of it.

This leads to a final cluster of three statements to be made chiefly and correctly about the Christological context of Christian ethics, but whose implications for ethics in that context are as yet uncertain. These are statements about "the divine behavior," Lehmann writes; and he adds immediately, "and thus also of human behavior" (ECC 105). (1) Christian ethics has a trinitarian basis; it is rooted in the triune *economy* of God's action. (2) Its context is redemption as this is understood under the Threefold Office of Christ; His prophetic, regal, and priestly functions. (3) The nature and direction of the human fulfillment of which Christians speak is oriented upon the Second Adam, the Second Advent. Together, these Christological affirmations indicate the environment and the prospect of Christian behavior.

Lehmann several times points out an advantage for the enterprise of Christian ethics in keeping these doctrines—or the reality to which they point—steadily in mind. The trinitarian formulation is "an important traditional safeguard against basing ethics upon *theological anthropology*" (ECC 109n., italics added). The significance of a theology and ethics of messianism is exactly that it protects against a "metaphysical surrender" (ECC 112n.), against a natural, ontological, or anthropological environment for ethics. The doctrine of the Second Adam, in particular, "fortifies the Christological focus" by removing "the last possibility of a surreptitious resort to *anthropology* in Christian ethical reflection" (ECC 120, italics added). And later Lehmann writes, he thinks tellingly, against John Bennett, that "a *theological anthropology* is simply insufficient to support the method and substance of Christian ethical reflection."[18]

[18] p. 154 (italics added). Lehmann's discussion at this point (pp. 148–59) "of the concept of middle axioms" developed by Dr. J. H. Oldham and Professor John Bennett (and his discussion of Bennett's unpublished paper "Principles and the Situation") is vitiated by his supposition that the *chief* point about the theory of natural law, or the concept of middle axioms, was to establish "a common link between the believer and the non-believer" (p. 148). I should have said that the chief point was how the believer himself and the community of believers are to arrive at any guidance for Christian moral and social action, whether or not this

He who would pick any bones with this must first understand it. Does Lehmann reject anthropology in general from among the bases of Christian ethical reflection, or only general anthropology? Does he only oppose surreptitious resort to anthropology, or as well any elaboration of *theological* anthropology? Among the options in theological anthropology is an elaboration of a Christocentric understanding of the nature of man; and Lehmann himself makes reference to Barth's *"special anthropology of Jesus Christ . . . the norm of all anthropology"* (ECC 119).

One can fruitfully inquire into the dependent or independent relationship, surreptitious or otherwise, between general anthropology and Barth's Christocentric theological anthropology as a basis for ethics. But since Lehmann develops no Christian doctrine of man as one ingredient in the environment of Christian ethics, this question cannot fruitfully be raised with him. He does refer to a "dialectical relation between the 'second Adam' and the 'first Adam' in the shaping of the new humanity" (ECC 154); but he nowhere tells us anything about the nature of one pole of that dialectic, namely, the "first Adam." This would require a statement concerning the nature of *the man* (Adam) as this may be understood of the "first" from the point of view of the "second Adam."

Here again, however, it may be observed that the fact that Lehmann elaborates no Christocentric theological anthropology does not mean that he is innocent of anthropological insights, or that these are without significant weight in his ethics. It only means that the anthropological underpinning of a secular theory of contextualism comes to fill the vacuum. Indeed, in his resolve to stick with the ultimates of a theology of messianism, Lehmann is without the protection against independent anthropological insights (which for him are the structures of a structureless understanding of the human situation) which Barth secures by unhesitatingly basing a large part of his ethics on a carefully

---

links them with non-believers in a common enterprise. The question, therefore, of Christian anthropology, or of a Christian doctrine of creation, or of the Christian natural law, or of the "orders" or of rule-agapism, etc., are questions *within* Christian theological ethics, not apologetic ethics.

worked-out theological anthropology. The wording "mature (whole)" was one indication of where Lehmann's meaning comes from. Another [mis-?] translation of a New Testament verse will indicate that, taken so alone, the Second Adam as the aim and prospect of "maturity" in its Christian ethical meaning fails quite definitely to remove the last possibility of a surreptitious resort to anthropology in Christian ethical reflection. "When God is everything to everyone (I Cor. 15:29) then men will be 'like God,' that is, everything to everyone" (ECC 106n.). Being like God means being everything to everyone; the advantage of saying it this way is that no one could possibly give you a pre-scription for that! Being like God in any Christian qualitative sense would, of course, immediately admit of preceptual under-standing of God's claim, of the prospect or *telos* of human ma-turity, of what God is doing in the world to make human life human.

In this connection, it may be noted that Lehmann makes the astonishing, and quite incorrect, statement: "Barth includes ethics under the doctrine of God, not the doctrine of man" (ECC 271). He knows better, assiduous student of Barth that he is; and anyone who knows of the existence of *C-D*, III/4 knows better. The fact is that there is an ethical articulation of *every* doctrine in Barth's *Dogmatics*; and that our knowledge *into God, into man,* and *into ethics* are all fully explored and fully Christocen-tric. Anthropology is no further removed from Christology than theology is, or for that matter ethics with its statements about actions and abstentions that Christians may and can and must perform insofar as they are disciples of Christ and members of His *koinonia.*

Here a final comment is in order. It is that Lehmann has particular need for that part of Barth's dogmatic ethics where he seems only to locate ethics within the doctrine of God. For here the freedom and uniqueness of the Divine command and claim are emphasized.[19] (Even here, the words "command" and "claim" are used, and not is-language alone.) In his *Dogmatics* taken as a whole, however, Barth stresses as well what is entailed for man in God's binding Himself to the world and the world

19 *Church Dogmatics,* II/2.

to Himself; he does not hesitate to discourse upon the doctrines of creation and the nature of man, and in this connection to elaborate a "special ethics" entailed in all this.[20] This "special ethics" gets quite specific, before ever Barth surrounds and locates an "exception" which is steadfastly preserved in its nature as an exception by its environment in Christian ethical analysis.

In a section entitled "The Protection of Life," Barth writes that "The command of respect for human life . . . is not a law but a direction for service."[21] It is, however, a *definite* directive, under which Barth analyzes such problems as suicide, killing another person, abortion, euthanasia, self-defense, capital punishment, and killing in war. "Thou shalt not kill," writes Barth, "reaches us in such a way that in all the detailed problems which may arise we cannot exclude the exceptional case and yet we cannot assert too sharply that it is genuinely exceptional. In other words, we cannot overemphasize the arguments against it . . ."[22] even when we judge that in an exception to the rule that life should always be sustained there may be a call of God. Moreover, even *in* the exception the rule is applied: "God as the Lord of life may further its protection even in the *strange form* of its conclusion and termination rather than in its [immediate?] preservation and advancement."[23] Even so, this exceptional service, "this exceptional case can and should be envisaged and accepted only as such, only as *ultima ratio*, only as highly exceptional, and only with the greatest reserve on the exhaustion of all other possibilities."[24] In other words, Barth asks and attempts to answer the question: What is the meaning of the forbidden self-destruction, or the prohibited killing? His answer to this question surrounds and locates the exception and sustains it as a genuine exception (so much so that the more one reads Barth and ponders his writings on special ethics, the more "the exception" itself will be discovered to be a case of specific application).

[20] III/4.
[21] III/4, p. 433.
[22] p. 400.
[23] p. 398 (italics added). What is this if it is not "love's casuistry" not seeking to overleap principles?
[24] p. 398.

By contrast, Lehmann can write, and does write, "Christianity *specializes* in the exception." He says that an exception which "suspends the rule" and does not "fall securely under normative generalization" is the truly significant case because it breaks challengingly with the surrounding normative context and "breaks fresh ethical ground" (ECC 243–44). In contrast, Barth's "exception" continues to bear the burden placed upon it by the acknowledged general validity of right conduct in the matter to which exception is allowed. Indeed, an ethical exception cannot, by definition, exist unless this is the case. No ethics can specialize in it. Lehmann, however, can write of "the 'rule' of forgiveness": "Here was a 'rule' which was not a rule"; it "could only be applied as a suspension of itself" (ECC 245)—thus building his ethics upon a plainly self-contradictory notion of an exception, and withdrawing everything he seemed to say when earlier he wrote: "The statement 'God forgives' is a theological statement that does imply necessarily an ethical statement, i.e. that 'Men should deal with one another as God deals with them,' viz. forgive one another" (ECC 239). That would seem not ever to be suspended in application, whether or not it is called a "rule" or a "rule which was not a rule" (whatever that may mean).

Here, however, the point is not the ethics that may be located under the doctrine of God, or such ultimates as justification. It is rather the question whether Christian ethics does not require also an ethics located under the doctrines of creation and man. It is the question whether there is a Christian ethic if about all that can be said by or to husband and wife who are in the depths of moral predicament is: "If what God is doing in the world has anything to do with what man is doing in the world, it is His next move!" (ECC 321).

Professor James M. Gustafson has written that Lehmann's book "could be reviewed instructively as an emendation of Barth's theology and ethics."[25] If it is an emendation, Barth's ethics is here considerably reduced—and not in length only but in indispensable moments for Christian ethical reflection. After the statement, near the end of the book, that "A context for conscience concludes with a conscience for that context," the

[25] *Union Seminary Quarterly Review*, XIX, 3 (March 1964), p. 262.

author was troubled for the second time by the apparent empti-
ness and circularity of his "conclusion" (which is surely ethically
impoverished whether this be conscience in a Christian or a secular context). He asked whimsically: "Has the mountain merely
labored to bring forth a mouse? Or is this the mouse which
gnaws the lion free?" (ECC 351 and 284n.1). He leans good-
humoredly to the latter opinion. Leaning as I do toward the
former one, I may say that the mouse has gnawed Christian conscience free from a good deal that is necessary if there is to be
any such thing as Christian ethics.

Lehmann's understanding of Christian ethics, however, may
be said to be a characteristically American statement of the subject. This is truly "A theology for . . ." the Committees on Christian Social Concerns. For in American Protestant theology we
do not so much resist "natural" justice as opposed to "revealed"
ethics, or revealed ethics as opposed to the ethics of natural law.
Behind this antinomy there is even greater resistance to any full-
scaled articulation of ethics whether on the basis of nature or
revelation or both. Barth's specific ethics and its theological
groundwork are not apt to prove any more acceptable than
moral theology with *its* "casuistry."

B. THE CONTEXTUAL CHARACTER
OF CHRISTIAN ETHICS

Lehmann's volume, then, is a book about the context. It is
a book on the doctrine of the church, on the methodology of
Christian ethics, on messianism or christology, on justification,
on divine and human freedom, on what God is doing in the
world making for maturity and the new humanity. The volume has to be assessed in terms of the adequacy with which
these theological doctrines and methods are set forth. It is only
quite subordinately a book about the nature and meaning of
ethics in this context.

The present writer is quite conscious of the fact that in the
foregoing he may have already reflected beyond warrant upon
the ethical implications that follow or do not follow from taking
Lehmann's approach to Christian ethics and from his under-

standing of its context. The author himself makes quite clear that:

> The elaboration of what is involved in the constructive substance of a *koinonia* ethic lies beyond the scope of the present inquiry and must presuppose the methodological analysis with which these pages are concerned. Only then can a systematic exposition of the content of a Christian ethic exhibit the distinctive orientation with which the gospel provides behavior. And only in the light of such an orientation can the meaning of forgiveness and love, of love and righteousness, of the role of law in Christian life, and of the difference which being a Christian makes in personal conduct and in social patterns and structures be intrinsically explained [ECC 224].

If this is forthcoming in the next volume, the present reviewer will be the first to be glad he was proved wrong. From a huge furnace of doubt my hosanna will break forth! For then Christian ethics will have made great advances both in theoretical formulation and in possible application.

Nevertheless, Lehmann serves up more than a morsel of what may be expected from an ethics within his understanding of its context and method. This he does in a chapter entitled, "The Contextual Character of Christian Ethics." We must now turn to this chapter and to a few other places in the present volume where Lehmann begins to do Christian ethics. I propose first to raise one general question about the contextual character of Christian ethics. Then we will examine what Lehmann has to say about (1) the problem of truth-telling, (2) sex ethics, and (3) a Christian's participation in war, which are the three substantive moral problems discussed in this chapter.

The first question to be asked is how, by what logic, and with what justification Lehmann moves from the title of his book, *Ethics in a Christian Context* to the title of this chapter, "The Contextual Character of Christian Ethics." This, of course, requires no demonstration if the transition from "context" to "contextual" is only grammatical. One can always turn a noun into an adjective, a substantive into a predicate, provided he means no more than and nothing different from the noun when he uses the adjectival form. In this sense, ethics in a Christian context is obviously contextual. One has said no more by using the word "contextual" than was contained in the statement, to which I suppose no one objects, that Christian ethics is ethics in a Christian theological context. In this sense, and this sense alone, there can be no objection to the assumption that Christian ethics has contextual character. Just so, a Tillich might affirm that ethics is rooted in ontology; and, after proving that, he could speak about the ontological character of ethics provided the predicate "ontological" contained no assumption about the content of that ethic beyond establishing the fact that "ontology" must be its basis. There may be a wide variety of possible ethical systems, and ways of dealing with specific moral problems, that can all be called ontological; and there may be a wide variety of Christian ethical systems that are possible, and ways of dealing with specific moral problems, that could be called "contextual" because they all agree that Christian ethics must be ethics in a Christian theological "context."

I am afraid, however, that Lehmann thinks he has said more than that about the nature of Christian ethics when he passes from using the noun "context" to using the adjective "contextual." He seems to assume that he has said something by the word "contextual" and yet that there is no more to prove in order to establish his notion of the contextual character of Christian ethics than has already been shown in establishing the fact that it is always ethics in a Christian context. In one sense—the grammatical sense—Christian ethics is obviously contextual; in any more significant sense, he who does not undertake to demonstrate begs the question. Is there not a simple logical and grammatical illation involved when Lehmann writes that "when the church is the context of ethical reflection, Christian ethics becomes contextual" (ECC 73)? This is evident in only the most inconsequential, grammatical sense. But Lehmann assumes that the word "contextual" as an attribute of Christian ethics says a good deal more than the nominative "context" requires, and more than has been shown to be required by the primacy of Christian theology to Christian ethics.

Great minds before Lehmann have made so simple yet crucial a mistake. John Stuart Mill, for example, reasoned that since we call something "visible" because it can be seen or "edible" because it is eaten, so the only reason for believing a thing is "desirable" is the fact that it is desired. If "desirable" means no more than "able to be desired," that is evidently established by the fact that someone desires it; but Mill clearly meant more than this by his use of the word. He meant "worth being desired." Just so, if "contextual" means no more than that the ethics we are talking about is in a Christian context, that is evidently established by the fact that we are speaking of Christian ethics. But Lehmann clearly means more than this by his use of the expression "the contextual character of Christian ethics." No one denies that something that is desired is, in that sense, "desirable"; or that ethics in a Christian context is, in that sense, "contextual" ethics. No more meaning can be obtained from the adjective than there is, in the first case, in the verb or, in the second case, in the noun. Such is the simple but glaring logical mis-step that has already been made when Lehmann begins his discussion of particular problems with the aim of illustrating the contextual character of Christian ethics.

1. *The bearing of Truth-telling upon truth-telling*

Lehmann opens his discussion of the question of truth-telling by reasserting that "a koinonia *ethic is concerned with relations and functions, not with principles and precepts.*" He reveals his unexamined assumption about "principles," in that this contrast promptly becomes a contrast between *contextual ethics* and *absolutist ethics* (ECC 124). He then further reveals his understanding of "absolutist ethics" by defining an "absolute" as "*a standard of conduct which can be and must be applied to all people in all situations in exactly the same way*" (ECC 125). If that is the meaning of absolutes in ethics, and still further if that is the meaning of principles and precepts, then very few absolutists in ethical theory have measured up to it, and almost no defenders of moral principles have done so. Because of these faulty assumptions, we are forewarned that Lehmann may be quite mistaken when he asserts that an affirmative answer to the question, Is the Christian required to tell the truth? can only be "based upon a conception or standard of truth which is foreign to the focus and foundations of a Christian ethic" (ECC 125). That will have to be proved—negatively by showing that truth-telling as a principle is foreign, and positively by a full exploration of the bearing, if any, of a Christian's Truth-telling upon his truth-telling.

Lehmann, of course, has no difficulty in disposing of the farcical situations in the stage-play *Nothing but the Truth* and in rejecting the pure formalism of Kant's essay *On the Supposed Right to Tell a Lie from Altruistic Motives.* He might have been led toward a sounder ethical analysis if he had taken up more seriously the position of the man Kant was trying to refute. That author believed that while it is generally a duty to tell the truth, this only applies to someone who has a right to it. Thus, he placed an *extrinsic* limitation upon the duty of truth-telling; he allowed that there were exceptions to this rule. A consideration of this viewpoint might have opened up an entire body of traditional teachings upon this subject which goes further than Kant's opponent and defines the *intrinsic* meaning of the truth in question by reference to those to whom it is due, and defines the forbidden lie as any denial of the truth (in the sense of verbal accuracy) to someone to whom the truth is due. This would have disclosed that there are very many great moral thinkers who affirm a principle of truth-telling but who are not "absolutist" in Lehmann's restricted—I might even say, abstract, absolutist, and non-contexual—meaning of that word.

Instead of asking after the meaning of truth-telling in the light of Truth-telling, or in the light of some other ethical reality, Lehmann tries "to get at it this way: Suppose a man has a car which he wants to sell." *Then* and only then does he ask "situationally," "What does it mean to tell the truth?" (ECC 128). From no number of suppositions about men who have cars to sell, or from other supposed situations of the same order, will an answer to the question of the meaning of telling the truth *arise.* Such "cases" help to clarify the meaning in application of telling the truth to someone to whom the truth is due. They may even make it plain that there are exceptions and that there is a problem of compromise, when, for example, one must withhold or deny the truth to someone to whom it is rightfully due under ordinary circumstances, for the sake of an unusual and overriding obligation (in the case of a man who has only one car to sell, no other way of securing funds and who must pay at once for his wife's emergency operation—her *burial*, Lehmann says!). So has Christian ethics in almost all ages "justified" theft under certain circumstances (since the right of property is not the absolute, but only charity), or assassination or war (since life is not the absolute).

Lehmann, however, begins and stays with "the exception" which then is, of course, no exception in any reasonable meaning of the term. Specializing in the exceptional (which is, when you think about it, a quite self-contradictory vocation), he has only rules which were never rules, principles which were never principles, and a meaning for truth-telling which was never the meaning of the truth to be told in ordinary transactions. This lands him in some extraordinarily naïve arguments. For example, who (since it was not Kant or Fichte or even that playful farce) ever defined truth-telling as *"optimum verbal veracity"* in such a fashion that it is pertinent even to mention the fact that "he might have forgotten something" about the car he is trying to sell?[26] This is not a trivial point to bring up, because Lehmann

[26] p. 129. Note that my question is: Who ever defined truth-telling as "optimum verbal veracity" *in such a fashion that it is pertinent even to mention the fact*, etc.? The italicized words are crucial; and Mr. Lehmann omitted and took no account of these words, which are crucial, in his reply ("Critic's Corner," *Theology Today*, April 1965) to this portion of the present essay (*Theology Today*, January 1965, pp. 466–75). The whole of ethics prior to Lehmann—so far as this literature has come to my attention—establishes a significant *relation* between personal integrity and verbal integrity, and from the former it articulates the latter requirement. *This* is the issue, if Lehmann will let it be joined. The issue is whether Truth-telling has any bearing on truth-telling; and, if so, what is entailed in Christ for our knowledge *into ethics* and for truth-telling in ordinary transactions. The issue is whether Lehmann did not first *attribute* to normative ethics the absurdity of defining truth-telling as verbal veracity *alone*; and then was himself propelled to a like absurdity, namely, defining truth-telling as personal integrity and openness *alone*. Heretofore it has been understood that there is an important connection between the integrities, i.e. between authentic interpersonal response and the correspondence of human speech with the mind's apprehension of (small letter) truths. It is not possible to avoid the normative requirement of (small letter) truth-telling without soaring with some assertedly "ethical" reality above life's situations.

places right after this supposed refutation of truth-telling as optimum verbal veracity a supposed refutation of one of "the most ingenious and tested and tried attempts to bring an absolutist ethic into line with the actual diversity and complexity of the ethical situation," namely the distinction between the *intention* and the *action* done, with greater importance assigned to the *intention* to do or say the right thing (ECC 128-29). But truth-telling is neither verbal veracity alone nor the intention alone, if it means actually communicating the truth (and, of course, intending to do so) to someone to whom the truth in question belongs.

This does mean, of course, that, in the words of Bonhoeffer, "telling the truth must be learned" and an "increasingly accurate knowledge of the situation is a necessary element of ethical action" (ECC 129). Knowledge of the situation may be a necessary element, even an indispensable one, if one is to learn to tell the truth. A knowledge of the truth to be told may, indeed, only "arise with" increased knowledge of the situation. From the situation I may also learn more about the range and depth of the truth-claims upon me. But truth-telling as a claim upon me does not "arise from" the situation; and *a fortiori* it does not arise from the variables in situations.

To tell the truth means, Lehmann says in Bonhoeffer's phrase, to speak "the right word" or better "the living word" (ECC 129). But what first and fundamentally gives meaning to the "right" and "living" word to be spoken is Lehmann's secular theory of contextualism. (Such it must be called, despite the author's disavowal.) In place of optimum verbal veracity, or a correspondence between thought and word, he puts situational coherence as the meaning of truth-telling. "What is *ethical* about the existing, concrete situation is that which holds it together"; and what holds the situation together, in turn, are words that make it "possible for human beings to be open *for* one another and *to* one another" (ECC 130). This is the meaning of the right and living word.

Of course, it is important to stress that "to communicate" does not mean idle talk, nor does the integrity of human communication consist solely in a correspondence between one's thought and one's words. Moreover, an aspect of integrity in communication, and perhaps the controlling dimension of it, is being "in an actual relationship with somebody in which you give yourself to him and he gives himself to you" (ECC 64). To tell the truth requires, it would seem, both a certain correspondence and integrity between thought and speech and a co-respondence and integrity between the speaker and other persons. Having defined an ethic of principle in this matter to mean verbal veracity alone, Lehmann proceeds to make the opposite mistake of defining truth-telling as personal co-respondence and openness alone.

This only states the problem of truth-telling, not an answer to it. The problem is whether to communicate with my neighbor, and in this sense to be true to him, I must tell him the truth in the sense that my words will need to match my thoughts and the facts. Lehmann is simply too obsessed with the exceptional case, in which in order to be true to my neighbor it may be that my words should not correspond exactly with my thoughts. There remains for him not even a derivative connection between co-respondence with or openness to the other person and correspondence between thought and speech, which surrounds and even makes logically and actually possible the exceptional case. In contrast, the well-established analysis of the problem of truth-telling in terms of telling the truth (verbal veracity) to persons to whom the truth is due has at least this to commend it: that the *ethical* problem or the problem of veracity in both senses and the bearing of the one upon the other has been directly addressed. It is simply too easy to dismiss "absolutism" and establish contextualism by ignoring this analysis of the meaning of telling the truth.

In passing, it may also be asked whence Lehmann gets the idea that whatever "holds the situation together" and makes it possible for persons to be open for one another and to one another is *right* or *living* in word or in fact. Suppose I don't want to hold things together, or don't want to be open, and would rather live otherwise. It is not obvious that I should do so. There can be no answer to this question that is not *normative* (theological or otherwise); nor can there be an answer to this question that does not open a gap between the actual concrete context and what the context *should* be. Ethics cannot be born out of any concrete "whole" without the moral requirement or claim of "wholeness." Nor, for that matter, does the *indicative* theological statement, "God forgives," imply the injunction, "Forgive one another" without the intervention of a *normative* statement in theological ethics, "Men *should* deal with one another as God deals with them" (cf. ECC 239). Neither in a secular context nor in a Christian context is it possible to formulate the ethical question as, What *am* I to do? Any ethics, in any context, must ask, What *ought* I to do?

Lehmann fails to explore the ultimate requirement of openness of human beings for one another and to one another in its implications for truth-telling with a small "t." If buyer and seller discover each other as human beings, "whether much or little is told about the car, *whatever is told is the truth*" (ECC 130, italics added). They "do not merely transact business." In fact it is difficult to see that they are transacting *business* at all. The transaction in which they are engaged is an ultimate one; it is interhuman communication, and in this they are true to one another.

The first thing to be said about this is that if the seller succeeds in withholding some "truth" about the car he must also try to hide the truth about his own human "predicament" which drove him to it; and it is hard to see how he is going to disclose or communicate himself to the other, or be open to the other, if he really succeeds in his dissimulation (which is the meaning of an effective withholding of the truth). Thus, integrity of speech and correspondence between word and thought would seem to be entailed in integrity of co-respondence between man and man, no matter how much more important the latter is than the former.

The second thing to be said is that such a radical shifting of the problem from truth-telling in "mere business" transactions to telling forth the truth in interpersonal openness comes as close to Lehmann's definition of an "absolute" as any principle that has ever been formulated preceptually. His language, of course, sounds thoroughly relevant, contextual, nay, even relativistic: "in all these relationships the truth in the words varies" (ECC 130). But what is the "truth" which is being communicated, what is this openness *for* and *to* one another, if it is not a standard for conduct which invariably can be and must be applied to all people and to every situation? This is the Truth that can and may and must be told unconditionally. No matter what is said in ordinary transactions, whether much or little is told about the car, whether speech is or is not an accurate reflection of the mind's apprehension of the facts about the little transactions of daily life, the fundamental thing can still be exhibited and "whatever is told is the truth." That last word should have been capitalized or the article italicized, to indicate the contextualist's absolute. This is abstracted from any *important* relevance to authenticity in spoken words or degrees of verbal integrity. Because Truth-telling is relevant to all it may find embodiment in many or in any ways. This is a statement of the problem of (small letter) truth-telling in human communication, no answer to it. If this is the meaning of the *koinonia* as a "laboratory of the living word" (ECC 131), there may be in it some or even rich *nourishment* for the seeds of truth, but little ethical clarification of its meaning.

Lehmann gives one instance of contextualism *in a Christian context* to illustrate a Christian's truth-telling. This was the case of the devout woman "who had come to be virtually a second mother" to the author, and who asked him in her extreme pain and terminal illness, "What do the doctors say? Is there anything to be done?" (ECC 132).

Now, there's a question to deal with, and with which to test the adequacy of one's theory! In dealing with the poignant problem posed for him by his friend, Lehmann comes closest to dealing with the real moral issue, and yet his analysis drives him to a place most removed from it. He says rightly that "the point at issue here is not the celebrated ethical problem of the right of the patient to the truth" (ECC 132). That was a reference to Joseph Fletcher's inter-personalistic—one might even say contextual—treatment of the problem of (small letter) truth-telling in his *Morals and Medicine*.[27] This would have been a far, far

[27] Princeton, N.J., 1954.

better position than Kant's for Lehmann to break his lances against, if he wanted to demonstrate that all the Christian knows to do is to "wade in and wade through" since that is what the God of the Bible who "places little importance upon human consistency" (or, it would seem, upon His own as well) is doing "to get His purposes accomplished" (ECC 133).

But Lehmann is quite correct when he says that the problem of (small letter) truth-telling is *not* (only) the patient's right to the truth. It is *not* interpersonal co-respondence. It is *not* one's openness to and for others, and of others to and for him. The point at issue is rather *"what,"* because of all this, *"is the truth to which the patient has a right"* (ECC 132–33, italics added).

Thus the decisive question was raised of the bearing of personal co-respondence upon correspondence between speech and thought about the final finite transaction of a person's dying. Now, there are far profounder sorts of veracity than verbal ones. It may be that Lehmann answered his friend's actual question but did not do so verbally. It may be that by tone or gesture or countenance he communicated that little truth she wanted to know. It may be that he knew that she knew he had done so; or that he knew she already knew her little truth.

But, except for these possibilities, it must be recorded to my great astonishment that Lehmann *writes* that he avoided her question and *changed the subject.* He said, ". . . when in the next days and weeks the going gets hard, remember you are not alone! Jesus Christ . . ." (ECC 133). Thus, he brought up the Truth when the truth was asked. He spoke of the "truth situation" all Christians know they are in, of the ultimates of the Christian context. Certainly not with the same intentionality as Pilate who, hard pressed as he was with the burdens of wading through, turned from the small question about justice and truth in his official acts to open the great question, "What is the Truth?" To Pilate's question Lehmann had a positive answer, and of this he spoke quietly with his friend. That was, of course, the most important thing to speak of in that hour, or at any hour! However, on the supposition that Lehmann left her little question unanswered (and did not answer it non-verbally) as he turned to the most important matter, it would seem that he (if he was the one to tell her) withheld the truth from someone to whom that truth belonged—that little truth as well as Christ the Truth. That *respect*, that truth, he still owed her in her mortality; and he ought not to have treated her dying as something to which she was merely *patient*, something to be passed over. She was the (small letter) *subject* of that dying and the honor owed her, in this regard also, ought not to have been avoided in their common devotion to *the* Subject of all Christian living and dying.

Nothing of present moment depends upon the correctness of this opinion of mine concerning the bearing of Truth-telling upon truth-telling. The point is that Lehmann has not undertaken to tell us what he thinks concerning this question, unless changing the subject is his answer to it. Therefore Truth-telling goes on above the situations—the hospital rooms, courts, and market-places—in which (small letter) truths must be told, and it has no stated or proven relevance to them. One wonders whether that justice and truth was so "non-preceptual" which the Hebrew prophets urged should be done "in the gate" and throughout all the relations among men.[28]

2. *Koinonia and porneia*[29]

Again we are placed on notice by Professor Lehmann that the "ethical meaning and guidance" provided for sexual behavior when it is set within the "liberating and humanizing context" of the *koinonia* cannot be fully set forth in a volume on the "methodology" of Christian ethics, but "belongs properly to the substance or content of Christian ethics"—to follow (ECC 139). Still sexual ethics, not itself random, seems to be more than a "random instance of contextual behavior" (ECC 132); and what is said on this subject in the present volume does not fail to

[28] The foregoing paragraphs, comprising sub-section 1. of this Chapter, were first published in *Theology Today*, January 1965.

[29] I use this sub-section title just for the fun of it. It is evident that *porneia* has already been ruled out. (See John A. T. Robinson, *Christian Morals Today*, p. 32, for a discussion of the meaning of this term.) My title should, however, draw attention to the fact and make it evident that an act-*koinonia* ethics establishes itself as an ethic without principles or rules or virtues by omitting to begin at the beginning with the precepts it certifies.

enter upon the substance and the content of Christian ethics which, in Lehmann's opinion, properly follows from adopting his methodology.

Lehmann's remarks about sex ethics are laudably motivated by the aim of avoiding a morality of venereal fears and tabus or a morality of venereal frivolity. He wants to avoid libidinal sexual repression without falling into the encouragement of enlightened libidinal indulgence with their distortions of the human spirit (ECC 136). In fact in this connection Lehmann makes what is for him a remarkably preceptual statement, nay, even a proscriptive statement, to the effect that in a Christian context promiscuous sexual acts (and not only prostitution) "simply have no place. They are *ab initio* sexual deviations" (ECC 138). From this not insignificant beginning, a fuller articulation of Christian sex ethics might be expected. This will be forthcoming provided the author sets some of his other thoughts in order, and if in particular he follows out the methodological consequences of the fact that he has just allowed that from *the ethical* in a wholly non-preceptual sense, from an ethics of "freedom in obedience," unqualified ethical imperatives, even if secondary ones, can somehow be derived. I shall not inquire into the consistency between the judgment that promiscuity, which is all over the place, has no place and the declaration that a Christian ethics can be written which permits no gap to open up between the ethical claim and the ethical act.

The important thing to note about Lehmann's treatment of sex ethics, however, is the fact that he accepts the most egregious error thoughtlessly propounded by the modern world "come of age" concerning the traditional Christian teachings in regard to marriage. He identifies the traditional theology of marriage with a theology of the marriage *ceremony*. In all but one instance of his use of the word "marriage," it means the ceremony or the legalities in the sphere of church or state. It must be said that *that* was never the church's teaching about sex and marriage, at least never before the bourgeois period (and not rightly even then). The bourgeois period did develop an ethics of social respectability as its highest norm for the sexual relation, along with its notion of absolute property right, which in turn helped to corrupt the traditional meaning of the marriage covenant to mean placing on record an exchange of absolute and exclusive rights of sexual dominion. Against this the present age has rebelled with its notion of marriage as "contract."[30] In any case, a bourgeois theology of the marriage ceremony shapes Lehmann's understanding of the traditional teaching. It also shapes, and misshapes, his understanding of a sex ethics of "freedom in obedience" which will set sexual behavior in "a liberating and humanizing context," not simply in the context of the ceremony (which Lehmann mistakenly calls "marriage").

The tradition of Christian ethics, Lehmann writes, "regarded marriage as the legitimization of the sexual act." It "exalted marriage as the norm of sexual permissiveness." It enforced "the marriage criterion," and insisted on "conformity" (ECC 136).

In contrast, Lehmann wants "the sexual act . . . loosed from the marriage criterion." This makes eminent sense if by "marriage" Lehmann means the ceremony. It makes almost none at all if he does not. For the sentence just quoted continues with the proposal that the sexual act be "anchored in the human reality of encounter between male and female under conditions of trust and fulfillment which such an encounter both nourishes and presupposes" (ECC 137). Take away the occasionalism that creeps in through the word "encounter" (and which has already been proscribed by the precept against promiscuity) and, of course, take away the assumption that what God is characteristically doing in the world to effectuate His purposes for the humanization of men and women is to act literally by the "moment," "day," or "year" in which they should follow Him. Take away that, I say, and Lehmann's statement comes close to affirming what the church has always meant by marriage.

In this interpretation of Lehmann, I confess that I have imposed a meaning upon the word "marriage" as he uses it, which remains obscure. It is, however, the least pejorative interpretation, since the alternative to assigning a legal and ceremonial meaning to "marriage" is to say that he has simply

---

[30] See my article "Marriage Law and Biblical Covenant," in *Religion and the Public Order,* ed. by D. Giannella (Chicago, Ill., 1964), pp. 41–77.

begged the question about (in lieu of a ceremony) what ought to be the meaning of that "openness" and consent to the being of one's partner, that "trust" and (*marital?*) "belonging" which in a Christian context should precede or accompany the sex act for this to be a fully responsible act.

The meaning of this is what should be articulated and debated among theological ethicists today in living dialogue with all that was ever said by the tradition about marriage and its perdurance as an ordinance made for man. Instead, Lehmann joins the present age in its feckless debate with a bourgeois theology of the marriage ceremony now no longer effectual among us, and which was never the church's meaning when it understood covenant-consent and covenant-responsibility to be the humanizing context of the sex act.

Lehmann struggles to free himself from such a degraded legalistic notion of marriage. His first formulation is: "*It is not marriage which legitimizes the sexual act but the sexual act which legitimizes marriage.*" But the word "legitimizes" (rightly connected as it is with the legalistic meaning of "marriage" in the first part of that sentence) does not seem to him quite apt for what he wants to affirm in the latter part. So he tries again, and writes: "*It is not marriage which fulfills the sexual act but the sexual act which fulfills marriage*" (ECC 137). Here is perhaps one instance in which the word "marriage" takes on more than ceremonial or legalistic meaning: he says *marriage,* and not simply the trusting sex act; and, in the sequence and connection exhibited in the assertion, it is "the sexual act which fulfills marriage." So always said the tradition. What does Lehmann think consummation means?

But Lehmann is not yet quite free in his apprehension of marriage as a relationship that is before and deeper than any ceremony and therefore fit to be before the sex act as its humanizing context which is then "fulfilled" by the conjugal act. The limitation of this formulation is most evident in what it leads Lehmann, in the first part of the statement, to attribute to the tradition in order to make it fit for rejection. No instructed Christian theologian of the past would have said that "marriage fulfills the sexual act," since this would mean that marriage is

87

made by copulation and comes only as its completion (which rather seems to be the modern view). The tradition would no more have said that "marriage fulfills the sexual act"—in any sense of the word "fulfills"—than Lehmann can feel comfortable about saying in his first attempted reversal, that it is the sexual act which legitimizes marriage.

In any case, to speak of "a complete and transforming partnership which can be neither complete nor transforming apart from what can be finely called "the communion of the body" (ECC 137) is not the radical reversal of traditional teachings *in regard to the marriage relation* which Lehmann imagines it to be, though it does suggest a radical improvement of ancient views about sexuality as among the "goods" of marriage.

Of course, Lehmann's approximation to the traditional understanding of the marriage relation is deficient. This is a fruit of his ceaseless polemic against an understanding of marriage that tradition never meant. This prevents him from making a significant contribution to a further understanding of this subject even by way of important corrections of the understanding of *marriage* which prevailed in former ages.

Instead, Lehmann, having approached the borders of "a complete and transforming partnership," does not continue with an exploration of that, but instead falls back into accenting (against marriage believed to be among the legalities) the fact that "such an ethic can offer no sexual guidance according to a blue print to apply to all sexual behavior in the same way" (ECC 137). He boldly includes "the sexual act among the risks of free obedience" (ECC 138), which of course it is. But that tells us little about the Christian meaning of free obedience, or obedient freedom, or the implications of this for marriage. Lehmann, however, "hopes" that his "axiom of reversal" (which we have seen to be no reversal) will lead "toward a heightening rather than a weakening of the integrity of the sexual relation and of fidelity in marriage" (ECC 139).

Thus he wants to have his Christian fidelity and also wants to play to the ear of the groundlings of the present age. Each of these concerns brunts the other. He wants "sexual intensity . . . creatively related to sexual sensitivity" without coming clear about what that means or to what it should lead. Or again, he writes about sexual experience "intrinsic to human wholeness in and through human belonging," and then immediately precludes an openminded exploration of what "belonging" may and can and should mean, by adding: "whether the sexual act occurs within the marriage relationship or on the way toward marriage" (ECC 138). Apparently these are equal alternatives for the free, sensitive, and obedient human heart; and that, of course, is *the* ethical question to which Lehmann presupposes an answer, or undertakes to give none. The tradition was much wiser in its ability to take into account sexual acts on the way to marriage without making a "principle" of it.

Moreover, Lehmann must simply be informed that it is later than he thinks in the social history of contextualism, and therefore too late for Christian contextualism to imagine that it is saying anything important by speaking of "sexual acts on the way to marriage" in either a bourgeois or a Christian sense, with no attempt to explicate the full Christian meaning of marriage which sexual behavior is supposed to be on its way toward. It is too late for this Christian contextualism because it is necessarily dependent upon the structural concepts to be supplied by and articulated in a Christian *ethos* and upon the silent assumptions of an age which gave Christian meaning to such words as "belonging," or to "wholeness" or integrity in marriage. The ethos and the assumptions are no longer there to place sexual behavior upon any particular route. The relevant sounding words about relating "the sexual act to human belonging" and "human belonging to marriage" actually are today suspended in mid-air. In this book, they express a *program* not seriously undertaken.

We are forced to conclude that Christian contextualism does not develop a positive account of norms because it secretly depends on them, and expects a Christian *ethos* to supply a moral context which it no longer is there to give. Lehmann's contextualism is decades too late.

For Lehmann to undertake to *set* sexual acts on the way to *marriage* (in any other sense than the arrangement, alongside "responsible" love, for breeding and educating children to which the current "sexual revolution" has reduced it while ignorantly

89

accusing the tradition of exactly that) will bring him into productive dialogue with traditional Christian teachings and into conflict with the present age with, in particular, its misunderstanding of that tradition. It will also bring him in touch with more elements and ethical implications of *the Christian context* than the single reference in which he places the "encounter" between a man and a woman into "encounter with him who reigns in forgiveness and renewal over human failure and defeat" (ECC 139). It will bring him into touch also with Ephesians 5 which determines and nourishes the Christian ethical (not necessarily sacramental) meaning of marriage by reference to Christ's inseverable love for the church as criterion. This is "the marriage criterion." This precludes specializing in the exception, to which the divine forgiveness and renewal after human failure are most directly pertinent when these are left standing alone. In fact, without other Christian teachings in regard to marriage, the word "failure" has no meaning given it by reference to Christ, and there remain only sexual acts along many ways in quest of wholeness.

3. *The justifiedness of Christian participation in war*

Here pacifism is the "absolutist" position Lehmann takes as the foil to show that a prescriptive approach is not "really consonant with a Christian ethic." There was, of course, a gap between the pacifist ethical claim and acts of war; and in the midst of war a turmoil, perhaps an unnecessary turmoil, was brought about in the consciences of Christian pacifists because of a "conflict between what they believed to be Christian teaching and what they found themselves unable to avoid" (ECC 140). But this introduction to the problem has to be set entirely aside as not necessarily pointing to the virtues of a contextual ethic. It may only be that "what they believed to be Christian teaching" was in error.

It is in connection with the morality of Christian participation in war, however, that Lehmann waxes most contextual and utters most brilliantly his theological absolutes in asserted relevance to an ethical problem. It is here that he asserts that "there is never any one way as against all others for dealing with any human situation," and here he brings in God's imagination. Here again he reiterates that *koinonia* ethics is "never a matter of having really done *the good*" (italics added); it is rather a matter of having really "been on the track of God's doing." I should not have said "really," for getting on the track of God's doing is as difficult as doing the good. So we must say it is never a matter of "having really" done either. *Koinonia* life in time of war (or peace) is "bracketed by the dynamics of God's political activity on the one hand and God's forgiveness on the other" (ECC 141).

All this is theology and I will not presume to assess whether it is a good or sufficient statement of Christian theology. But it is not ethics, even if these are wholly valid perspectives and however much they may have *indirectly* to do with ethics. The moral response required and made possible in wartime by this understanding of the Christian context is simply "taking in trust the risk of trust" (ECC 141). But that is not ethics either, however much more ultimate and important it may be. It is rather a religious attitude appropriate to all our works, from which of course important consequences may flow for the moral life. To take in trust the risk of trust is relevant to all choices; it has therefore little or no light to shed upon any particular choice or upon the *problem* of *choice* itself. It does not tell us how to get on the track (or do the good), but only sustains our trust and hope that we are, or, if not, God is.

Lehmann next writes, as he must, that "such an ethic" will sound "puzzling, even ridiculous" to anyone who has not the "eyes to see the signs of the times." In face of this appeal to the hiddenness of the *koinonia* behind the eyes of faith and to the hiddenness of "the times," or of the track God is on, behind the choices before us in actual politics, it becomes difficult to remember that a strength of this whole approach to Christian ethics is said to be its relevance. And in face of the gap here that is far greater than any between ethical claim and act, it is impossible even to understand that ethics was said to have now become a *descriptive* discipline and not an imperative one (ECC 14).

Lehmann not only makes this "ridiculous" point. He insists upon it, and proves it by the fact that "even so sophisticated a daily as the *New York Times* could not understand what the theologians were saying in the 1950 report on *The Christian Conscience and Weapons of Mass Destruction.* What the theologians communicated to journalists and other intelligent people in the actual world of political choices was clear enough,[31] but what, according to Lehmann, the journalists should have received and what the theologians intended to say was utterly ambiguous. No journalist can be expected to understand that, not because of the nature of journalists but because of the nature of ambiguity!

In Lehmann's view, what the Federal Council of Churches document declared was actually an ambiguous "Yes" and "No." It declared that "war is *never* a Christian possibility and on the other hand that war is *always* a possibility which a Christian may not be able ultimately to avoid" (ECC 142). Was this double-talk? No, says Lehmann. "A *koinonia* ethic would insist" the FCC "was not engaged in double-talk but in speaking the right or living word" (ECC 142).

This requires explication. It means that "war is ethically ambiguous"—with which no one, I suppose, disagrees. But then the ambiguity is explained to mean that "war *both* contradicts what God is doing in the world to bring about a new humanity and is instrumental to this activity" (ECC 143, italics added). Since Lehmann cannot be making generalizations about war in general, but is thinking contextually (as did the document in question) about a particular action of war under given circumstances, our journalist may be excused from seeing how a particular act of war can at the same time be both contradictory to and instrumental to what God is doing. Perhaps he might dimly apprehend that there is some profound religious meaning in these assertions that is hidden in God's inscrutable rulership, upon which it is significant for human life to be oriented through an acknowledgment that His purposes overarch the whole of man's political decisions and destiny. But the document and Christian ethics and church political pronouncements will seem to him de-

---

[31] The *New York Times* got the point very well indeed, when to the headline "Church Unit Backs Use of Atom Bomb" is added (as any newspaper reader knows to be proper form) the subhead: "Nuclear Attack on U.S. or Allies Made Condition of Sanction" (November 28, 1950).

signed to go to the point of clarifying what a nation or a Christian should do or not do in politics when there are options for choice before us.

Lost in the desert of ambiguity, a man may well yearn for "the irrelevance of ethical absolutism" or else yield to "the expediency of ethical relativism" instead of finding the way to overcome these "dismal alternatives" (ECC 143). A man will want to know what *thrust* to make with his life when he takes "in trust the risk of trust" (ECC 141). Acknowledging that he cannot make his actions *right*, and that their *rightness* depends on their potential instrumentality within God's purposes, he will still want to know, if he can do anything, what can make one decision rather than another somewhat more "*potentially instrumental* to the divine activity in the world." To this question, which is the Christian ethical question, it helps not at all to say that "the freedom of the divine initiative cannot be abrogated by any human decision"; or for a man to be told that it is "a matter of the Christian's *hope*" whether and how far his actions "actually served the purposes of God in fashioning a new humanity" (ECC 144, first italics added). All this is true and profound and important, but it is neither relevant nor expedient nor Christian enough to be all that there is to the living word that needs to be spoken in politics.

While emphasizing that "the ethical originality of Christianity lies in its refusal to ignore or to weaken ambiguity," however, Lehmann does not fail to indicate "the considerations which make such decisions possible" (ECC 144). Insofar as these considerations are references to the ultimate context of all human action, they tell us how uninstructed "decisions in obedience" may be expected and religiously sustained in the midst of ambiguity. Insofar, however, as these are considerations of a Christian *ethical* order, they do provide some direction for choice and action. They tell us something about the *thrust* of trust in politics.

In his discussion of the Federal Council of Churches document, *The Christian Conscience and Weapons of Mass Destruction*, I find two such considerations or thrusts. (1) In support of that document's defense of U.S. responsibility to mount a nuclear deterrent and use, or at least threaten to use, it in response to an attack upon our allies or ourselves, Lehmann writes: "American Christians . . . could not live out their lives in this world in disregard of fellow Christians and fellow human beings in other parts of the world" (ECC 142–43). Lest we forsake our neighbors and leave them defenseless, there could be no "categorical prohibition of the use of nuclear weapons" (ECC 143). This is a love-derived justification of U.S. responsibility for massive deterrence (perhaps for an actual second strike— though Lehmann does not go into being ambiguous about *that*). (2) "*It is plain,*" Lehmann writes, "that the love of neighbor as a principle of action derived from the love of God excludes acts which *initiate* war or lead to war" (ECC 143, italics added).

That is a correct statement, under the first point, of the source and meaning of the justifiedness of Christian responsibility in military decisions. Moreover, if "American Christians could not live out their lives in this world in disregard of fellow Christians and fellow human beings in other parts of the world," it is *not at all plain* that they should make a categorical prohibition of this nation's positive or first use of its power, in interventions or other acts that may *initiate* war. Lehmann says the right thing under the first point, but not enough of critical import about what a Christian should ever do; and he says too much in his second about what a Christian should never do.

Thus, insofar as this *koinonia* ethics does not dwell in ambiguity, the twin implications to be found in it for the guidance of Christian political action in regard to participation in war turn out to be precisely those contained in the American ethos, which came to fill the vacuum. This is the American aggressor-defender doctrine of the "just war," the final product of which was our massive deterrence military policy coupled with an immobilized foreign policy. No considerations are articulated which govern what should be done in defense, no morality of war; and no considerations would seem ever to justify war's start. Prior to war's occasion in unjustified aggression, nothing stirs Christian responsibility so far as the use of force is concerned; after war's start, there are only technical problems to be solved and no moral issues about what should be done in war, or in deterrence.

Lehmann's "Yes" is too unqualified on his first point and his "No" is too emphatic on the second. This happens when the "Yes-No" of ambiguous obedience in faith is unlocked: without further ethical reflection, one has no protection against saying "Yes" or "No" whenever common opinion says "Yes" or "No," and in its manner. Are we called in such wise to take in trust the risk of trust that our decisions and actions may still by God's grace be found potentially instrumental to His activity in the world? The traditional just war doctrine, to which Lehmann has refused to listen, did better than that on both points.

Lehmann repeats the canard[32] that traditional Christian teachings about the "just war" are a peculiar Roman Catholic possession and that its criteria are supposed to entail "precise distinctions" between events and situations in history (ECC 142). Yet in 1961 I tried to demonstrate that in essential respects this theory came to birth in Christian moral reflection because of the pressures of and the refinements required by Christian love-in-action.[33] Insofar as Lehmann articulates considerations that provide minimum guidance for political action, these too are suggestions about the meaning of responsible action in war time that are the requirements of Christian love for neighbor. That is Lehmann's language too. It can be affirmed that the teachings about the just war, in their recurrence in Christian conscience and their continuity through time, were a product of the *agapé* meaning of *koinonia* ethics almost from its beginning until now. This is the oldest *koinonia* ethics on the subject of the justifiedness of Christian participation in the uses of power. A sign of this is the fact that this matter was always discussed by theologians in all ages under the treatise on charity. However much the expression "just war" may be an inadequate one, or even offensive, and however much no Christian today should be rigidly bound by the conclusions of the past, the task is to try to see with the

32 The dictionary I use defines this to mean "an extravagant or absurd report or story set afloat to delude the public."

33 See my *War and the Christian Conscience* (Durham, N.C.,1961), Chap. 3. This chapter examines, in fact, a prime example of rule-agapism in the history of Christian ethics. This book also contains (pp. 141–47) an analysis of *The Christian Conscience and Weapons of Mass Destruction* which may be compared with Lehmann's treatment of the same document.

eyes of faith and love at least as deeply into what is entailed in Christian ethics itself for and into contemporary political realities. This task can only be avoided by setting the just war theory outside the *koinonia* (which, aside from its consequence in denying to ourselves a source for the sensitizing and instruction of our consciences, is simply a gross error in the historical and systematic interpretation of Christian ethics).

Observe what happens when Lehmann makes too fresh a beginning in *koinonia* ethics, or when he does not persevere in the articulation, the questioning and correction of the considerations he begins to set forth. Just as before he substituted Truth-telling for truth-telling, so now he substitutes Reconciliation at the moment of decision in question for the work of graceful reason and love-in-action seeking to determine and do "justice" in actual concrete political choices.

This is the upshot of his discussion of Hiroshima and Nagasaki. Lehmann asks: "What were the ethical considerations involved in the judgment and the action taken *at that time?*" (ECC 241). The *intention* was to end the war and to save lives. If these good intentions and a concern for consequences was all that was involved at that time in the decision, or culpably absent from it, then of course Lehmann is correct in his observation that "the destructive consequences of the use of nuclear weapons could not be limited by the normative judgment in terms of which the decision was taken." He concludes from this: "Here was a conspicuous exception to a conspicuous ethical norm," namely, that "human life is a good which must be safe-guarded rather than destroyed" (ECC 242). Why this was a "conspicuous exception" is not clear, if these terms are an adequate analysis of the decision-making process at the time, since I suppose the risk of trust was taken in trust and with some reasonable calculation that more lives would be saved by dropping the bomb than by fighting on the beaches of Japan. The bombs that fell over these cities were in no sense "exceptions to the logic of ethical generalization" (ECC 242), but cases of it, the generalizations being limited to determining the actions that should be chosen because of their conduciveness to choiceworthy consequences.

In any case, there was more involved in the decision at that time. President Truman said not only "Save the greater number lives," but also "Drop it on a *military* target," i.e. *an open city.* Robert Batchelder has shown that the option of dropping it on a large military installation was *not even considered* as an alternative, just as earlier the destruction of Japan's intricate system of railroads was not considered as a target possibly to be preferred over using our bombers to set fire to Tokyo night after night.[34] The very meaning of *legitimate* military objectives had been completely eroded from the minds of men during the course of the war. *That* was a factor decisive at the time the decision was made, *missing* from it.

Lehmann gives himself this "conspicuous exception" to ethical norms by, first, forgetting that the logic of ethical generalization from the norm of saving rather than destroying human life requires and is not at all contradicted by an act that it is believed will save more while destroying many lives; and, second, by passing over the conspicuous absence *at the time* of ethical norms governing warfare that had been the fruit of the most ancient and widely held *koinonia* ethics of them all, namely, the just war theory. He would have had to go into that, or something like it of the same order of political relevance, in order to speak the truth about or to that situation.

Instead he speaks the Truth. He seeks to find in Hiroshima and Nagasaki evidence for reading the situation *at that time* as a "transvaluational exception" in which "Christianity specializes." He even seems to compare these events, or what God was (*sic*) doing in them, with the man healed on the Sabbath day, the woman taken in adultery, the good Samaritan, and the prodigal son as all vivid instances of "an exception that suspends the rule" and "challenges previously accepted ethical judgments and patterns of behavior and breaks fresh ethical ground" (ECC 243). Actually the ingredient missing from the decision to drop the bombs was any memory of what was implied in precisely these transvaluational exceptions in Jesus' teaching for man's concrete political and military conduct.

Lehmann continues to *assert* that there was "*at that time,* another possibility which is still an ethical option"—and not only

[34] *The Irreversible Decision* (Boston, 1962).

that there was *at that time* ethical ambiguity concerning what to do at Hiroshima (ECC 244). Yet this is plainly retrospective interpretation of what God *was* doing in the world, overruling man's evil, and of course is still doing in the age inaugurated by the first and last use of atomic power as an instrument of war. He finds in the devastation of these cities "signs of God's pressure toward a global implementation of the full humanity of man" and declares their destruction "to that extent ethically significant and defensible" (ECC 244). Now, one can perhaps say that God may do or permit evil that good may come of it. He can certainly say that God overrules the good and evil actions of men so that good comes of it. But one ought not to say that now, at this time, a proper response to what God *is* doing in the world is that we should do evil (or do ambiguity where it is possible to come to greater clarity) in order that He may bring good out of it. Only retrospectively, when reflecting on what we now can see God *was* doing, is it proper to see in such events the ethical significance that from them God has brought forth a new possibility and need for the global implementation of the full humanity of man.

Lehmann actually has no more to say that could have been said or done at that time than U.S. policy said and did. He fills in the gap by reference to the "transvaluation" of all the norms we violated which God *was* doing in the world. True, he *says* that there was another possibility *at that time*: the particular convergences upon that "single moment of decision *could have been* ethically understood and explained as requiring an action which moved the concrete human situation to a new level of freedom, power, and order" (ECC 244). Surely he is here reading a possibility back into that situation. The army among the Japanese services *wanted* to fight on the beaches, and they almost succeeded in assassinating the Emperor when after Hiroshima he unconstitutionally intervened to begin to bring the war to an end. Lehmann cannot possibly be taken seriously to mean as an ethical and political judgment that the bearing of Truth upon truth, of Reconciliation upon political choices, could have produced at that time and in that moment a new political ordering of mankind. Yet this is what he says, in order to make a

Christian contextualism that is devoid of any structural elements of ethical or political reflection (i.e. devoid of any examination of the morality of war itself) seem relevant to the situation. That this was a quite impossible possibility is as much as admitted: "the existing political sovereignties and structures *were incommensurate and unprepared*" for the "bold re-examination of the ethical foundation and use of power" which was "required" (ECC 243, italics added). So what God *is* doing in the world goes on over the heads of men and nations; and from insight into this Christians seem unable to say more about political decisions in wartime than the nations do. The gap here between *the ethical reality* (as Lehmann prefers to call it) and the choices for action open for men is far greater than in any so-called preceptual ethics.

It may be true, of course, that the bold venture required of mankind in the nuclear age cannot be ventured without crossing the boundary from ethics and politics into religion. But as the proposal of an option for the warring nations *at that time* this would have required crossing the boundary again from religion into political miracle. Of course, it is *now* possible to see that what God *was* doing at Hiroshima and still is doing in His politics is to require of mankind a thorough-going revision of the uses and institutions of power. But then this will still mean an application of the *agapé* and *koinonia* ethics enshrined in the principles governing the just uses of power. For the global domestication of force, it can be demonstrated, requires the legalization or institutional ordering of world politics in accord with the principles of the just war theory. That body of teachings only states the bearing of Reconciliation upon reconciliation among men insofar as this requires that the force which must be used to preserve human life and tolerable community be surrounded by specifiable limits upon its exercise. Perhaps mankind will one day make this response to what God is doing in the world. But a Christian ethics which does not know enough to say more than this contextualism about Hiroshima at the time is not apt to prove able to fulfill its responsibility toward the present and future life of mankind by articulating from the interior of its religious insights the ingredients of a political ethic for *this* time, A.H. (after Hiroshima). Thus alone can "reconciliation become a political reality" (ECC 244).

A not insignificant point may be added to the above. Just as Lehmann understands the decision at Hiroshima to be one of inward intention oriented upon the end of saving lives (and not also one misshapen exteriorly by the absence of any limits upon conduct or means), so also he understands Roman Catholic moral theology to be primarily concerned about the intention (and not beyond this also concerned with the shape of actual conduct). This is a principal feature in the traditional Christian morality in regard to the conduct of war that it is important to understand. Lehmann explains a Roman Catholic theologian to mean, in what he wrote about intending the good effect and not the evil effect of an action, that the good effects which are intended justify putting forth the action, not only in the face of foreseeable evil consequences, but also in the face of avoidable evil consequences, and furthermore, it seems, without shaping the actions so as to avoid these consequences if they can be avoided. "If an action ought to have been pursued" because of the good intended, he writes, "even though the evil effects of the action could have been foreseen, and could [*sic*] have been prevented, the action is good and not evil" (ECC 293). The truth is that the word "not" should be inserted in that sentence where my "sic" is. I am ready to believe this a typographical error rather than to believe Lehmann mistaken, except for the fact that the same crucial omission occurs five lines above this one.

Christian love shaped itself for action, and it shaped *action* —and not the intention alone—in surrounding non-combatants with moral immunity from *direct* attack. This does not simply mean from intended attack. The foreseen evil effect that was allowed was always understood to be an *unavoidable* one. No amount of good intention justified doing avoidable evil. Reinhold Niebuhr is in agreement with this celebrated rule of "double effect" when in his "responsibilist" ethic he includes within the meaning of political and military responsibility a course of action which chooses the greater good in the midst of also doing a lesser evil. Only he does not say this so exactly, and his language is different. Niebuhr says "it is responsible," where the

Catholic moralist says "it is permitted," to adopt a course of action which can achieve a greater good (or a lesser evil than the one prevented), even when there are also comparatively lesser evils unavoidably consequent upon this same course of action. Both positions result from Christian love-in-action, and love-shaping-action, on the part of persons who, as Lehmann wrote, "could not live out their lives in this world in disregard of their fellow human beings" even though to live in this world means to be engaged in action that always unavoidably has multiple good and evil consequences (ECC 142–43).

It was pointed out that in his "special ethics" Karl Barth surrounds and locates an "exception" which is then steadfastly preserved in its nature as an exception (or as an instance of application) by its environment in Christian ethical understanding into what God is doing in the world to make and keep human life human. It was also pointed out that Barth's "exception" continues to bear the burden placed upon it by knowledge of the claim God has placed on human life in the matter to which exception is called for in a complete ethics of freedom in obedience. In conclusion, I might point out that a great many (though not all) of Barth's "exceptions" for choice are susceptible of illumination or "solution" in terms of the so-called rule of double effect, which is only an extension of the analysis of right Christian conduct in terms of love-in-action and love-shaping-action (and not only or mainly an application of "natural justice"). Barth's exceptions fall within his discussion of "respect for life," "the protection of life," etc.; and here he finds some very hard choices, some of which involve the conflict of life with life. It was precisely through thinking about such situations that traditional Christian ethics and Roman Catholic moral theology extended the requirements of obedient love in concrete contexts and in the difficult decisions of men to one step beyond the point to which this expressly brought Barth.[35] This is to say, Roman Catholic moral theology would *in principle* surround and locate

[35] See, however, *Church Dogmatics*, III/4, pp. 425 and 427, for points at which Barth's thinking about the service of life in cases of the conflict of life with life is itself forced to distinguish between direct and indirect killing and thus to begin to take the shape of service in accord wth the love-inspired rule of double effect.

the exceptional choice which may be uniquely obedient to God's claim one step removed from where Barth locates this. The forbidden self-destruction and the prohibited murder are *defined* as *direct* killing. *Theoretically*, there may still be cases that fall outside this refinement of how a Christian can and may and must serve life. It would therefore *in principle* be possible to say of exceptions to the *agapé-* and *koinonia*-shaped "rule of double effect"—or to say of decisions that fall outside the guidance that this supplies for conscience—all the great things Barth says about exceptional obedience under the call and permission of God. It is simply that Roman Catholic moral theologians discover no such exceptional cases—in which sovereign charity should prevail in freely determining the good to be done—apart from the principles by which divine charity regulated life in the past thinking of the *koinonia* concerning these matters. In this they are mistaken.

It will indeed be an anomaly if Lehmann's *koinonia* ethics were to become the mind of the Protestant churches in this age, and if our thinking about Christian ethics were to assume a shape much further removed than is Barth's from fruitful dialogue with the Christian ethics done in the Roman Catholic tradition. For this is an era in which it is widely supposed that there is something to be gained from a reexamination of the Protestant tradition and—by doing so and in doing so—from an ecumenical dialogue with Roman Catholicism at the supersonic (and doubtless more important) levels of our respective, yet possibly common, understanding of church, tradition, and theology. Is this to be programmatically ruled out in the realm of ethics?

One might quarrel with Paul Lehmann about whether "the clarification of ethical principles . . . is a *logical* enterprise." One might ask who ever believed that there is a way "*in logic* of closing the gap between the abstract and the concrete" (ECC 152, italics added)? Certainly the "expendable" natural law with its emphasis on the need for practical wisdom never taught any such thing. And one might ask whether the error of the "middle axiom" people was not precisely that they agreed with Lehmann that there should be a way *in logic* of closing the gap between ethical claims and ethical action.

But all that would be of secondary importance, however instructive it might prove to the author. Far more important it is to point out the far, far greater gap in Lehmann's system of ethics between the Christian context and any actual context, bridged as this is by very little ethical clarification; and to call attention to the alternative ways in which this gap must necessarily disguise itself. It is far more important to point out what happens when ethics in a Christian context is defined as "being what it has been given me to be," being and doing "what I am" in the context of "the Truth" (ECC 159), without an enormous amount of solid clarifying Christian ethical reflection about what this means for the direction of action. Without such clarification, Christian contextualism swings high above the social context— or else unsorted-out elements of the secular context are elevated into identification with it. Doing the Truth becomes without more ado the only truth to be done and so the Christian context is really irrelevant to actual behavior—or else something that is going on in the secular context, whether its ideals or its actuality, is absolutized and becomes the Truth. One might venture to predict, for example, what "organic interrelational differentiation" (ECC 66) will produce when that is taken as a clue to what God is doing in the world in the matter of racial integration. Will this not be a highly relevant-sounding instance of postulating "at the same time the free expression of the individual and . . . absolute social cohesion," which J. L. Talmon defined as the nature of all utopianism?[36]

Doubtless "the indicative character of the Christian ethos . . . underlies every ethical imperative." Doubtless this "underlines the provisional character of such imperatives." And doubtless it "ultimately suspends them" (cf. ECC 161) because God is merciful. But to fail to underline the imperatives, to underline their provisional character too heavily, or to presume to suspend them too quickly ourselves, raises no question more certainly than whether there is any light to our feet or any guide along the pathways of life. This in turn raises no question more certainly than whether there is any such thing as Christian ethics, or only religious solace for the absence of it.

[36] *Utopianism and Politics* (London, 1957), p. 13.

V

An Unfinished Agenda

In a recent essay, "Love and Principle in Christian Ethics"[1] Professor William K. Frankena continues to chide the theologians for failing to say clearly what they mean by Christian normative ethics. He believes that "its theological proponents may be selling Christian ethics short by their manner of expounding and defending it."[2] A philosopher, he writes, reading in the literature of Christian ethics, "is bound to be struck, not only by the topics discussed and the claims made, but by the relative absence of careful definition, clear statement, or cogent and rigorous argument, as these are judged by the standards with which he is familiar in his own field (even if he does not himself always conform to them)."[3] Frankena wants to do something toward remedying the situation. He proposes to do this by again indicating positions "that are possible."[4] With a number of wry comments about his own proclivity for multiplying categories and upon the fact that like all mankind he "has sought out many inventions,"[5] he proposes a dozen or more types when you take account of the combinations that are possible.

Thus, this essay contains a fuller delineation of the options

[1] In *Faith and Philosophy*, ed. by Alvin Plantinga (Grand Rapids, Mich., 1964). It will be unfortunate if, because it was published in a *Festschrift*, this essay does not receive the attention it deserves.

[2] p. 204.

[3] p. 203.

[4] p. 204.

[5] p. 219.

in Christian ethical theory than those he began to set forth in his book on *Ethics*, with which I launched the present analysis of doing Christian ethics. Again, I believe that Frankena's types may prove helpful if these are brought into consideration; and, in particular, that a somewhat simplified review of his suggestions may assist us in identifying or projecting an unfinished agenda for Christian normative ethics.[6]

The following, according to Frankena, are the several distinguishable types that are possible or actual.

1. *Pure agapism*

This general position "assigns to the 'law of love' the same position that utilitarianism assigns to the principle of utility; it allows no *basic* ethical principles other than or independent of 'the law of love.' "[7] In order that the point of Frankena's suggestions for the doing of constructive Christian ethics be not blunted, it should be noted that his typology sits loose within the terminology he employs, and would be repeated if a Christian ethicist judges that it is better to use some other root word in place of *agapé*. Someone may object to using love as the "primitive idea" in Christian ethics; or someone may object to calling love a "principle." To them Frankena replies: 'What interests me here is not so much the question whether love or the love-command is itself a rule or principle[8] as the question whether there are *other* rules or principles which do not mention love, what their status is, and how they are related to love (whether this is conceived as a principle or not). . . . Some take faith or commitment to God as the basic virtue or posture of Christian ethics, rather than love, but even then most of what I say will hold with 'faith' or 'commitment to God' substituted where I say 'love.' "[9]

---

[6] In contrast to the analysis of particular moral or social problems, on the one hand, or, on the other, Christian meta-ethics, which searches out the justification of the principle or principles of normative ethics.

[7] p. 208.

[8] Frankena has already specified (p. 206) that, while a distinction between a "rule" and a "principle" may be important in some contexts, he proposes to use these words interchangeably in the present context.

[9] p. 206.

Pure agapism, which allows no *basic* ethical principles other than or independent of love,[10] may take *four* forms:

(*a*) Pure act-agapism. This view holds that "one is to discover or decide what one's right or duty in a particular situation is solely by confronting one's loving will with the facts of that situation . . . ."[11] The facts of other similar situations, or generalizations drawn from such situations, or from previous moments of loving obedience, are simply irrelevant or misleading. This is "circumstance," or "situational," ethics in its purest form. This view, of course, may be formulated without using "*agapé*": it holds that "each moral decision about what to do is to be a direct function of faith, . . . or the experience of God together with a knowledge of the facts of the case, with no other ethical principles coming into the matter."[12]

(*b*) Summary rule-agapism or modified act-agapism. Here I deliberately reverse the sequence of Frankena's two expressions for this position, in order to emphasize and make more prominent its reliance on "summary rules." This view holds that there are rules of conduct. These rules are summaries of past experience, perhaps of past acts of loving obedience; but "it cannot allow that a rule [or principle] may ever be followed in a situation when it seems to conflict with what love dictates in that situation. For, if rules are to be followed only in so far as they are helpful as aids to love, they cannot constrain or constrict love in any way."[13] We have had an example of this position under scrutiny insofar as Robinson modifies his act-agapism to include a considerable concern for "working rules," or insofar as his "working rules" are not intended and cannot be shown to be rules that have general validity. Frankena himself says that perhaps some of the so-called contextualists, or "circumstance" moralists, actually belong in this category; and he cites Joseph Sittler's *The Structure of Christian Ethics* as an example.[14]

(*c*) Pure rule-agapism. This view maintains that "we are always to tell what we are to do in particular situations by referring to a set of rules, and that what rules are to prevail and

[10] p. 208.
[11] p. 211.
[12] p. 205.
[13] p. 212.
[14] Baton Rouge, La., 1958.

be followed is to be determined by seeing what rules (not what acts) best or most fully embody love."[15]

To these three types of pure agapism there should at once be added a fourth classification:

(*d*) Combinations of act-agapism and rule-agapism,[16] or combinations of act-agapism, summary rule-agapism, and rule-agapism. *Vide*, John A. T. Robinson. This final type of pure agapism arises from the fact that act-agapism may be believed to apply in certain kinds of particular cases or situations while rule-agapism applies to other kinds of situations or moral problems.[17] (Someone *might* say, for example, that act-agapism, or its modification as summary rule-agapism, governs private morality, while pure rule-agapism to a very great extent governs public morality or social ethics.) Combinations also arise from the fact that summary rule-agapism may be believed to be the correct interpretation of certain principles of conduct, while pure rule-agapism is required for an adequate understanding of certain other principles.[18] It would seem, in fact, that if a Christian ethicist is going to be a pure agapist he would find this fourth possibility to be the most fruitful one, and most in accord with the freedom of *agapé* both to act through the firmest principles and to act, if need be, without them.

Let us at this point call a halt in our exposition of Frankena's types in order to pose for ourselves, as well as for him, some exceedingly important questions.

In introducing this typology in his book on *Ethics*, Frankena seemed to locate agapism as a possible normative ethical theory between or beyond *teleology* and *deontology*. The reference to act- and rule-utilitarianism (which is the prime example of teleological ethics in the modern period) was only an analogy to aid in the construction of the sub-types. His own view was, it is true, that *agapé* should be identified with "the principle of benevolence, that is, of doing good,"[19] and that meant to reduce agapism

[15] p. 212. Below, I shall object to the primacy given, in this description of Christian moral judgments, to "referring to a set of rules."

[16] p. 214.

[17] Cf. p. 208 for this assertion about utilitarianism.

[18] Cf. p. 221.

[19] *Ethics*, p. 44: to be supplemented (as also utilitarianism must be, according to Frankena) by a principle of distributive justice or equality.

to a form of teleological ethics. That was to take away what was granted in the first place, namely, that Christian ethics may be a third type of normative theory that is neither teleology nor deontology.

In the present essay Frankena seems to me to associate agapism from the beginning even more closely with utilitarianism, with teleological ethics, or with the principle of benevolence (doing good in the sense of ends or consequences)—which, of course, is his own constructive position. This is a debatable point. As the discussion of Christian ethics proceeds it will be necessary, in order to restore the balance, for a possible closer relation with deontological theories to be explored. Analogies for possible sub-types of pure agapism can also be found here: there is an act-deontology, a summary rule-deontology, and a pure rule-deontology, as Frankena points out.[20] If agapism is *not* a third and a distinctive type of normative theory which is neither *teleology* (goal-seeking) nor *deontology* (an ethics of duty), then it seems to me more true to say that it is a type of deontology than to say that it is a type of teleology. *Agapé* defines for the Christian what is right, righteous, obligatory to be done among men; it is not a Christian's definition of the good that better be done and much less is it a definition of the right way to the good. This is a fundamental problem that has hardly begun to be debated among Christian ethicists, since it is generally supposed, without that cogent and rigorous argument for which he calls, that Frankena's opinion about love and the principle of benevolence must be correct.

Eschatology has at least this significance for Christian ethics in all ages: that reliance on producing *teloi*, or on doing good consequences, or on goal-seeking, has been decisively set aside. The meaning of obligation or of right action is not to be derived from any of these ends-in-view in an age that is fast being liquidated. The Christian understanding of righteousness is therefore radically non-teleological. It means ready obedience to the *present* reign of God, the alignment of the human will with the

---

[20] p. 209. It is on this page that Frankena begs the question about the teleological orientation of *agapé* when he brings in deontology in the course of showing that Christian "schemes of morality need not be wholly agapistic."

Divine will that men should live together in covenant-love no matter what the morrow brings, even if it brings nothing. When Christ comes he will ask whether there is any faith and love in the earth, not whether there is any practice of "the principle of benevolence," i.e. doing good.

Of course, after the waning of the Christian expectation of an early end, when the years continued to come without ceasing one after another, this understanding of righteousness took on the character of "doing good" in the sense that the results of any action should be calculated for as far ahead as the mind can see. Maintaining the social order, and reconstructing it, replaced the simpler ideal of giving a cup of cold water as more significant ways to exhibit righteousness. But these are still witnessing actions. They manifest covenant-righteousness, or make this more possible among men. The benefits of these actions, the good they do, is a *service*; it is never a *reliance* in the Christian life. Therefore Christian normative ethics cannot primarily be a type of teleology. It cannot derive its notion of what's right from a notion of what's good, or from goals that are worth seeking. A teleological calculus (no matter how *ideal*) can be included in Christian ethics only in the service of its definition of righteousness, and subordinate to its view of obedient love. Whether this means that Christian ethics is a form of deontology, or is a third type of normative theory that is neither deontology nor teleology, remains unresolved. But the reduction of Christian ethics to teleology is nearly the same thing as abandoning it.

A second set of basic questions that should be raised concerns the nature of the decision in Christian ethics (if choice must be made) between summary rule- and pure rule-agapism.[21] If one takes the latter viewpoint, he must say, for example, "Keeping-promises-always is love-fulfilling." This will be a principle that has general validity even if it is a derived or secondary principle. It is one of those "classes of things" the violation of which Bishop Robinson said, could not conceivably express love. Breaking-promises is wrong however, *for this reason*, that it is never love-fulfilling. Moreover, love itself has entered and will

---

[21] Pure act-agapism seems to be a possibility only because a good many people think the unexamined life is worth living!

continue to enter into the determination of the meaning of the promise-keeping that is enjoined because this will always be love-fulfilling, even as it helps to define the meaning of the prohibited breaches of promise which can never express love.

In contrast, summary rule-agapism will say, "Keeping promises is 'generally' love-fulfilling."[22] The difference, according to Frankena, is that according to pure rule-agapism "we may and sometimes must obey a rule in a particular situation even though the action it calls for is seen not to be what love itself would directly require";[23] while proponents of summary rule-agapism "cannot allow that a rule may ever be followed in a particular situation when following it is known not to have the best possible [or love-fulfilling] consequences in this particular case."[24]

This draws the contrast too sharply, and in a way that would require a Christian to govern his actions if by rules at all by

[22] On p. 212 of this essay, Frankena opposes "Keeping promises is always love-fulfilling" (summary rule) to "Keeping-promises-always is love-fulfilling" (pure rule-agapism). The first formulation does not seem to be correct. If the word "always" means what it says, there is little difference between the first and the second formulation. I correct this and also Frankena's rule for summary rule-utilitarianism ("Keeping promises is always for the greatest general good"). This correction is supported by the line two lines above that utilitarian formulation (on p. 208), where Frankena writes: "it is *always or generally* for the greatest good to act in a certain way in such situations" (italics added); and by the contrast he draws between "Telling the truth is *generally* for the greatest good," and "Our *always* telling the truth is for the greatest good," in his *Ethics*, p. 31.

[23] p. 212.

[24] p. 208. In the text above I criticize Frankena's statement of the pure rule position as a model for a possible form of agapism. In addition to this it may be observed that the pure rule theory, as this is debated among philosophers, has affinity, and perhaps consanguinity, with an argument in utilitarianism that not only set up "the general happiness" as the criterion but also presupposed a "general subject" to will it according to the rules of utility. "We have not only all the proof which the case admits of," wrote J. S. Mill (*Utilitarianism*, Chap. 4), "but all which it is possible to require, that happiness is a good: that each person's happiness is a good to that person, and the general happiness, therefore, a good to the aggregate of persons." I am not now concerned with Mill's error in supposing that good=desired=desirable, but with the two tracks along which desire runs: (1) one person—his happiness; (2) "the aggregate of persons"—the general happiness. On this view there are bound to be rules which embody *the general will's* way of aiming at general happiness which should always be obeyed *by the generality* even though the action these rules call for is seen not to be directly required by the principle of utility in an individual's calculus of *his* happiness. Pure rule-agapism, to the contrary, will be a matter of each person 'doing what love requires or, if you please, each person himself willing generally what love requires, and therefore the rules (if rules there are) will *be* what love requires.

summary rules only, since he should always do what love requires. Perhaps those Christian ethicists who endorse acts or only summary rules have a similar if inarticulate understanding of the nature of pure rule-agapism. To correct Frankena will be to correct them also. It will be to join the issue where it should be joined; and, possibly in some combination of summary and pure rule-agapism, to establish the fact that *pure* agapism may take two possible forms each of which *equally* may be expressions of love in that very decision to be made, i.e. in the novel and exceptional, or in the ruled action to be performed. There may be kinds of situations or kinds of principles in which love implies rules summarizing love's past obedience or experience and there may be situations or principles in which love implies rules that have general validity. The discussion is prejudiced from the very beginning if pure rule-agapism is defined in such fashion that this means that a Christian should obey a rule "even though the action it calls for is seen not to be what love itself would directly require." That would be to do less or something other than love requires.

I cannot speak for the pure rule-utilitarian, or for how philosophers are accustomed to speak about rules. But the Christian does not believe that he lives in a world structured by rules, or that there is a "general subject" of moral agency acting in accord with these rules, or that he should tell what he should do in particular situations (as Frankena seems to suggest) *by referring to a set of rules* and choosing from among them those that are to be followed by seeing what rules best or most fully embody love.[25]

The pure rule-agapist does not follow the rule thus selected even when he knows very well that not to do so would lead to particular actions that embody love better than would other actions that he might have performed.

Pure rule-agapism, if there is such a position in Christian normative ethics, proceeds rather the other way around. It begins with persons and then devolves or discerns the rules. And yet, I believe, it can and may and must arrive at more than summary rules. There is such a thing as pure rule-agapism, and this covers

25 Cf. p. 212.

a good part of the moral decisions and problems in the midst of which the Christian life must find its direction. The Christian— and this includes the pure rule-agapist—starts with people and not rules. He starts with the multiple claims and needs of his neighbors for whom Christ died. If then, among the directives in which love manifests its direction and service there are any that are discovered to have general validity, this would precisely mean that when a man omits to act in accord with these rules or principles, or when he acts contrary to them, he would fail to do what love requires in that situation and would act contrary to the requirement of love in that situation. Starting with persons in all the actuality of their concrete beings (but without the blinkers of momentalism on his eyes), a Christian with unswerving compassion asks: What does love require? It is indifferent whether this leads to particular acts and summary rules only or also to general principles of conduct. If love leads to them, it leads to them. A Christian should still do what love requires.

If it could be shown that to act in accord with one of these love-formed principles of conduct is in a particular situation not what love itself directly requires, then that was not a general principle of conduct but a summary rule only. A Christian, however, will be particularly careful lest for "what love directly requires" he has put "what love (or sentiment) *immediately* requires"; and he foreknows that such unruly behavior may not be what love requires.

This is the only way to *join* the issue between summary rule- and pure rule-agapism; and it is the only way for there to be any collaboration between them in the whole of Christian ethics. The question is simply whether there *are* any general rules or principles or virtues or styles of life that embody love, and if so what these may be. Answers that have been given to this question include the characteristics of love peerlessly set forth in I Corinthians 13 (which are all, so far as I can see, *universal* statements about what *agapé* requires); the qualities called the "fruits," "works," and "gifts" of the Spirit by St. Paul; the qualities called "theological virtues," "infused moral virtues," "gifts," "fruits," and "Beatitudes" in Thomistic ethics; what Christ teaches us concerning the broadest and deepest meaning of justice; the bond of marriage tempered to the meaning and strength indicated in Ephesians 5; order, or the orders, in dialectical relation with justice and with love; truth-telling and promise-keeping; and (as the floor below which love can not and may not and must not fall) those works of sin in the flesh listed in Scripture, the more or less than seven more or less deadly sins, or those "classes of things" like murder, theft, rape, promiscuity, pillage, adultery, and sexual relations that are genuinely and therefore irresponsibly premarital. Some of these things may not be quite general, and there may be more to be added that will always and everywhere form the conscience and the life of the Christian man.[26] But the point to be made in a discussion of the methods of ethics is simply that pure rule-agapism cannot be ruled out once its definition is corrected as I have suggested. To do so, or to accept Frankena's definition (which is that of a legalism that does less than love requires), would be like saying that love cannot will in every situation what in fact it does will to do or to not do. Doubtless what *agapé* requires can always be resolved into what love finds itself required to do, and what is pleasing to love can be resolved into what love ever finds it pleasing to do (if that is proper speaking). But to rule out from this any concern for general principles of conduct (or to say that in following these rules love's concrete requirements are violated) arbitrarily limits the freedom of love in determining the right. It says that "Love, and do as you *then* please" can mean almost anything, *except* that it *cannot* mean that anything will be found to be generally pleasing. Of course, the rule-agapist says that one ought not act wide of the rule *for this reason*, because of the love that is in it and which would be violated by any departure from it. But this for him is only to invoke or fall back upon his most basic theory of normative ethics. This does not make him a situationalist who does not know beforehand this much, or very much else, about the requirements of love. Nor does he expect ever to support action in accord with rules even though they can be "seen" to mean doing in a particular situation less than love requires. *He sees no such thing*, and that is why he is a proponent of pure rule-agapism in some matters.

One final and a related point. This has to do with the

---

[26] I would add the *agapé koinonia* ethics concerning justice in war and in the use of political power generally.

openness of act-agapism, or a situational ethic that is truly based on *agapé* and not upon some other foundation, to the fashioning of rules of conduct. The point to be made is that act-agapism drives on to rule-agapism of some sort, just as we have shown in the above that summary rule-agapism drives on, or is open, to pure rule-agapism as part of the truth to be discerned by the Christian.

At one point Frankena describes pure act-utilitarianism in a way to which we must take strong exception, if this was meant to hold also for its analogue in Christian ethical theory. "One is to tell," Frankena writes, "what is one's right or duty in a particular situation simply by an appeal to the principle of utility, that is, by looking to see what action will produce or probably produce the greatest balance of good over evil, counting all of the consequences which it itself causes or will probably cause and no others, and in particular ignoring the consequences which might be brought about if the same thing were done in similar situations (i.e. if it were made a rule to do that act in such situations)."[27] Because of the limitation that statement (perhaps correctly) places—in its latter portion—upon how a utilitarian should count the consequences, Frankena himself believes that the principle of benevolence, or doing good, has to be supplemented by an independent principle of just distribution, or equality. Certainly a proponent of act-agapism should take exception to any such description of his position in ethics, not because *agapé* is in need of supplement but because it contains in itself the corrective of the individualism of this calculus of doing good. Act-agapism, if it is truly grounded in *agapé*, cannot remain content with restricting its concern to the *direct* consequences of its own single action. I grant that Frankena's statement may be logically quite exact as also a formulation of act-agapism, in excluding consideration of any *explicit* rule that men should act generally as the agapist acts unusually. The statement itself would be difficult for the act-agapist to object to. He would not know, for example, whether to *deny* that he means to ignore the consequences which might be brought about if the same thing were done in similar situations (the *indirect* consequences of his action and example upon the accepted ethic), or

[27] p. 207.

whether to *enlarge* the conception of the consequences of his action that are to be counted to include those indirectly caused or occasioned by his action. But one way or another the Christian will know that an exceptional action of his (which may be the most loving thing to do in all its own *direct* consequences and probable consequences) may still as a side-effect tend to break down the social practice of a rule of behavior which "generally" embodies love, and thus lead in the end and on balance to a totality of less loving actions than if he had not made an exception of himself and his single action (which, however, it cannot be denied, *was* justified in terms of an individualistic act-calculus). This is just to say that even the Christian who thinks of himself as an act-agapist has, or should have, an *implicit* concern for the social consequences that are not in the direct line of his action for the social fabric in which all men must dwell, for the most fellowship-producing general rules of action. Thus does *agapé* in the form of act-agapism drive on and open the way to summary rule-agapism, and the *agapé* at work in summary rules drives on and opens the way, so far as may be, to pure rule-agapism. This for Christian ethics is the meaning of being ready for Jesus Christ to reign over human life and the meaning of being ready to do everything that love requires—everything without a single exception (not even excepting general rules).

At this point it may be pertinent to insert a comment upon the notion of "order," or "the orders," in Christian social ethics. This notion cannot but be puzzling to a philosopher who does ethics in terms that are all exclusively *ethical*, as the notion of "order," or "the orders," seems not to be. Yet (and despite the fact that the notion of "the orders" in any profound system Christian ethics is a complex one containing more than one ingredient) this is also a form of rule-governing love. Christian ethics does not get to the notion of "the orders" exclusively through the concept of justice, as philosophical ethics tends to do. It does not prize order simply for the justice there may be in it; or begin to upset order or withdraw its moral warrant at the point where injustice appears. Order is not only for the sake of justice. Instead, in some measure justice is also for the sake of order, since a social order can only endure so long as men adhere to it or love it for the degree of justice there is in it. They will not sustain order unless there is a tolerable justice. Therefore justice is for the sake of order as well as order for the sake of justice. Order and justice are both "values"; both are rules of love. Order may be a conditional value and justice a higher value; but order is not merely menial in the service of justice. Order is a good in itself, in that the orders provide the fabric in which men may dwell. This means that no Christian, not even an act-agapist, if he is at all sensitive to the concrete requirements of love, should justify a revolution (violent *or non-violent*) in the social order simply or only because a greater justice belongs also among the requirements of love. Habits of upheaval and disobedience to law on one's own determination that it is unjust are not easily slacked. Order and justice are dialectically related rules of love; and a Christian will be alert to the indirect consequences of even those acts of his that are motivated by a loving justice in destroying the accepted ethic, the rules of social due process, the social habit of compliance with law, etc.

I should say that this wisdom was forgotten by a great many of the leaders of Christian opinion and action in the United States during our national ordeal of struggling for greater interracial justice, who substituted for it the categories of a dynamic secular idealism with its resultant utopianism and Manichaeanism (the Negro "revolution," the "white power structure," "the struggle," "direct action," "an unjust law is no law at all") which no Christian should let become primary in his view of social relations. If it is *agapé*, and not something else masquerading under this label, that is at work seeking to discover all that love requires, there will be an inner pressure within acts that seek to be concretely loving also toward order (and not only order so far as it is just) as among the fundamental needs of men. This too will be seen to be among the rules of love that are generally valid. An act that goes wide of this rule because it is "seen" to be the most love-fulfilling thing to do can only seem so. Order is a provision of pure rule-agapism that has general validity; and, within this, obedience to law is certainly a summary rule.

I should say that the exceptional disobedience to law, if it is properly surrounded and located by all that love requires, is to be inversely determined by the possibilities in social due process and in the momentum of the social forces for reforming or changing that law; and that from the beginning of the current civil rights movement in the United States the duty of compliance with law has been vastly underestimated by many of the leaders of Christian opinion and action. People often say that social disorganization is only a symptom of injustice and of the alienation and resentment that results from this. But when society becomes dis-ordered it will not be *only* for lack of justice. This will also be because of a lack of respect for the value of order itself, for the majesty of political rulership as such, and for the service of human life these things perform. And this in turn will be not only because the "worse elements" (the *Lumpenproletariat*) fall below obedience to social due process and the compliance required for social peace and required by a consideration for the unadjudicated and still legal rights of others. It will also, and especially in the modern liberal period, be because the "better elements" aspire too highly (or too narrowly) in taking the sole standard and goal of community life to be "at the same time the free expression of the individual and . . . absolute social cohesion" (which was J. L. Tolman's definition of utopianism).

It is time now for us to get back on Frankena's track.

2. *Mixed agapism*

There may be theologians who regard love as *one* of the principles to be used in the elaboration of Christian ethics, but not as the only basic one. Such a normative theory of ethics Frankena calls "mixed agapism," in contrast to the types of pure agapism that we have so far considered. For views of this second sort there are judgments about right and wrong which are independent of love and of love-derived rules or acts. It is important that mixed agapism not be restricted to theories that combine agapism with natural or rational morality. This type says only that there *are* principles or precepts that are *not* derived from the law of love in any such way as pure agapists believed to be the nature and source of all their principles. There may be non-agapistic norms that are known to us from *revelation* no less than there may be norms that are naturally known.[28] The conclusion that either is also basic within Christian ethics would produce an instance of mixed agapism. Frankena takes C. H. Dodd's *Gospel and Law* to illustrate this; and he is correct if Dodd believes that there are "ethical precepts" in the Gospels which are neither the summary nor the general rules of love but which still govern the Christian life.[29] The conservative Christian ethics written in America by Carl F. H. Henry[30] would be another example. So also would Bonhoeffer's doctrine of the biblical "mandates" (even if one would never gain this impression from the purveyors of Bonhoeffer in the English-speaking world).[31] Thus, theories of divine law as well as theories of Christian natural law may be classified under mixed agapism.

Still, theories of the "Christian natural law" and an ethics of the "orders of creation" are the more usual examples of what Frankena calls mixed agapism. Perhaps an American theologian can say what few Protestant theologians on the continent of Europe can yet say concerning these possibilities; so let me now

[28] p. 216.

[29] p. 223, n. 24. If the Christian ethicist wants to begin at the beginning and with the "given" in Christian ethics, he will have systematically to come to terms with W. D. Davies' *The Setting of the Sermon on the Mount* (Cambridge, Eng., 1964). Taking into account the fact that this admirable study is a historical work and not as such a constructive statement of Christian ethics, the evidence Professor Davies gathers, and the reasonable interpretation he gives, of the foundational New Testament documents comes close to excluding act-agapism from among positions in Christian ethics on the part of anyone who wants to be faithful to the Source and to the sources of our faith. Whether pure rule-agapism receives the more support from this study, or some form of mixed agapism (there being authoritative teachings of the Christ that are not reducible to forms or expressions of love)—this question I will simply place on the agenda.

[30] *Christian Personal Ethics* (Grand Rapids, Mich., 1957).

[31] It is possible, of course, that both Henry and Bonhoeffer are instances of *non*-agapism (or of *derived* agapism), depending on the degree of primacy and independence assigned to love in their systems. For that matter, if love is at all a source of the Christian life for Bonhoeffer, he may be a *mixed* agapist—although, again, no one is apt to gain the impression from the purveyors of Bonhoeffer to the English-speaking world that he actually makes extensive use of a category of the "unnatural" or the "inhumane" in his probing description of man's plight in this world that has come of age. Moreover, the disciples of Bonhoeffer in the United States do not grapple with him in the matter of his "special ethics" (which often contains some quite conservative opinions)—no more than Lehmann deserves to be called a Barthian (or a learner from him) so long as he ignores Barth's doctrines of creation and man and the "special ethics" built on this.

say it. In the discussion of Christian ethical principles of explanation and interpretation, it is high time we returned to a bit of wisdom that is so old the Latins had an axiom for it: *abusus non tollit usum*. Of course, the "German Christians" grossly abused the notion that in part God's will may be immanent within the created order. So also did the divine-right monarchs grossly abuse the notion that God's will is extrinsic and comes from above to impose righteousness upon the world. To correct the one abuse the Confessing Church appealed to the sovereignty of God over the entire creation, and to correct the other abuse Calvinists of the left wing appealed to an immanent justice in support of wars of civil and religious liberty. In any case, *abusus non tollit usum*, and history settles nothing.

Protestant theological ethics will hardly set its house in order until it learns this lesson, and begins to debate issues without prejudice. What, for example, are we to make of the efforts present-day theologians make to avoid at all cost the use of the word "orders" while saying the same thing by means of a different term that should puzzle any reader to tell the difference? Thus, at the outset of his "special ethics," Karl Barth speaks of the "contours" of the event or field of obedience, and of a "formed reference" to the ethical event. The reader has reason to suppose that these are Christologically penetrated orders of creation until Barth disavows this. Or does he? Does he *succeed* in doing so merely by saying so when he writes: "These might very well be called *orders* or *ordinances*. But then there would always be the possibility of misunderstanding them as laws, prescriptions and imperatives. They are *spheres* in which God commands and man is obedient or disobedient. . . ."[32] There where Dietrich Bonhoeffer introduces his discussion of the "mandates of God in the world," which He imposes on all men, we are suddenly warned that something terribly important is at stake in *not* calling these "orders": "We speak of divine mandates rather than of divine orders because the word mandate refers most clearly to a divinely imposed task rather than a determination of being."[33] Who does not know that Emil Brunner's "orders" are divinely imposed tasks rather than determinations of

[32] *Church Dogmatics* III/4, §52, pp. 29-30 (italics added).
[33] *Ethics*, p. 73.

being, that they are orders of God's governance of the world rather than orders of created being apart from the Creator, Governor, Preserver, and Redeemer of the world?

There remain legitimate and important differences among these systems of theological ethics, but these differences are confused and not focused by all this effort to avoid using the word "order" or even "order of creation." The question is not the usefulness or the need for these categories in any full elaboration of Christian ethics. The question to be debated is rather whether the "orders" are to be understood only Christologically (pure agapism) or *also* in some degree by natural reason (mixed agapism). The latter possibility would seem to be entailed in the conviction that when Christ came He came to "His own."

3. *Non-agapism*

Finally Frankena introduces a third generic type. For him to do so may be somewhat inconsistent with his earlier statements that seemed to use the term *agapé* in such a large and loose sense that it was said either that this includes "faith," or "the experience of God," or "God's commands," etc., as primary ethical categories or that an ethics that uses any such primary ethical term in place of *agapé* would be productive of the same typology as the one Frankena elaborates by means of this root word. Still it may be important for us to take note of the fact that Frankena finds in the literature of Christian ethics normative theories which make use of "the imitation of God" or "gratitude to God," etc., to refer to the primary posture of the Christian life and the primary norm to be used in Christian ethical reflection and which seem not to use the term "love" at all, or at all significantly. These views he calls non-agapism.

Some of these views, however, may use the norm of love *derivatively*. For example, A. C. Garnett's normative theory is self-realization, but Christian agapism tells him the way this can and may and must be accomplished. This is an example of *derived agapism* within a non-agapistic normative theory.[34] So also

34 p. 218.

a working or derived agapism may be the way to obey God's commands or imitate Him or show gratitude or do His will.

It may be long past time to call a halt to Frankena's inventions. But since our purpose is the preparation of an agenda for the possible clarification of the tasks and methods of Christian ethics, we ought finally to note a few of Frankena's notations concerning certain celebrated and less than celebrated Christian theologians he has read who are doing ethics today.

Emil Brunner's position, Frankena writes, "seems to me to be quite ambiguous; sometimes it looks like a form of act-agapism, but at others like a form of mixed agapism or even like a species of non-agapism."[35] As for Reinhold Niebuhr, "he appears to me to suggest, in one place or another, almost every one of the positions I have described; whether this spells richness or confusion of mind I shall leave for others to judge."[36] "Paul Ramsey . . . has been attacking such theories [pure act-agapism] lately, but in *Basic Christian Ethics* he appeared to come very close to agreeing with them."[37] "Presumably what Ramsey calls 'in-principled love-ethics' falls under one [of the forms of rule-agapism], but I have not been able to tell which."[38] "I have mentioned Ramsey, but am not clear just what his position is. It seems to be a form of pure agapism—or possibly of derived agapism—but it is not clear just what kind of pure agapism it is and it may even be a kind of impure or mixed agapism."[39]

None of the above mentioned writers ought too readily to reply that Frankena's puzzlement only shows that his typology is too abstract and therefore not suited to the purpose of enabling him the better to see the meaning of Christian ethics.

As for myself, I have already indicated that if one is going to be a proponent of pure agapism, it would seem that some combination [1 (d) above] of act-agapism, summary rule-, and pure rule-agapism will prove the most fruitful procedure and theory to explore in regard to the situations, moral problems,

[35] p. 220.
[36] p. 220.
[37] pp. 211–12.
[38] p. 214.
[39] p. 219.

or principles that may turn out to be corrigible to adequate interpretation by one or another of these procedures within the normative ethic of pure agapism.

It remains for me to say that, on account of the diversity in the practical wisdom that may be needed for the guidance of moral and political action, it seems to me that if a Christian ethicist is going to be so far a pure agapist, and is going to go as far as this will take him in throwing light upon the path of action, still there can be no sufficient reason for him programmatically to exclude the possibility that there may be rules, principles, or precepts whose source is man's natural competence to make moral judgments.[40] An inhabitant of Jerusalem need not rely on messages from Athens, but he should not refuse them: he might even go to see if there are any. This would be mixed agapism—a combination of *agapé* with man's sense of natural justice or injustice which, however, contains an internal asymmetry that I indicate by the expression "love transforming natural justice."[41]

[40] This says nothing about *how* and *why* love leads to principles or *how* and *why* natural moral knowledge arises. These questions come much later on the agenda; and they may fall within meta-ethics, and not at all within normative ethics. For the record, I will only indicate that Frankena (pp. 213–14) makes some interesting remarks upon the question *why* "love is thus constrained to express itself through rules or principles rather than by doing in each case the act which is most loving in that case."

[41] See my *Nine Modern Moralists* (Englewood Cliffs, N.J., 1962) and *Christian Ethics and the Sit-In* (New York, 1961), esp. pp. 124–28. I do not see how Frankena can conclude that my *Basic Christian Ethics* (New York, 1950) exhibited in the whole of it the position of act-agapism. True, that book was concerned to clarify what I regard to be both *primary* and also *distinctive* in Christian ethics. I freely concede that *agapé* itself was so analyzed as to leave standing the assumption that this could itself come to full and faithful expression in acts only, and never in rules also; and that such principles, moral bonds, and structures as there may be would derive from some source secondary to this. But to say that only *agapé* is primary and distinctive does not deny that there may be independent secondary and non-distinctive principles (mixed agapism). That book not only allowed for this possibility in what was said about *"enlightened* disinterestedness," and (as to the source of such enlightenment) in the stated indifference, so far as the primacy of *agapé* is concerned, between whether love finds that there are only social case studies to compile in telling what to do or finds that there are principles of the natural law. It only denied that natural justice is primary or distinctive in Christian ethics, thus putting natural justice, if there are such principles, in the quite secondary position where it may be subject to elevation and transformation by love. The book also made generous use of the principle of generalization in ethics and of the truth to be drawn from idealistic social philosophy in elaborating a Christian social policy.

VI

Two Concepts of General Rules in Christian Ethics[1]

Ten years ago, Professor John Rawls of Harvard University published a crucial and much-discussed article entitled "Two Concepts of Rules."[2] This article has had considerable influence upon philosophical ethics. In fact, it has become something of a classic in its own time. Yet it has had almost no impact on Christian ethics, although its allegations and demonstrations, being quite general ones, apply to the methods of Christian ethics as well as to any other. In particular, the logic of his article goes to the question of how there can be a Christian *social* ethics.

Rawls's undertaking is the repair and defense of utilitarianism in ethics. Since, however, what he says applies as well to other normative ethical theories, I shall state his contentions and argument in terms of the ethics of Christian love.[3]

Summary rules are reports that cases of a certain sort have been found to be most love-fulfilling. They are summaries of

[1] This chapter was originally presented as the Presidential Address at the annual meeting of the American Theological Society in April 1965, and has been revised and reprinted, with permission of the editor, from *Ethics*, Vol. LXXVI, No. 3 (April 1966), pp. 192–207.

[2] *Philosophical Review*, LXIV, No. 1 (January 1955), pp. 3–32.

[3] In what follows I am probably too dependent on Rawls's article. Yet it is necessary to transpose his argument into the terms of Christian ethics by means of extensive paraphrase in order to confront Christian ethicists with a logic of ethics they have too long ignored.

past decisions that have been made by a *direct* application of *agapé* to particular cases. Thus, judgments concerning rules of behavior arise proximately and judgments concerning the right in particular cases arise immediately from the same source: the discernment of what love implies or requires in particular deeds. The decisions made in particular cases are logically prior to the rules.

On this view, each person is in principle always entitled to reconsider the correctness of a rule and to question whether it is proper to follow it in any particular case. This he does by making a fresh application of the general norm of *agapé* to the case in point. The rules of behavior simply describe how in fact persons behave or have behaved when they are activated by *agapé*. A rule is simply a report that they always or usually have acted *as if* they were obeying a rule under which the case falls. One has, in principle, full option to use the guides or to discard them as the situation warrants without one's "moral office" being changed in any way. In this view, there is in fact only one moral office, and this is a universal one. This universal moral office may be defined as doing in every act what love requires. Sometimes this leads to action that falls under the summary rule; it may with equal propriety lead to action that violates the rule.

It may be assumed that Christian ethics, if there is any such view, finds its basis in the righteousness of God, in the *agapé* of Christ. For this position in ethics we have used the term "agapism."[4] Then it is possible to discern how the Christian "way in" to ethics leads by two steps to certain rules of behavior.[5] The first move we have called "act-agapism." When taking this first step we say (and ethicists who get locked-in at this position continue to say) that we are to tell what we should do in a particular situation simply by getting clear about the facts of that situation and then asking what is the loving (or the most loving) thing to do. A serious intention, however, thus to "home in" upon persons and to determine what the righteousness of God requires in regard to them leads to a second move, which

---

[4] If some term other than "*agapé*" is believed to be more fecund in references to the basis of Christian ethics, the issues to be raised still remain the same.

[5] If any other term is believed to be more fitting than "rules," the issues I shall raise still have to be addressed.

we may call "summary rule-agapism." This view holds that there are rules of conduct to which *agapé* leads us, but that these rules are only summaries of experience, records of past acts of loving obedience. There is a shape which the engendered deeds take from the engendering event of Christ; and the contours of the Christian life may be articulated in terms of certain rules, principles, or styles of conduct. Nevertheless, the proponent of summary rule-agapism still believes that *all* (and not only *some* or *many* or *most*) rules or principles threaten to constrain or constrict love. While he uses principles to guide conduct, still he gets himself ready to violate those same principles in situations in which to follow them would conflict with what love dictates in that situation.

In this view, it follows, also, that a society of fully rational and sensitive Christians would be a society without any rules or accepted obligatory practices, in which each and every person applies the insights or requirements of *agapé* directly and smoothly, and without error, case by case. The reason for rules is that we know not every Christian—nor any of us all the time —is able to apply the law of love effortlessly and flawlessly. We need rules to save time, to post a guide, to jog our consciences. At most, summary rules should be called "rules of thumb." They pronounce nothing that a person with an alert conscience instructed by *agapé* would not gather simply from the case in front of him and do on that occasion. As Rawls affirms, it is doubtful that any such notion should be called a rule, or a practice, or an institution: "Arguing as if one regarded rules in this way is a mistake one makes while doing philosophy."[6]

Yet in this view it is possible to have general rules in the sense of "generalizations" which, in advance, one knows there can never be sufficient reason to violate. At this point contemporary philosophers help themselves on the way toward unbreakable rules by two arguments which need to be drawn to the attention of anyone who thinks it proper to compose his account of the Christian life out of acts only plus summary rules also. (1) The first is a contention advanced by G. E. Moore.[7] Given that the summaries of past acts of obedience still lead, by and

6 Rawls, *op. cit.*, p. 23.

7 *Principia Ethica* (Cambridge, Eng., 1929), pp. 162–64.

large, to the correct decision, one has only to estimate that the likelihood of making a mistake by applying *agapé* directly on one's own in particular cases of a given sort is greater than the likelihood of making a mistake by following the rule. Then there would be sufficient reason to urge upon oneself and others the adoption, in cases of this sort, of a general rule governing all particular acts that fall under it. (2) Second, a Christian (who is concerned solely and soberly with an effectual love in particular actions) will know that an exceptional action of his (which may be the most loving thing to do in all its own *direct* and its probable *direct* consequences) may still, because of its side effects, its *indirect* results, tend to break down the social practice of a rule of behavior which "generally" embodies love. This might lead in the end and on balance to a totality of less loving actions than if he had not made an exception of himself and his single deed (which, however, it cannot be denied, may have been justified in terms of a single-track act-calculus). A Christian who thinks of himself as an act-agapist has, or should have, concern for the social consequences that are not in the direct line of his action, for the social fabric in which all men must dwell, for the most fellowship-producing general rules of action.[8]

Thus does *agapé* express itself in particular acts, and then it opens the way to summary rules; and in turn the *agapé* at work in summary rules establishes a beachhead upon the territory of general rules of conduct. In fact, it would be surprising if the Christian life could be held back from rules as generalizations, since the most loving general social practice would seem to be implied in readiness for Jesus Christ to reign over human life, and this would seem to be a part of the meaning of being ready to do everything that love requires—everything without a single exception (not even excepting the most loving general behavior).

1. *Rules from agapé-knowing "the human"*
and the good for men

Still, on this interpretation of general rules as "generalizations" in the sense explained, there is only one "moral office,"

---

[8] See above, pp. 114–15. It is evident that by either or both of these arguments an act-agapist or a summary rule-agapist can, without ceasing to be one, give himself general rules *to obey.*

that is, doing what love requires in each and every decision or deed as this might be determined by a fresh assessment in each case. Therefore, there are no moral offices such as are established by Rawls's second conception of rules.

Before turning to that, however, a question should be raised concerning whether Christian ethics, when it takes this first "way in" upon the needs and care of the persons who are our neighbors and companions in Christ, has any reason to come to rest in a Humean probabilism which holds that all moral principles are at most positivistic or statistical generalizations in the sense explained. According to philosophers like Wilfred Sellars, it is now possible to overcome the bondage of modern thought to Humean empiricism and to the Kantian view that judgments (which are not merely analytic and uninformative) must necessarily be either synthetic a priori judgments or empirical generalizations that are less than universally valid. If in "natural philosophy" it is now possible to say that a proposition may be both a priori (i.e., *universally* true *ex vi terminorum*) and also synthetic (i.e., *true of objective reality*, and not of phenomena only), why should we still be bound to notions of probabilism and statistical generalization in "moral philosophy" or in theological ethics? I should not myself deny that man's natural sense of justice and injustice is able to penetrate to the person and into the meaning of the good for him deeply enough to discern some quite general principles that discriminate between the humane and the inhumane. But even if this were false, surely Christian theologians ought not to dismiss out of hand—rather it is their specific business to explore—the possibility that Christian faith and love affords mankind more than *probable knowledge* into ethics. A position we might call "pure or general rule-agapism" would seem to be entailed in any conviction that in Jesus Christ the righteousness of God and the mystery of the ages, the meaning of the creation, of mature manhood, and the destination of man toward unfailing covenant with God and with fellowman, have been made manifest. An unbinding love would seem the least likely conclusion one would reach if he seriously regarded the freedom of God's love in binding Himself to the world as the model for all covenants between men. Could anyone who perceives that God in total love and total freedom bound

Himself to the world possibly view the implications of this love as unbinding on men? Love seems to have only a dissolving or relativizing power when the *freedom of agapé* is taken to mean love's *inability* to bind itself one way and not another or in no way except in acts that are the immediate response of one person's depth to another's depth.

I have shown earlier that the writings of Bishop J. A. T. Robinson on Christian ethics are a signal demonstration of the fact that, just as *agapé* in deeds drives on to *agapé* in summary rules, so we are driven on from summary rule-agapism to pure or general rules of conduct—provided only that it is the searching claims of *agapé* of which we are speaking and not some sentimental attitude. Here I will say only that if one places Robinson's notion of "working rules" under scrutiny, this can clearly be shown to be a quite inaccurate expression for all that he means. It has to be replaced by a notion of "general rules," even though Robinson insists that things that are "always wrong" are wrong for this reason: "that it is so inconceivable that they could ever be an expression of love."[9] That does not alter the fact that these things (*cruelty* and *rape*) are inherently wrong, wrong in themselves, because of the lovelessness that is *always* in them.

To say otherwise would be rather like a rule-utilitarian who felt bound always to be singing the praises of the principle of utility and who, as a consequence, refuses ever to talk about rules of action except to explain that anything that is wrong is wrong for the reason that it is inconceivable that under any circumstances it could be an expression of utility. Such a man would simply not be getting on with the business of doing utilitarian ethics. Similarly, a proponent of agapism in normative ethical theory may, in the course of doing special ethics and at the point where this has led him to general rules of conduct, invoke his general principle of justification. Again and again in his writings he will tip his hat to the single norm of Christian love or *koinonia*. This logically means nothing, except that it has the apparent and illicit effect of seeming to weaken the rules to which he has been driven when he was seriously engaged in determining all that love implies and all that it requires.

[9] John A. T. Robinson, *Christian Morals Today* (Philadelphia, Pa., 1964), p. 16.

The fact that nothing other than *agapé* makes a thing right or wrong does not mean that nothing is made right or wrong. The fact that there is only one commandment [to love] and that every other injunction depends on it and is an explication or application of it, does not mean that there are no generally valid explications and applications in "special ethics" of that one norm of general ethics. The fact that apart from *agapé* there are no unbreakable rules does not mean that there are no unbreakable rules. Quite the contrary, since the Christian never interprets the moral life apart from *agapé*. There are some things that are as unconditionally wrong as love is unconditionally right. One is driven from "working rules" to general rules by simply observing that if there is anything that is *ab initio* a violation of love, then the view that *agapé* can be best exhibited in acts plus only summary rules can sustain its plausibility only by the device of neglecting to begin *ab initio*. A single exception to act-agapism and to summary rule-agapism would be sufficient to destroy these positions utterly and to establish general rule-agapism in at least some types of action. Not only does the pious reiteration of the premise of Christian ethics establish nothing, it is also apt to disestablish a good deal of past moral wisdom and leave contemporary Christians with an understanding of the Christian life that will not provide a proper posture for the accumulation of any new wisdom. This is the consequence when we forget that the premise of general ethics does not of itself lead to one conclusion only: righteousness in deeds only. It may also lead to summary rules and thence to general rules, if we are not slovenly in ethical reflection.

Still, the "general rules" which we now have under consideration would "arise from" love's penetration to the nature of persons and from experience of at least some sequence of acts of loving obedience and care for them. The mode of justification would be by always justifying the act and finding no possible genuine exception to the rule. These would be general rules sufficiently established, if you will, by "generalization" from an analysis of the requirements of love in particular actions; but these need not be imperfect generalizations, an exception to which is logically possible but simply has not yet occurred.

If, for example, promise-keeping-always is a rule with general validity, it is a general rule whose validity arises, not from any comparison of systems of rules, or social practices, with one another, but secondarily and derivatively from penetration to the moral constitution of persons in their communication with one another. This would be one of those "classes of things" of which Bishop Robinson said that it is so inconceivable they could ever express love that for the Christian they can never be right. Breaking promises would be wrong, however, *for this reason*, that it is never love-fulfilling in a personal sense (and not in the sense of a social practice, which is another "way in" on the problem of general rules of behavior which must be taken up later). Moreover, *agapé* itself has already entered, and it will continue to enter, into the determination of the meaning of the love-fulfilling promise-keeping that is enjoined by this rule, into the determination of the reservations and qualifications any general rule must be taken to include, and into defining those prohibited breaches of promise which can never express love.

It is incorrect to set up the choice between proponents of less than generally valid summary rules in Christian ethics and proponents of general rule-agapism as if the latter must always believe concerning *every* general rule that a person should obey the rule even though the action it calls for is seen not to be what love itself would directly require. This draws the contrast sharply in the case of every rule, and in a way that would require a Christian to govern his actions, if by rules at all, by less than generally valid summary rules only, since he should always do what love requires. This would be to fail to join the issue as it should be joined. It would be to rule out general rule-agapism *ab initio*, by definition and without argument, by arbitrarily debarring *agapé*, in its perception of the need of persons, from reaching conclusions that have general validity for the reason that action in accord with them will always be seen to be the most love-fulfilling.

Prima facie a more humble approach is to be commended. There may be kinds of situations or kinds of principles in which love implies rules that have general validity. The discussion is prejudiced from the very beginning if general rule-agapism is defined in such fashion that a Christian's obedience to rules or principles has only *one* meaning, namely, that a man should act in accord with the rule "even though the action it calls for is seen not to be what love itself would directly require."[10] That would be to do less or something other than love requires in that act. It is the second, and not the first, concept of general rules in Christian ethics that *may* entail or often entails one's doing what love requires *as a social practice* or as a rule of practice even when this may not accord with what love requires in a particular deed.

The Christian does not believe (as his first "way in" upon the problem of social ethics) that he lives in a world populated by rules, or that he should tell what he should do in particular situations *by referring to a set of rules* and choosing from among them those that are to be followed by seeing which rules most fully embody love. The general rule-agapist does not always follow the rule thus selected even when he knows very well that this leads to particular actions that do not embody love as well as would other actions that he might have performed.

General rule-agapism, if there is such a position in Christian ethics, proceeds rather the other way around in its first and always most basic discernment of how Christian conduct should be governed by unbreakable rules. It begins with persons and then devolves or discerns the rules. And yet it can and may and does arrive at more than summary rules that have less than general validity. There is such a thing as general rule-agapism, and this covers a good part of the moral decisions and problems in the midst of which the Christian life must find its direction. The Christian starts with people and not rules. He starts with the

[10] William K. Frankena: "Love and Principle in Christian Ethics," in Alvin Plantinga, ed., *Faith and Philosophy* (Grand Rapids, Mich., 1964). This is also the view of J. D. Mabbott, "Moral Rules," *Proceedings of the British Academy*, XXXIX, (February 1953), p. 107: "When I approve a rule because its general observance would have good consequences, I approve a particular act which falls under the rule even in those cases where the particular act does less good than some alternative open to me." This is, of course, the case with regard to the second concept of general rules—Rawls's rules of practices or Mabbott's rules that are approved *because* their general observance would have good consequences. But this is not the case with regard to general rules (if there are any) that are approved because of some natural-law judgment or *agapé* insight into essential humanity. In such a case, the general rule states what will be found in action to be fulfilling of the human being or of *agapé*. These are rules whose particular and whose general observance will have "good consequences."

multiple claims and needs of his neighbors for whom Christ died. If then, among the directives in which love manifests its direction and service, there are any that are discovered to have general validity, this would mean precisely that when a man omits to act in accord with these rules or principles, or when he acts contrary to them, he would fail to do what love requires in that situation or would act contrary to the requirement of love in that situation. Starting with persons in all the actuality of their concrete beings (but without the blinkers of momentalism or probabilism on his eyes), a Christian with unswerving compassion asks: What does love require? It is indifferent whether this leads to particular acts and summary rules only or also to general principles of conduct. If love leads to them, it leads to them. A Christian should still do what love requires.

If it could be shown that to act in accord with one of these love-formed principles of conduct is in a particular situation not what love itself directly requires, then one way out (corresponding to this first "way in" to general rules) would be to say that *that* was not a general principle of conduct but a less than generally valid summary rule only. A Christian, however, will be particularly careful lest for "what love directly requires" he has put "what love (or sentiment) *immediately* requires and he foreknows that such unruly (or only summary) behavior may not in fact be what love requires. Moreover, he will not neglect a second possible meaning of a rule required by love *as a general practice*.

Nevertheless, this first is the most basic way to *join* the issue between summary rule and pure rule-agapism; and it is the most significant way for there to be any collaboration between them in the whole of Christian ethics. The question is simply whether there *are* any general rules or principles or virtues or styles of life that embody love for fellowman, and if so what these may be.

But the point to be made in discussion of the methods of ethics is simply that, even upon this first approach to the needs of men alone, general rule-agapism cannot be ruled out. To do so, or to define general rules *ab initio* as necessarily and always legalistic, resulting in less than love requires, would be like saying that love cannot will in every situation what in fact it does will to do or not to do. Doubtless what *agapé* requires can always be resolved into what love finds itself required to do, and what is pleasing to love can be resolved into what love ever finds it pleasing to do (if that is proper speaking). But to rule out from this any concern for general principles of conduct (or to say that in following such rules love's concrete requirements must always be violated) arbitrarily limits the freedom of love in determining the right. It says that "Love, and do as you *then* please" can mean almost anything, except that it *cannot* mean that anything will be found to be generally pleasing. Of course, the general rule-agapist says that one ought not act wide of the rule *for this reason*, because of the love that is in it which would be violated by any departure from it. But this for him is only to invoke or fall back upon his most basic theory of normative ethics. This does not make him a situationalist who does not know beforehand certain general principles that are among the requirements of love. And he may never expect to support action in accord with rules even though they can be "seen" to mean doing in a particular situation less than love requires. *He sees no such thing*, and that is why, in the first instance, he is a proponent of general rules in some matters.

2. Rules of practice

There is, however, another move in establishing a place for general rules in Christian ethics. Indeed, I would argue that whether there is such a thing as Christian "social" ethics depends upon whether this second possible justification of general rules has a legitimate place in the enterprise of systematic reflection upon the nature of the Christian life.

Rawls's principal aim (in the article mentioned above) was to call attention to the importance of the distinction between justifying a societal rule and justifying an action, between justifying a *practice* and justifying an action falling under it, between the justification of an institution and the justification of a particular action the institution requires. His secondary undertaking was to explain why this seemingly simple distinction is so often overlooked altogether, and to account for the tendency to fail to appreciate its importance in social ethics. The explanation is that it is widely supposed that there are less-than-general summary rules only, rules that are only generalizations from particular good actions—in which case, of course, the distinction between justifying a practice and justifying an action is of no crucial importance. Rawls's recommendation is that we take note of the fact that there are at least two types of rules in social ethics: summary rules and *rules of practices* (or general rules, properly so-called). He calls attention to the fact that in the latter case the justification of the practice must be explicitly different from the justification of an action falling under it.

I shall again state Rawls's contentions and argument in terms of the ethics of Christian love. This procedure is warranted because what he says applies as well to any normative ethical theory. Rawls's own intention was, as has been pointed out, to strengthen the case for utilitarianism in ethics by expressly reformulating that position in terms of the distinction between two concepts of rules. For the edification of Christian ethicists, Rawls's intention can be more strictly stated: this was to draw attention to the fact that the classical utilitarians understood quite well the distinction between summary rules and general rules, and they were most concerned with the justification of general rules, or rules of practice. No one before G. E. Moore confused the statement: "I am morally bound to perform this action," with the statement: "*This* action will produce the greatest possible amount of good in the Universe."[11] Many Protestant ethical writings in the contemporary period follow G. E. Moore in making this move. The result has been the destruction of Christian social ethics, or the production of Protestant casuistry without prior principles or without rules of practice.

Rules of practices (Rawls's only sort of general rules, or his only justification for any general rules, strictly so-called) specify that to engage in a practice demands the performance of those actions required by the practice. *The practice* itself is to be justified by a direct application of Christian love. One asks *which practice* most embodies or fulfills love. But then one justifies an action falling under it by appeal to the practice.

[11] Moore, p. 147 (italics added); and Rawls, p. 18, n. 21.

A practice or institution may be compared to a game with its established rules. If one wants to play a game, he doesn't treat the rules of the game as mere summaries or guides as to what is usually best in particular cases. "In a game of baseball if a batter were to ask, 'Can I have four strikes?' it would be assumed that he was asking what the rule was; and if, when told what the rule was, he were to say that he meant that on this occasion he thought it would be best on the whole for him to have four strikes rather than three, this would be most kindly taken as a joke."[12]

A person can, of course, adopt the office of a reformer and challenge the practice. Then the appeal is to whether the game wouldn't be better on the whole if the rules were changed. Here, citing the rules is of no avail. There must now be an appeal to one's standard for justifying all practices. But so long as one functions in the office of baseball player, there is nothing one can do or should do but refer to the rules when justifying particular actions. Rules of practice necessarily involve the abdication of full liberty to guide one's action case by case by making immediate appeals to what love (or utility) requires in each particular case. The point of a practice is to annul anyone's title to act, on his individual judgment, in accordance with ultimate utilitarian or prudential considerations, or from considerations of Christian love in that one instance alone. Yet, since there are obviously advantages in having a practice or institution which denies to the participant, as a defense, any direct general appeal case by case to doing what love implies, the practice itself may be justified by precisely this appeal to *agapé*. If the practice itself is warranted as the most loving practice, then the participant must in fact not have complete liberty to define his duty in particular actions falling under the practice by making repeated appeals to what

---

[12] Rawls, p. 26. Rawls's principal contention had already been stated but not as fully or cogently argued by J. D. Mabbott, *op. cit.*, pp. 106–7, 115: "There is a crucial difference between accepting the utilitarian validation of a rule and accepting the utilitarian account of the rightness of a particular action. . . . [It is] vital to distinguish between the good done in general by the adoption of a rule and the good done by following a rule in a particular case. . . . [A] good reason (and the only good reason) for approving a particular action is that it is the carrying-out of a rule; and a good reason (and the only good reason) for approving a rule is that its general adoption would do good on the whole."

alone justifies the practice—to the end that, perhaps, he gives himself warrant to violate it. The practice forbids this general defense, and it is the purpose of the practice to do this. Weighing his case on the merits is not open to him, so long as the practice is the most love-fulfilling socially accepted ethic or institution (and so long as he does not challenge this judgment by taking full social responsibility for a fresh application of *agapé* in the derivation or formulation of a new practice with which to replace it).

This does not mean that there is no deliberation about the actions that are to be done within the rules of practices. It means only, assuming that there are *moral* practices (and not games only), that the deliberation that falls under these practices must take the form of thinking about the meaning of the practice, the meaning of an application of it in this instance, and about the qualifications and exceptions that should be understood to fall under the rules themselves. One can deliberate whether and how the various excuses, exceptions, and defenses, which are understood by and which constitute an important part of the practice, apply to one's own case. A person should think about the meaning of promise-keeping, the meaning of the forbidden lie, the meaning of the proscribed theft, the meaning of murder as distinct from killing. This is how an individual contributes to the accumulation of moral wisdom in the practice. It is also an account of judge-made law.[13] In both cases, the "uniqueness" of an individual case falls under the practice and is a qualification and a further specification of the rule. This is a matter of prudence or equity in the application of law, or a matter of a

[13] Rawls makes too complete a distinction between a legislator (who enacts some practice) and a judge (who applies rules of practice to cases falling under them). Judicial interpretation, which he omits to take up, can be viewed as a further probing of the meaning a practice may be believed already to contain in the course of applying it to some new case that can be brought under it. Alternatively, judge-made law might be regarded as a permanent institution for the reform of practices by a general appeal to ultimate norms. The former interpretation is to be preferred because of the control exerted by the rules, precedents, and constitutional categories that are there in the practice. Yet it cannot be denied that case-law is a point in our social system where fresh assessment of cases is made by *some degree* of direct appeal to what can only justify practices or reform (according to Rawls) *and* by appeal to the precedents already in the practice. This takes place in the course of bringing cases under already established rules.

love-informed justice expanding or deepening the meaning of a practice. If there are any Christian moral or social practices, there cannot be exceptions that depart from them by direct general appeals to *agapé* overriding the rules in particular cases in which the agent does not take the weighty responsibility of criticizing the practice as a whole and attempting to replace it with another. *Agapé* justifies no exception within a practice. One must rather undertake to reform the accepted practice as a whole in some fundamental respect which, he ventures to say, would render it generally a more loving practice.

Supposing a man considers himself in the office of one empowered to criticize and change the social practice in some fundamental respect; he then must consider general agapistic arguments as applied to the old and to the new practice (and not as applied to acts only). When he does this he will see that, if there is a general argument for the new practice as more love-fulfilling, then (upon its institution) particular actions falling under the reformed social institution will be justifiable only by referring to the practice, and not by raising the general question case by case whether an exception can be justified directly on the grounds that this would be best on the whole. Just so, if baseball would be a better game with a rule permitting four strikes, anyone who then asks whether it would not be better on the whole if he were allowed five strikes instead of four may be suspected of not having understood the nature of a social practice or of his own social responsibility. He does not know the meaning of "social ethics" or of social institutions.

Perhaps one can illustrate and discuss rules of practice best by taking up again the practice of truth-telling or promise-keeping, and among promises the marriage-promise. These must be understood as rules of practices if one is to understand them correctly and thoroughly.

If promise-keeping is a moral practice which Christian love justifies as such because it is *the practice* that best exhibits and expresses what love requires in keeping true covenants among men, then the justification of a particular act of keeping one's promise must refer to and be upheld by the practice. Keeping one's promise cannot be said to have its only or main ground in the fact that in this particular case one will realize the most good on the whole. The purpose of the practice is to rule out this general appeal case by case, and thus to coordinate human actions and expectations. The general defense that breaking one's promise did more good on the whole is not open to the promisor. In the case of a promise made by a son to his dying father, or in the case of being told something in confidence by someone who subsequently dies, there may be very few unlovely consequences that follow from a breach of these promises.[14] Yet we would not say that the obligation is to that degree suspended. We would say instead that the promisor may deliberate about the meaning of such promises within the practice of promise-keeping, or upon how far into the future their writ runs, or what revisions of these particular promises the promisor is entitled to assume without in spirit or in actuality breaking the practice of promise-keeping.

No one is entitled without restriction to bring prudential or agapistic considerations to bear directly and immediately upon the particular case in deciding whether to keep *his* promise. Whoever says that he is entitled to break his promise because that was in this instance the most loving thing to do or because it was best on the whole may be suspected of not understanding what it means to say "I promise" and of not understanding the defenses the practice, which defines the promise, allows to him. He remains *obliged* so long as it is the case that utilitarian considerations are sufficient to establish promise-keeping as the best of all practices, or so long as considerations of Christian love are sufficient to establish this as the most love-embodying practice. Under this understanding, whoever keeps promises simply does what love requires, and he does not do otherwise than what love requires, *as a practice*. If, to the question, "Why did you do that?" a person replies, "Because I promised," that is clear and sufficient evidence that he understands the nature of promise-keeping as a rule of practice, which as a Christian he justifies because *that* is what love requires *as a practice*.

---

[14] Rawls, p. 15. Cf. Mabbott, p. 103: "I promise a friend who is going to the wars that I will help to look after his children if he does not come back. He has told no one else of this arrangement. If he does not return, why, on utilitarian grounds, should I help his children rather than other children who need help more?"

Indeed, a particular action would not be described as keeping a promise or breaking a promise unless there was the practice. In the case of actions specified by practices or as violations of practices, it is logically impossible to perform them outside of the "moral net" (Robinson) provided by the practice; for unless there is the practice, having general validity, whatever one does will fail to count either as a form of action required by the practice or as an action in violation of it. A man can slide into a bag of sawdust any time and anywhere he pleases; but he can slide into first base only in a game of baseball. "No matter what a person did, what he did would not be described as stealing a base or striking out or drawing a walk unless he could be described as playing baseball, and for him to be doing this [or for him to make errors!] presupposes the rulelike practice which constitutes the game."[15] Just so, no matter what a person does, what he does would not count as promise-keeping or promise-breaking unless he may be described as engaged in the rulelike practice of promise-keeping. If there is a moral practice of promise-keeping, the very notion of a justifiable "exception" to it makes no sense except as a qualification within the practice itself and a specification or deepening of its meaning.

On the other hand, if promise-keeping is only a summary rule without general validity, then there are only acts that are justified because they do the greatest good on the whole or spread love abroad in the world. The performance accords with or violates the most general moral office only, and not the office of a promisor. What one did would not count as breaking a promise, but doing good. It is only *as if* certain acts are required by a rule of fidelity to promises and *as if* certain other acts are in violation of it. On the one hand, if there is in this matter a rule of practice, there are no exceptions; there are only qualifications and applications of the practice. On the other hand, if there is only

[15] Rawls, p. 25. Cf. Mabbott, pp. 100–01: "This theory, that moral rules are empirical generalizations, seems to me the one theory about them which is certainly false. . . . If the agent approved of returning the book to Jones *because* it was borrowed or if he dissuaded Jill from pin-sticking *because* it would cause pain, then the connection between "right" and returning borrowed articles or between "wrong" and causing pain would NOT have been an empirical generalization nor inductively established."

a less-than-general rule, there is still no exception but only the most love-embodying actions. In neither case can there be an ethics erected upon a so-called exception.

The reason this is a correct account of some, at least, of the moral rules of practice is because words like "I promise" are "performative" utterances. "I promise" establishes a moral relationship among men, it creates a bond. Performative language is to be contrasted with statements like "I am well intentioned toward you," or "I love you," or "there is *agapé* in my heart which means that, no matter what I do, *agapé* will be expressed." The latter more or less correctly report an already existing (or possibly existing) and an alterable state of affairs. The words "I promise," however, are performative in the sense that they create and establish the relationship or moral bond to which they refer and that did not exist before. Saying the words "I promise" will be performative, they will be promising words, *only given the existence* of the practice. This is why it would be absurd to interpret the rules about promising, and the moral office which promising establishes, in accordance with the less-than-general summary conception of rules. "It would be absurd to say, for example, that the rule that promises should be kept could have arisen from its being found in past cases [even in past cases of openness and of loving response of persons to one another] to be best on the whole to keep one's promise; for unless there were already the understanding that one keeps one's promises as part of the practice itself there couldn't have been any cases of promising."[16] Therefore a person who responds to the question, "Why are you in a hurry to pay him?" by saying, "Because I promised to pay him today," is the man who knows the meaning of promise-keeping. Only he is in position to accumulate from experience moral wisdom about the meaning of keeping promises. Fidelity among men specifies itself into the moral office of promisor, which assumes the practice. "I promise" creates and establishes a moral bond between two particular persons whose whole meaning is referred to the practice or to the general love-derived obligation of promise-keeping among men.

In the same way, a man who answers the question, "Why don't you make love to Mary?" by answering, "Because I'm mar-

[16] Rawls, p. 30.

ried to Jane," may be supposed to understand the nature of marriage as a practice. To understand this he need not have been instructed by contemporary philosophers[17] in the meaning and function of performative statements such as "I take thee" in contrast to the meaning and function of such roughly verifiable and therefore variable statements as "I love you," or "I am open to you," or "I am honest with you," which describe or summarize (more or less correctly) something about the world of moral and personal experience before it is given shape by the performatory power of the promise. Moreover, no matter what he does, a man does not do anything that counts as conjugal fidelity unless there is the rulelike practice of marriage; and no matter what he does he does not commit adultery—unless we are to say foolishly (as do so many today) that chastity before and within marriage means "honesty" in sexual relations. To say that sliding into bed somewhere without authenticity of personal feeling is the meaning of adultery or of unchastity would be like saying that dropping a ball thrown at you anywhere is the meaning of making an "error" in baseball; and it would mean little or nothing for the institutions of social ethics to say that both sorts of actions are forbidden because on the whole it is not best or love-fulfilling to do them.

Recent Protestant ethicists (Otto Piper, Emil Brunner, Derrick Sherwin Bailey, Karl Barth, and Helmut Thielicke) have probed deeply the meaning of human sexuality, of one-flesh unity, of man-womanhood, of the created nature of human sexuality as the external basis and condition of the possibility of the marriage covenant. But ordinarily they have assumed that an extension or exercise of these realities in the world makes marriage in its moral and human meaning, and that statements summarizing these things are accounts of marriage. While denying that marriage is constituted by "romantic love," they nevertheless suggest that it is made by one-flesh unity and by personal authen-

[17] Donald Evans, *The Logic of Self-Involvement* (London, 1963), gives an extensive analysis of "performative" utterances with special reference to the Christian use of language about God the Creator. The covenant language of the Bible is thoroughly performative in character; and I venture to predict that an examination of the meaning and logic of performative speech, as this has been elaborated by Austin and Evans, will be even more fruitful in comprehending the biblical and Christian meaning of moral relations, obligation, and the law than in the exploration of theological questions.

ticity in sexual relations or by our man-womanhood. But these are more or less correct statements about the moral constitution of human beings as they exist bisexually in the man-woman relation before any performative promise enters to shape, create, and establish a moral bond between them, whereinafter the very meanings of fidelity and infidelity are derived from marriage as a rule of practice. The stress on marriage *consent* in Roman Catholic ethics, and in the civil law of domestic relations, presumes, of course, marriage as a practice and not as a mere summary of how, on the whole, love implies men and women should live together case by case, loving deed following loving deed. Kierkegaard, of course, made marriage *resolve* and the steady determination of the will definitive of the ethical stage; but he placed this before the Christian stage or mode of existence. And if Karl Barth had emphasized somewhat more the nature of man as a promise-making and covenant-keeping animal, and marriage as a practice, as a covenant, touched by the divine covenant, he might have helped us men of the West to resume again our connection with that "consent" which, in our entire traditional understanding of marriage as a rulelike practice, had the power to pre-form and to perform, to make, and establish marriage as a moral bond between men and women. Until this is the direction taken by Protestant Christian ethics, and until this understanding of marriage as a practice tempered to the *agapé* of Christ becomes more actual in the *ethos* of the church, then it just has to be said that there is more understanding of marriage still left as a relic in our civil law (though not, of course, in what goes on in law courts, which usually consists of a series of frauds perpetrated upon our actual law of marriage relations) than there is in our liberal Protestant churches where marriage as a summary of particular actions that best embody love goes without challenge. Clearly it is the case that sometimes this direct general appeal to *agapé* in justifying particular decisions or deeds may lead to actions that fall under marriage as a summary rule, but this might with equal propriety lead to actions that violate and dissolve the practice.

The preceding remarks on the methods of Christian ethics are not intended to solve all problems, not even those raised by my analysis itself. It may be objected that I have not spoken of "two concepts of general rules" but of two possible sources or justifications of general rules in Christian ethics, that is, first, general rules that are derived from Christian and from rational penetrations to the meaning of essential humanity and, secondly, rules that are rules of practices derived from Christian ethical or from rational penetrations of the conditions of the best possible social existence. Yet if these are two ways in which general rules function or work in a system of thought, two different approaches to the justification of general principles of conduct, it may not be illegitimate to call them two "concepts" of general rules. If there is more than one way how a word means, there is more than one meaning to the word.

If, second, it is objected that I have not shown two concepts, or two sorts of possible justification of general rules, but two different "ways in" upon the *same* general rules (e.g., promise-keeping), the answer must be to hold this an open question. It may be that there are principles that at one and the same time express generally what love requires in particular acts and what love requires as a practice. But this may not always be so. There may be rules of practices that are always the most love-fulfilling practices *anyone* can think of *and* can get established as a social institution, but which seem to require less than what love alone would lead to in particular deeds that irresponsibly prescind from questions of social ethics.

Someone may ask how long it takes an action to become a practice. This is a genetic question—having nothing to do with the logic of rules of practices or with the conditions of the possibility of there being any such thing as a *Christian* social ethic. My primary intention has been to explore the latter question. Or, it may be asked how we are to tell when the moral responsibilities, the values, or the situations calling for action, are governed primarily by act-agapism, or by summary rule-agapism, or by general rule-agapism (all of which have their place in any adequate account of Christian ethics). If this too is an open question, it is the question calling for the most careful and disciplined reflection and exchange of opinion among theological moralists.

In any case, to be born means to be born among practices. To be a moral agent means, among other things, to be an agent responsible for the attitude he takes up and the actions he posits in regard to rules of practices. Everywhere, and at all recorded times, practices precede individual choice. It is never a question of getting to the point where the logic of rules of practices begins to apply, or of getting to the crux of either justifying actions by the practices they fall under or else undertaking the reform of a practice as a whole. Every man already stands at this point. It may be that to be born among practices is to be born in the midst of dangers, as Luther said of being born among ceremonies. Still "the freedom of the Christian man" cannot remain only inward. Though that is the heart of the matter, such a man is no true reformer (in the social, not necessarily the religious, sense), and as yet he says or does nothing that can be called a social ethic. Nor can the freedom of the Christian man remain to be expressed only in *gratuitous* deeds (in either or both senses of that predicate). Sooner or later one must go out into the midst of the practices into which he was born.

When this happens it will be discovered that the justification of a practice is one thing, the justification of an action falling under it is another. Some of the justifications of practices or the reform of practices will be such that a Christian in adhering to them does so as (only) a man among men (perhaps as Rawls's utilitarian). There may be other practices or reforms whose content is in important respects required by *agapé* itself as the most love-fulfilling institution or customary practice it is possible to devise. Only if this latter move can be shown to be necessary can there be such a thing as a Christian social ethics. If this final step is not logically possible and required in Christian ethical reflection, or if it is eschewed by an undifferentiated rejection of "legalism," then it has to be admitted that there is no such thing as Christian social ethics, but only policy-making exercises.

VII

The Case of Joseph Fletcher and Joseph Fletcher's Cases

Professor Joseph Fletcher defines situational ethics in such a way that it falls between the two extremes of legalism, or "prefabricated" morality, on one side and antinomianism or existentialism on the other.

Legalism begins with law, or rules, or principles; it "encumbers" moral decision-making with "a whole apparatus of prefabricated rules and regulations."[1] Legalism lives by a program, not by a norm, even when it "listens to love" and develops a casuistry to correct its grossest rigidities (SE 19, 21). Protestant scriptural legalism and Roman Catholic "natural law" legalism "treat principles as rules rather than maxims," Fletcher wrote in the *Commonweal* discussion of the "new morality," and "legalism treats many of its rules idolatrously by making them into absolutes."[2]

---

[1] *Situation Ethics* (Philadelphia, Pa., 1966), p. 18. Reference to this volume will hereafter be indicated by "SE" followed by a page number in parentheses in the text. Thus: (SE 18).

[2] Joseph Fletcher and Herbert McCabe, "The New Morality," in *Commonweal*, Vol. LXXXIII, No. 14 (January 14, 1966), p. 428. Reference to this discussion will hereafter be indicated by "C" followed by a page number in parentheses in the text. Thus: (C 428). The discerning reader will know already from these

At the other extreme, antinomianism in its various historical expressions and in present-day existentialism teaches that a person goes into a situation calling for some responsible decision "armed with no principles or maxims whatsoever, to say nothing of *rules*" (SE 22). Antinomians and existentialists "follow no forecastable course from one situation to another" (SE 23). Such people are "sheer extemporizers" in their moral decisions; their actions are always "impromptu" (SE 23), arbitrary, gratuitous. Such persons "make their moral decisions with "autonomy" and "instantaneity," i.e. without help from general maxims, unpredictably, wholly within the situation [*sic!*], in the belief that one "moment" of existence is entirely discontinuous from others—so that we cannot generalize about our decision-making" (C 427).

It is important to emphasize that this viewpoint in ethics is not, according to its adherents, *adopted* arbitrarily and imposed upon moral experience. Instead, according to these views, there is in fact no forecastable course to follow from one situation to another. Moral reality and moral experience *are* quite incoherent; there are no continuities and "no connective tissue between one situation or moment of experience and another" (SE 24, 25). Since there are only instantaneities, there can be no generalizations from moral choices made in the past that might be helpful to future decisions. One lives wholly within the momentary situation. Therefore moral decisions must be impromptu if they are to accord with actual life.

Now, formally speaking, Fletcher locates situation ethics in between these two extremes. We shall have to inquire whether materially his ethics can be located in this middle position; whether his own polemics do not drive him to a position indistinguishable in practice from antinomianism with its denial that there is any connective tissue between one situation or moment of experience and another; whether from case to case the deeds

---

descriptions that there are a number more than "at bottom just [these] three lines of approach to moral decision-making" (C 427). It is incredible how Fletcher, learned man that he undoubtedly is, can actually believe that on his overly simplified definitions the only alternatives to his own ethical theory are legalists who "absolutize" ethical principles and extemporists who make decisions without any principles at all (C 428).

said to be possible responsible decisions do not in fact turn out to be impromptu. The first question to be raised is whether (to put the best complexion on it) Fletcher's ethics does not fall, within the range of the territory situationists might occupy, so very close to the borders of antinomianism that there are other positions falling under this method's formal definition and having as good or better claim to being situational which the author neglects to elucidate. These other accounts of the situation and all its ingredients may give a better account of the connecting tissue between one situation, or moment of experience, and another and follow a more forecastable course from one situation to another. Such views would qualify as "situational" under Fletcher's definition, no matter how much connective tissue was discovered or how strong the generalizations about ethics. Yet our author uniformly suspects in them that "intrinsicalism" and "absolutism" are about to be revived.

Still the author's intentions are evident enough. He means, in formally defining the method of situation ethics, to come between these two extremes. The situationist does not go into a situation unarmed; instead, he approaches a moral decision *"fully armed* with the ethical maxims of his community and its heritage" (SE 26, italics added). These he respects as "illuminators" of his problems, even if not as "directors" of his decision (SE 31). "The situationist," Fletcher writes with as yet no prejudice either way, "follows a moral law or violates it according to love's need" (SE 26). He aims to do whatever is fully appropriate, the fitting thing to do (SE 28). This might mean the law-observing thing quite as well as it could mean some departure from a tradition of morality, so far as concerns any of the entailments of this formal definition or description of the method of situation ethics. In *Commonweal* Fletcher wrote that the situationist is "armed with principles," just as the legalist is; and, while he calls these principles "maxims," they are "maxims of *general* or frequent validity" (C 428, italics added).

Yet Fletcher right away treats as encumbrances, or at best as of very little use, the accumulated moral wisdom which, in his formal definition of this method, he says "fully arms" the situationist for responsible decision-making. Asserting even-handedly that "in actual problems of conscience the situational variables are to be weighed as heavily as the normative or 'general' constants," he immediately corrects the balance: "The situational factors are so primary that we may even say 'circumstances alter rules and principles' " (SE 29). This seems already to say more than that the situation is "the governing consideration" in the application of principles that may have general or frequent validity (C 428). The situation is brought against the maxims so that the latter are not apt to exert any probative or prohibitive power. Thus the alleged illuminators (but not the directors) of action turn out always to threaten to obscure our moral vision and to hamper action unless they are corrected. With what, then, is the situationist fully armed that distinguishes this ethics from antinomianism, if anythng from outside the immediate situation which indicates the connecting tissue between moral decisions and forecasts some course of action always threatens to un-man us and to depersonalize moral action?

In actual fact Fletcher's operating ethical method is an extreme and exclusive act-agapism; if not *antinomian*, it is certainly *anomia*, no matter how he formally defines situation ethics and attempts to locate it in between extremes. Abstract definitions aside, there is not a single line in *Situation Ethics* to compare with many statements of Bishop J. A. T. Robinson which indicate that his position is, in the main, a *modified* act-agapism or *summary* rule-agapism (i.e. which indicate that Robinson's situationalism meets the conditions laid down by Fletcher's definition of this method of ethics).

Bishop Robinson pays high tribute to the need for law and for the net of a good moral ethos that exhibits and preserves the connecting tissue between moral events and experiences. "The deeper one's concern for persons, the more effectively one wants to see love buttressed by law," he writes.[3] "Christians must be to the fore in every age helping to construct it [the moral net requisite in any society], criticize it, and keep it in repair."[4] "The more he [the Christian] loves his neighbor, the more he will be concerned that the whole *ethos* of his society [its 'accepted ethics']

[3] *Christian Morals Today*, p. 26.
[4] p. 18.

. . . is a good one, preserving personality rather than destroying it."[5] Fletcher himself quotes from Robinson's earlier book, *Honest to God*, a statement to the same effect as the foregoing—except that in this instance it is not simply *the neighbor's* need for person-upholding institutions, laws, customs, and established rules and principles of conduct, but *the agent's* need as well for these things if he is to act rightly: "It is this bank of experience ['the cumulative experience of one's own and other people's obedience'] which gives us our working rules of "right" and "wrong," and without them we could not but flounder."[6] The sparse meaning Fletcher takes from this, however, or the vanishing effect such considerations have on his way of doing ethics, is shown by his statement, immediately before this quotation from Robinson, that "situationists ask, very seriously, if there ever are enough cases enough alike to validate a law or to support anything more than a *cautious* generalization" (SE 32, italics added). He does not tell us how one can be "fully armed" with a "cautious generalization"; nor how this assertion and myriads like it in this volume comports with the postulated contrast between existentialism, or antinomianism, and situationalism in that the latter acknowledges, while the former does not acknowledge, the connecting tissue between one situation or moment of experience and another, and launches upon some forecastable and dependable course of action. In the contrast between Fletcher's "cautious generalization," which is a dispensable moment, and Robinson's bank of experience without which Christian moral agents "could not but flounder" no matter how much they have Christian love and reason in exercise, one sees the difference between an almost pure act-agapism (or as Fletcher calls it, an almost pure antinomianism, or anomianism) and summary rule-agapism (or as Fletcher *defines* but does not practice it, situation ethics). To say the least, this locates Fletcher in the upper left hand corner of the kingdom of situationalism, from which when pressed he can readily take sanctuary across the border into an ethics of the unique moment without taking responsibility for the defense of the inhabitants of that territory.

[5] p. 12.
[6] *Honest to God*, pp. 119–20 (italics added), and SE 32.

This may only be a matter of stress or emphasis, to be accounted for by differences in the nationalities, personalities, and individual biographies of these two authors (if one wanted to have resort to *ad hominem* explanations). Even if this is only a matter of emphasis, let us see how extensive it is in Fletcher's writings, in order to tell the degree to which he does or does not amplify the meaning he himself assigns to this method of ethics.

While ordinarily Fletcher does not distinguish between principles and rules and while ordinarily he couples them together to be pushed aside, there is one sub-section bearing the title "Principles, Yes, but not Rules" (SE 31). Here he uses the language of "principled relativism" and indicates situational *willingness* "to make full and respectful use of principles." This, it is immediately explained, means: "principles, to be treated as maxims . . ."; and that in turn means that "*only* love and reason really count when the chips are down!" and not the armament of any tradition of ethics. Nor is any concern expressed for the upbuilding of a better ethos than the traditional one. "Love decides *there and then*" is one of Fletcher's main propositions (SE Chap. 8). How remote from "instantaneity" is this? Far from "relying, in deep humility, upon guiding rules" (Robinson), Fletcher makes every *sophia* of church or culture *subservient* in the moment of decision, it would seem, to an ethos-free act of love and an ethos-free calculation of reason. Situationists "cannot give to any principle less than love more than *tentative* consideration . . ." (SE 33). To catch the ear of the groundlings of the present age, Fletcher ridicules "the fixity and *establishment-mindedness* of all law ethics as contrasted to love ethics" (SE 53, italics added). "We follow law, *if at all*, for love's sake" (SE 70, Fletcher's italics); our author can therefore say that Emil Brunner's explanation of the traditional threefold use of the law as "discipline, repentance, and guidance" is not the same as his (Fletcher's) *use* of it, even though this threefold use (e.g. "guidance") would seem compatible with the initial *definition* of this method of ethics, and some degree of discipline and repentance would seem on occasion to be forthcoming from entering humbly into dialogue with a tradition of Christian ethics. "We [situationalists] are willing to follow principles and precepts *if* they serve love, *when* they do" (SE 71, Fletcher's italics); does this emphasis not differ a great deal even if only by degrees from Robinson's recognition that without principles and precepts we could not but flounder? Instead of salutary reference to the community's thinking on ethical questions, and to its deposit of ethos, the stress falls upon the fact that "every man is his own casuist when the decision-making chips are down." High premium is placed upon "our knowing what's what when we act," even if we are free to consult expert advice *"if we choose"* (SE 84, Fletcher's italics), and choose also, presumably, or choose not to choose to consult the *sophia* of church, or culture, or the cumulative experience of loving obedience (Robinson).

In the effort to "find *absolute love's relative course*" (SE 90), Fletcher's propulsion is not away from *both* the extremes stated in his definition of this method of ethics, but always away from one only: to "prevent law's Procrusteanly squeezing down an iron system of prefabricated decisions upon free people in living situations" (SE 84–85). "Situation ethics welcomes law for love's sake *sometimes, all depending*" (SE 100, italics added). Robinson said that the moral net of good laws and good customs are always needed both for the neighbor's sake and to sustain the moral agent even while he goes about criticizing the legal system and keeping it in repair. Fletcher is simply, as he himself said, "allergic to law" (SE 152), which is hardly a condition for doing any kind of social ethics. He therefore constantly uses such emotion-laden and question-begging language for the position he chiefly opposes, indiscriminately lumped together, as wanting "to lean on strong, unyielding rules," or "wallow and cower in the security of the law" (SE 134), the "ethical establishment," "a growing hunger for law," a "neurotic security device to simplify moral decisions" (SE 137), "childish rules" (SE 140), which is no way to engage with disciplined reflection in the doing of ethics of any sort. Having described extemporizers as "anarchic —i.e. without a rule" (SE 23), Fletcher later says that his own situationalism "is not anarchic (i.e. without an *arché*, an ordering principle)" (SE 45). If, however, the one and only *arché* is love and there are no pieces of behavior or any subordinate principles that count for love, wherein does this position differ from

Christian antinomianism throughout the ages? If "neocasuistry" repudiates any attempt not only to "prescribe" but to "anticipate" real-life situations (SE 29), and if conscience in its exclusive prospective function only engages in "first-guessing" (SE 154), where are the continuities between one moment of moral experience and another, or the basis for any forecastable course of action? It comes as something of an afterthought, therefore, for Fletcher to write: "Love can even love law . . ." (SE 144). This required amplification and full employment throughout if Fletcher meant to execute a situational ethic as this was *defined* at the outset.

It is noteworthy that when Fletcher undertook to frame a concluding summary of everything he had been saying in this volume he put it this way: "Christian ethics or moral theology is not a scheme of living according to a code but a continuous effort to relate love to a world of relativities through a casuistry obedient to love; its constant task is to work out the strategy and tactics of love, for Christ's sake" (SE 158). There is not a word in that "single, simple formula" for *Situation Ethics* which discriminates Fletcher's ethics from antinomianism, anomianism, or existential situationalism. There is not a word to indicate that the Christian life has or can find any forecastable course. There is not a word to indicate that Christian love has it in its own power to effect any continuities in the devolution of its responsibilities, or can find in moral experience any connecting tissue between one situation and another. It is this summary and not the initial demarcation of the meaning of situational ethics that has to be taken seriously if one wants to assay Fletcher's ethics.[7]

---

[7] Professor Fletcher affirms (SE 34–35) that the present writer is "a distinguished perpetrator of this misplaced argument in America," i.e. the argument against situationalism that mistakenly assumes it is the same as antinomianism. He cites in evidence my article, "Faith Effective Through In-Principled Love," *Christianity and Crisis*, Vol. XX, No. 9 (May 30, 1960), pp. 76–78. That article dealt with one by the late Alexander Miller entitled "Unprincipled Living: The Ethics of Obligation," published in *Christianity and Crisis*, March 21, 1960. Since the objection raised in my article was not so much against Miller's call for "unprincipled living" as against his inconsistency in at the same time elaborating (albeit briefly) a number of signal basic principles of ethics and making significant use of them, I was not, then or now, under the illusion that situation ethics *needs* to be identical with antinomianism. Miller affirmed that we need

It is tempting to resort to an explanation of Fletcher's constant emphasis (when placed beside some of Robinson's) in terms of nationality, personal factors, or biography; and, even if that would be *ad hominem*, there is certainly something here that requires explaining. In Great Britain when that nation's most celebrated situationist, and others, go about reforming the law out of compassion, they seek enactment of a statute that no longer defines as a "crime" homosexual acts between consenting adults done in private. In the United States, we organize the Mattachine Society, which in New York City claims public recognition for homosexuals as an *nth* minority; and Christian compassion is inclined to pass over the importance of a moral ethos in this regard. Fletcher declares flatly, and without undertaking the far more elaborate moral reasoning that might be sufficient to demonstrate the point, that "whether any form of sex (hetero, homo, or auto) is good or evil depends on whether love is served" (SE 139). That statement, in any case, passes over in complete silence the problem of constructing an ethos of some or of any sort in areas of human life that have important social dimensions; and it ignores the need for concern about public display of the privately permissible.

Or again, the explanation might be found not in national cultural differences at the moment, but in where on the spectrum Fletcher and Robinson are to be located as Anglicans. The genius of that tradition has been, to date, that the three factors, Christian faith (love), reason, and tradition, are held in living triologue, with no one of them, or no two, usurping the final authority without the others sharing with some degree of real

---

"a morphology of man," that Christians have "ushered Aristotle out too summarily," that "one marriage is in significant respects much like another"; he spoke of Christian morality as a "style of life," of "habits" of personal life, of an "ethics that represents the mutual obligations of a covenant folk," the ethos of a people whom God has "enmeshed"; and he directed the attention of moralists upon *these* things. In short, Miller was a situationalist according to Fletcher's initial *definition* of this position; and, in the main, there was no other sort among Christian ethicists in 1960. Now it is Fletcher who in the execution of his ethics is a distinguished perpetrator of the notion that one can make an ethical method out of one norm only by speaking always only of love and never decisively of the morphology, or style, or habits of the Christian life to which love leads. If not before, one might now not without reason identify situational ethics with anomianism.

independence in determining the meaning of Christian faith and life. By this standard, Robinson is an Anglican in whom his tradition in theological ethics is still intact in some measure, while Fletcher is an Anglican in whom this tradition has broken down, and Christian faith (love) and reason have seized hegemony. This is the interpretation that must be placed upon statements of Fletcher's to the effect that "acknowledging our heritage of canonical and civil principles of right and wrong," we can choose to be situationists free to decide for ourselves in all situations *which* principles are to be followed, or to reject the relevant principles (C 428–29), as if our tradition of ethics contained in itself no guidance on *these* questions that should be respected.

Moreover, the extremity of Fletcher's polemic, telling as it is against any but the most tentative conclusions as to the requirements in meaningful behavior of love itself, might require explanation in terms of individual idiosyncrasies in addition to the inveterate cultural individualism, pragmatism, and utopianism of American life, or in addition to Fletcher's departure from the genius of Anglicanism. If invoked, this more individual explanation might also make sense out of the astonishing remarks our author makes about other moralists in order both to class them as "situationalists" and at the same time to charge that somehow most of his predecessors and colleagues in this "movement" failed to be *consistent* situationalists (act-agapists?).

The three B's (Bonhoeffer, Brunner, and Barth) are listed among the company Fletcher wishes to keep. These three were "clearheaded and plainspoken about the thesis of situation ethics" (SE 149). Dietrich Bonhoeffer would seem to be a charter member of the society of situationalists (if such a society were possible) because he once wrote that "principles are only tools in God's hands, soon to be thrown away as unserviceable" (SE 28)—with no mention of the divine mandates which are also in God's hand ordering and imposing authority upon human life, and imposing authority also within the mandated regularities. Then, ten pages on, Fletcher is bound to disavow Bonhoeffer because "inexplicably, shockingly" he believed that there were two lives and not one only that have sanctity in cases of abortion, and because he knew the moral difference between direct-killing and dying, or allowing to die (SE 38).[8] Bonhoeffer "came close to seeing the 'property versus predicate issue' but he fell short, he missed it" (SE 58). There are no intrinsic values, Brunner says, "being a blunt situationist" (SE 50)—with no mention of Brunner's ethics of the orders of God's creation and preservation which is the definitive locus, positively accepted, of love's responsible action even while it also acts, some have charged, interstitially—and in particular with no mention of Brunner's argument for the *monos* of marriage. Karl Barth, while truly a landmark also in the inevitable march of modern situationalism, put himself "in an untenable corner with the intrinsic fallacy." This is Fletcher's astounding comment upon Barth's prolongation of the ethics of faith in the divine command and of love of neighbor into respect for life and the protection of life in his special ethics. Barth then only becomes an almost-situationalist when "finally he blurts out" (SE 62) that about the *ultima ratio* of the singular exceptional deed. To which it can here be said simply that any serious examination of Barth's special ethics, and especially a serious examination of all that he says about the *Grenzfall*, will demonstrate conclusively the difference between this and situational ethics in general and Fletcher's in particular.

Lesser lights perhaps than the three B's are gathered together so that the spirit of situationalism can make one in their midst. The publication of Reinhold Niebuhr's *Moral Man and Immoral Society* and Emil Brunner's *The Divine Imperative* simultaneously in 1932 was a great moment for the invasion of ethical relativism into Christian ethics (SE 45): only love is constant, these thinkers are asserted to have said, everything else is relative. Or again, Reinhold Niebuhr "is closer to situationism than to any other ethical method" (SE 61); but like Brunner and all the others he too never quite made it home. Kenneth Kirk "came close to an extrinsic, situational view," but he "failed to reach home. . . . His bid for freedom was too fainthearted" (SE 129, 130). Paul Lehmann "muddies the water" (SE 14) because

---

[8] Bonhoeffer would have known one reply to give to the man in one of Fletcher's concluding cases who said: "If I don't take the pills, I'm killing myself same as if I commit suicide with a razor or gas, seems to me" (SE 166). Fletcher also has need of this distinction between killing and allowing to die, in the case of the obstetrician (SE 138).

by "context" he means the full substance of the Christian context, as he understands this to be theologically viewed, and not the secular context only. Even Edgar Brightman proves comforting, because he once wrote that "in personality is the only true intrinsic value"—which is enough to permit Fletcher to turn this into support for the view that "there are no 'values' at all; there are only things . . . which happen to be valued by persons" (SE 58), where Brightman would certainly have said that there *are* values because there *are* things that are valuable to persons (and not only valued by them) and that God has *valued*.

There may be at work in all this a craving for security in numbers and movement as grave as any legalist ever felt in regard to his code-morality. In any case, there is in Fletcher's ethics an evident hunger for contemporareity, nay, even for *avant-gardism*. To say *this* is not to make use of an *ad hominem* argument or to commit the genetic fallacy so often used by Fletcher to assert his position. This is only to indicate the ethics by "declaratory policy" that Fletcher achieves, since he nowhere undertakes consecutive demonstration of the elements of modernity he everywhere eloquently espouses.

Our author calls his own pragmatism "neopragmatism" (SE 41) largely because he has come again to hold this view, which is evidently progress. To be plainspoken, pragmatism is "a *practical* or *success* posture" (SE 42), and that seems enough to warrant the posture. ". . . Our attempt to be situational" is described in apposition to our attempt "to be contemporary . . ." (SE 43). "Our milieu and era" are unfriendly to law (SE 46). Four theories of conscience lie side by side in all thought upon this subject, but "situationalism takes none of them seriously" (SE 53) —not even seriously enough to refute them before adopting a purely prospective view of the function of conscience, which I suppose is equivalent to saying that this is correct because prospective. "The whole mind-set of the modern man, *our* mind-set, is on the nominalists' side" (SE 58), which is enough said in behalf of mind-set even if it could be demonstrated to be a species of thoughtlessness. The words "benevolence-malevolence" have sometimes heretofore been used with "a more direct and deliberate meaning than Christian situation ethics *cares to adopt*" (SE

63, italics added). Our "normative relativism . . . waves goodby to legalism and dogmatism" (SE 67). "No twentieth-century man of even average training will turn his back on the anthropological and psychological evidence for relativity in morals" (SE 76). None should, of course, turn his back upon or wave goodby to such evidence; but a number of twentieth-century men of more than average training have not thought the evidence conclusive, and certainly not conclusive to the ethics Fletcher wishes to declare to be the policy of every true inmate of the twentieth century. Where Cicero affirmed that "only a madman could maintain the distinction between the honorable and the dishonorable . . . is a matter of opinion, not of nature,"[9] Fletcher counter-declares: "This is nevertheless precisely and exactly what

[9] This is as good a point as any to indicate a glaring dyslogic in Fletcher's book, and one that is a rather characteristic misstep made by theologians who wish to protect some revealed norm of ethics from any admixture or connection with an ethics based on "natural" justice. "The attempt to study nature and discern God's will in it," Fletcher writes, "is only a hoary old sample of the 'naturalistic fallacy' of deriving *ought* from *is*." (SE 76. The author had himself just derived *the relativity of morals* from anthropological and psychological evidence!) Now, if the naturalistic fallacy *is* a fallacy it counts as well against the foundation of Fletcher's ethics. It counts against his statement that "the key category of love (*agapé*) as the axiomatic value is established by *deciding* to say 'Yea' to the faith assertion that 'God is love' and *thence by logic's inference to the value assertion* that love is the highest good" (SE 49, italics added). The case is not altered by using more pious expressions such as "we understand love in terms of Jesus Christ"; or by using the jargon of pre- or meta-ethics: "before we ask the ethical question, 'What shall I do?' comes the *preethical* question, 'What has God done?'" (SE 157). Philosophers from David Hume to G. E. Moore who have been proponents of the naturalistic fallacy have known that it counts against any type of theological ethics as well as against so-called "naturalistic" ethics. One has either (1) to refute or otherwise reject the naturalistic fallacy (and then the way is open for either a Christological or theological ethics *or* for an ethics of "nature") or (2) to accept the naturalistic fallacy and then develop an ethics wholly upon some normative foundation, because the way is closed to either a supernaturalistic or a naturalistic ethics of any sort. One cannot be a theological moralist and at the same time invoke the naturalistic fallacy to get rid of hoary old opponents; that weapon would cut the ground from under one's own position. Yet this is a device used by both Joseph Fletcher and N. H. Søe, both Barthians of some sort who, however, refuse to engage seriously in the "prolongation" of *agapé* into special ethics lest "nature" or intrinsicalism be admitted.

If the fact that God is love is one good reason why I should love and if the fact that Jesus Christ first loved us is one good reason why I should be thankful and why Christian ethics is a *eucharistic* ethics (SE 156), then the deep propensities of human nature, etc., may be one good reason why I should do X. The naturalistic fallacy admits of none of these statements; it happens also to be by no means unanimously admitted to be a fallacy.

situation ethics maintains" (SE 77). The new morality is "the emerging contemporary Christian conscience" (SE 77); "people are, in any case, going to have to grow up into situation ethics, no doubt about it" (SE 82), since, I suppose, this is the wave of the future. The "generalization argument" is a "fundamentally antisituational gambit . . . a form of obstructionism, a delaying action of static morality" (SE 131), even though Fletcher should know that a number of reputable philosophers believe this to be a fundamental principle of ethics.[10] "Modern Christians ought not to be naïve enough to accept any other view of Jesus' ethics than the situational one (SE 139), even though W. D. Davies' monumental study of the Sermon on the Mount contains, with no *systematic* ax to grind, a great deal of historical evidence to the contrary.[11] Still, "*Situations-ethik* more and more openly wins a place . . ." (SE 146) not only among non-fundamentalist Protestants, but, when you think about it, "in effect most men are situationists and always have been!" (SE 147). After that sweeping, comforting statement, a better truth is told, advertently or inadvertently: "Situationism . . . is the crystal precipitated in Christian ethics by our era's pragmatism and relativism," to which acculturation of Christian ethics Fletcher pays his highest tribute: "It is an age of honesty, this age of anxiety is" (SE 147).

We can, then, riposte upon Fletcher his own account of classical Christian ethics' resistance to the situational love ethic: "by any and every tactic" (SE 36). This volume's exhibition of the situation in theological ethics could best be described as a stand-off, an opposition of declaratory policies or of persuasive appeals, and not a grappling with one another over intellectual issues and ethical warrants. I myself have a higher opinion of traditional ethics than to suppose that, say, its sexual ethics can appropriately be dealt with by making any use of the label "marital monopoly" (SE 80), but evidently Fletcher does not. This would still not be the way to do Christian ethics even if we had to give ourselves rational arguments where before there were none.

The foregoing excursus upon "the case of Joseph Fletcher" is by no means an inappropriate introduction to his ethics or to

---

[10] See, for example, Marcus George Singer, *Generalization in Ethics* (New York, 1961).

[11] *The Setting of the Sermon on the Mount* (Cambridge, Eng., 1964).

his cases, since so much depends for this book's suasion upon appeals to the reader's like-minded prejudices in favor of individualistic freedom, normlessness, traditionless contemporaneity, and modern technical reason.[12] I would be the first to grant, however, that there is little to incline the mind toward rational conviction one way or another insofar as I have simply riposted *ad hominem* explanations of Fletcher's ethics to his own *ad hominem* charges against all legalists and intrinsicalists, and insofar as I have suggested various cultural or personal idiosyncratic reasons why his ethics fails to fulfill the promise of his initial definition of situationalism and in fact turns out to be an act-situationalism.

1. *The slippery slopes of summation ethics*

My next and more serious purpose is to go deeper into the matter before us by asking the question: Why has Joseph Fletcher, *intellectually*, set his feet on slippery places? How are we to *interpret* the data that is before us in Fletcher's actual ethics? Why does his actual ethics fail to fall in between legalism and antinomianism? Is there a *reason* why he did not execute a situational ethics as this was defined? Is there a *rational* explanation (apart from personal or cultural propensities either way) that is a necessary and sufficient explanation of his slip so often in the direction of singular deeds only?

I think there is; and the answer is to be found in the nature and meaning, or in the *logic*, of "summary" rules or "summary" principles. This is only my expression for what Robinson called "the cumulative experience of one's own and other people's obedience," "this bank of experience which gives us our working rules of 'right' and 'wrong,' and without which we could not but flounder."[13] "Summary" rules would be among the components of situational ethics as Fletcher originally defined it; they would amply exhibit the fact that one moment of human existence is not entirely discontinuous from others and forecast a generally dependable course ahead for the Christian life.

Now, is there something about a summary rule that ration-

<hr/>

[12] "The temper of situation ethics is in keeping with the attempt to quantify qualities" (SE 118).
[13] *Honest to God*, pp. 119–20.

ally explains why this was a road not taken, or at least not mainly taken, in the execution of this ethics? Is there something in the logic of summary rule-agapism or summary principle-agapism that, if one seriously attempts to erect a Christian ethics upon this one type of Christian moral wisdom alone, is bound to prove a slippery place on which to tread? What is it in the nature of merely summary principles or rules that will invariably lead an ethicist to singular act-agapism the more implacably he pursues the question of the Christian determination of right and wrong?

This is the first systematic question to be taken up. Then, secondly, evidence will be adduced to show that while Fletcher very obviously moves from summary principle-agapism to act-agapism, he moves at the same time and less noticeably in the opposite direction, toward general, or pure rule-agapism. This raises a second systematic question: Is it in the nature of merely summary principles, or rules, that they will prove insufficiently imperative, and not general enough, the more earnestly one pursues the question of the Christian determination of right and wrong? On the one hand, one is led away from mere summations by trying to be faithful to the unique features of moral situations. On the other hand, one is led away from mere summations the more he takes faithfully into account the general features of moral situations and the similarities in the moral experience of persons, their needs and claims. Thus, summary principle-agapism (or situationism as Fletcher *defines* it) is evidently an insecure position on which to try to erect the entirety of Christian ethics.

1. Our first question, then, is: What is it in the nature of merely summary principles or rules that invariably leads a serious ethicist in the direction of singular act-agapism? Summary principles or rules are only reports that certain actions have been found to be most love-fulfilling. The decisions made in particular cases remain always logically prior to all talk about the illuminating power of principles "generally," or frequently, valid. Their foundation rests upon having asked and never ceasing to ask, what *action* would be most love-fulfilling? One is always acting, therefore, *as if* he were following a principle (maxim) under which his action falls. Perhaps we would flounder if amid the

pressures of the moral life we did not often do this. Still, if we did a right and good thing, we acted only *as if* some summary principle entered as an important component into shaping our action. This jogged our memory, and we noticed continuities we might have neglected. Still that jogging was only contingent; it was not in principle necessary in determining some aspect of right conduct. All that was necessary was faith (love) and the facts; a summary principle or rule only helped. If a man was fully loving and fully rational all the time, he would have absolutely no need for summary principles of any sort. A society composed entirely of fully rational and sensitive Christians who are fully loving and fully rational all the time would be a society that needed no principles of conduct, no rules of social behavior, and no accepted ethics. (Indeed, if a believer in only summary rules believes also in morally obliging continuities between moments and moral bonds between persons, this is simply by a "leap" of the optimistic faith of "philosophical anarchism.")

Thus, it does not matter essentially whether in a man's definition of types of ethical method he distinguishes between antinomianism and situationalism, or not. It does not matter essentially whether he asserts as a general philosophical proposition that one moment of moral experience is continuous or discontinuous with others. If he is a summary rule-agapist or a Fletcher situationalist on the best construction of it, he still acts *as if* all decisions are discontinuous even if in every action he seeks with all his heart to lay his deeds each to each in simple piety. Whether he follows or violates a summary rule or principle, he still goes about deciding in that act of self-elected sovereignty, by a *direct* application of *agapé* to that particular case, what is the right thing to do, to wit, whether to extemporize or not. He *singularly* decides whether he should *choose* to regard as relevant and important one of the summary principles in his tradition of canonical or civic righteousness—or in his own or his community's "bank of experience"—or should choose not to do so. Just as it can be said that, in choosing to follow some summary rule or principle, a man acts only *as if* he is doing so, so also it can be said that on this interpretation of the moral life one can only act *as if* there is some forecastable course of life and *as if* there are pieces of behavior that generally count for love. This has still to be determined each time, as love acts then and there, to say so or not.

This is why Fletcher was impelled to execute, contrary to plan, an ethics of act-agapism. The rational explanation, apart from the propensities of men, is to be found in the *logic* of the exclusive summary rule or summary principle position that was first announced. This is the reason, I suppose, that Professor William K. Frankena preferred to call summary rule-agapism by the name of *modified act*-agapism. It is already exactly that; and as proponents of this exclusive method in Christian ethics proceed the "modification" becomes less and less important (subject only to personal temperament or emphasis). This is because the generalizations of such an ethics arise as insights from singular acts of loving obedience, and to such acts they in the very nature of the case may always return. Summary rules are only acts of *agapé* taken together. Every such summary rule may in the nature of the case be dispersed again into its elements. This is why situational ethics as originally defined by Fletcher, and distinguished from extremes both to the right and to the left, was already on the way to becoming a Christian antinomianism dwelling only in love and wholly within the particular situation with no "accepted ethics" round about to buttress that noble experiment.

The present writer does not doubt that "summary principles" or "summary rules" comprise a great part of the Christian life, or of the moral life of any man; perhaps the greater part. Neither summary rule-agapism nor unique act-agapism are to be called in question, or sought to be removed. It is the exclusive claim made for summary principles that needs to be rejected. Not the notion of summary principles but the notion that every principle, or norm, or relevant moral matter other than love itself, is of this kind: this unproven assertion or declaratory program has to be rejected if one wishes in moral science to plant his feet on anything other than (intellectually) altogether slippery places. It is doubtful if we would have learned to call such moral generalizations "principles" if there were no other kind.

Merely summary rules or principles are known as such probably by analogy; theirs is a borrowed worth, and we have seen what mere summations of moral wisdom come to in the end when these alone are sent out to instruct the sovereign freedom of man who is notably inclined to overestimate the little time of his decision. To make a program of this and to affirm that each time one has to choose whether any of the elements in a civilized moral tradition is to be obeyed is to say that one is really obliged by none of these things.

Certainly it is doubtful that this notion of summary principles or rules can ever be a sufficient account of rules of social practice, a sufficient philosophy of law or of man's communities, or an adequate doctrine of justice and human rights, or a sufficient interpretation of the covenants of life with life enacted and mandated by God's covenant with men. Not so were we "enmeshed" when God created out of nothing his covenant folk, or when he saw that man was alone. There is obligation pertaining to man's response, responsiveness, and responsibility. There are moral bonds of life with and for other men. There is a cause between them made that is greater than their electable individual decisions determining whether this shall be so or not. There is God's governance and ordering, the divine mandates by whatever name. Only obligation can *oblige* one moment to be connected with another, or reliably forecast any route. Obedience to the divine command through love of neighbor can and may and must be prolonged into specifiable requirements for the respect, preservation, and protection of life for love to have any significant meaning or relevance. Love must be able to adduce, produce, or discover these universal requirements, even if one or another of them may be situationally rebuttable in bordercases. This is the meaning of Barth's *ultima ratio*, and it is quite different from Fletcher's situationalism. In Barth, the moral agent is bound, obliged; in Fletcher, he chooses, if he does, to be bound (which is to say he is not bound at all) by any specifiable requirements of love. But God stooped to the condition of the isolated and free moral agent. We are placed on notice that we can not and may not and must not be alone with the act *in situ.*

It is not simply that we have "noted," in a cautious (albeit firm) generalization, that every marriage is in important respects like any other, sometimes; and that we can remain as free as before (Rousseau) in deciding whether in this instance to treat the similarities or the dissimilarities as essential. It is not simply that we have "noted" that sometimes in some respects one moment of moral activity is like another, and this raises for us the question whether this shall continue to be so here and now. It is rather that this is found to be among the requirements of a searching, responsible love, or that such love finds this to be so in actual life, if love is not programmatically deprived of anything by which to *mean* love, of everything that *means* love, except love itself. One's individual existence is significantly affected when he gets married, or makes a promise, or when a needy neighbor claims him. One is bound to other persons in a *specifiable* way. One is established in a particular moral office—that of husband, or promiser, or neighbor—within the general Christian moral office of doing in each action anything that on the whole will make this a more loving universe. Maybe in heaven that will be all that needs to be said about living; but there is needed on earth more than summaries of that heavenly love. God knew better the requirements of creaturely life. We need not, we should not, storm the *eschaton*. This side resurrection, the question before us is: What are we to be as the creatures of God's ordinances, to be in being-with one another in the communities *we live?* not What are we to do occasionally, frequently, or "generally"? There may be in our creation traces of our creation toward *steadfast* covenant, toward the image of Christ. In any case, love finds many ways faithfulness means and perdurably means. Forms of steadfastness in responsibility and accountability one to another would seem to be the most likely inference from Christlike love, if that has any relevance at all to the affairs of men. The idea that there are on earth only summaries of the meaning of steadfast love would hardly occur to an unprejudiced theologian; neither would he imagine that all the entailments of steadfastness for the Christian life lead only to cautious or firm generalizations that are frequently to be followed.

There are structures of life into which we are called; and practices into which every man is born who ever was born. Into the rightfulness of these things and the specifiable requirements of love, if anything ever counts for love, must be our inquiry. Among the requirements of love only a mind prejudiced by instantaneity and contemporaneity would say programmatically that there can be no general principles or rules other than love itself that are indicative of the good for the people of God always. The idea that one has at his disposal only summary principles is a mistake one makes while doing ethics. It is a mistake one makes while preaching the gospel without preaching the gospel contained in the Law and Ordinances. It is, in fact, a mistake one makes while preaching the gospel that the gospel is whatever is easily preachable under the conditions of "worldly Christianity."

2. On the other hand, one can slip in the other direction from attempting to erect a Christian ethics solely upon the foundation of summary principles or summary rules. If an ethicist is serious in reflecting upon the requirements of love, the more serious and searching he is, the more he will not only be alert to particular situational factors that may rebut a summary of previous love-embodying actions in like situations—he will also be at the same time more sensitive to quite general features in moral experience and in moral relationships which, if not neglected or abridged, would render human behavior and institutions more love-fulfilling and more unswervingly devoted to persons. Whatever may have been the situationist declaratory program, it will likely be found that he does not exclude every general moral verdict from his system. Advertently or inadvertently, he will not be able to stick to his resolve arbitrarily to exclude the possibility that something may always be among the requirements of love, or always prohibited, because it could not possibly be loving, and not only frequently or sometimes. This would be to move in the direction of pure or general rule-agapism or pure or general principle-agapism. There is also a "logic" in this movement of thought about the Christian moral life, so much so that this slip can be avoided only by relaxing one's efforts to prolong love into life. *One* quite general rule, or principle of conduct, or rule of social practice, would be quite sufficient to subvert the exclusive claims of situational ethics.

Again, the ethics Professor Joseph Fletcher has actually executed can be brought in evidence. It is not evident that the main drift of his book on *Situation Ethics* toward single act-agapism is consistent with other writings of his, or entirely consistent with itself. There are also general rules adduced. In *Morals and Medicine* Fletcher affirmed that a quite general moral rule or principle should govern medical practice where there is any due respect for "The Patient's Right to Know the Truth."[14] If a doctor has proper understanding of the person and regard for the freedom of a dying man whom he is attending in his death, he will never permit himself to make a situational decision that the truth discovered in diagnosis (the patient's truth) should perhaps be withheld from him. Simply from asking what action in relation to persons who are the subjects of their own dying would most express and exhibit a searching love and profound respect for them, a physician has ample reason for always abstaining from medical lying in critical or terminal cases. There is also in this chapter abundant secondary argument for this rule *as a practice*.[15] From asking which sort of actions would, as a general professional practice, be most love-fulfilling, the physician also has sufficient ground for abstaining from lying to dying men, or from not telling them the truth. In this *kind* of situation the two questions: What does a caring love for this human being require? and, What does love require of doctors

---

[14] (Princeton, N.J., 1954), Chap. 2.

[15] One paragraph (SE 28) makes it evident that Fletcher does not understand the meaning of a *rule of practice*, or *rule of the game*. Quoting a "competent situationist" E. LaB. Cherbonnier, he compares societal rules to such rules of thumb as "Punt on fourth down" in football, or "Second hand low" in the game of bridge. Certainly "Punt on fourth down" is only a piece of useful advice, to be ignored, for example, if your team is within ten yards of the opponent's goal line and has only one yard to go for a first down. In this case, as with other instances of practical advice summed up in proverbial guidelines, one should make independent appeal to the *purpose* of the game and its goal, and not think simply of justifying one's action in terms of the rule, "Punt. . . ." But this sort of maxim is precisely *not* a rule of *the game*; it is a maxim concerning how a good *player* will act *within* the real rules of the game. Because there is a game with its own rules, one is *not* permitted to say, "I think that on this down it would be best on the whole for our team to have thirteen players on the field, or five downs before losing the ball." If there is a game at all, if there is a social practice, one is precisely barred from making an independent appeal to the purpose of the game and its goal; instead individual actions are justified or not by rules that express the nature or structure of the game which holds the players together and defines for them the moral office of players.

as a practice? lead to the same answer. Thus a general rule or principle[16] governing behavior can be stated; and this will be the moral judgment arising from fullest sensitivity in loving care for and respect for the freedom of the dying man *and also* from a thorough consideration of the medical practice that would be most love-embodying *as a practice* in these *kinds* of cases.

This is not a conclusion that awaits, or would vary according to the particularities of, an individual medical or personal diagnosis. Moreover, the fact that a given patient may not want to hear the truth about his condition, and that it should then not be told to him, would be no exception to this rule. No one asserts that the truth should be thrust upon him. If from some notion of purely verbal integrity this has been asserted by some philosophers, it is not the question that Fletcher raised about the physician's obligation always to tell a dying patient the truth that belongs to him. This clearly only deprives the doctor of the right on his own part to make a "situational" decision about what would be "good" for the patient. Professor Fletcher has not withdrawn, and he does not now reject, this judgment. Yet it is, of course, quite inconsistent with the *exclusive* act-agapism or summary rule ethics set forth in *Situation Ethics*.[17]

In Fletcher's recent volume, with its undifferentiated, blockbuster rejection of all "legalism," there are many sweeping assertions that Christians "cannot give to any principle less than love more than tentative consideration" (SE 33). It is a "slip" to fall into "the error of deriving universals from universals" (SE 32). "We cannot milk universals from a universal [love]" (SE 27). These are mostly unproven assertions; one might ask who ever said either "milking" or logical "derivation" was the procedure by which a Christian "special ethics" is to be adduced

---

[16] In some discussions of ethics it is necessary to distinguish between "rules" and "principles," but not in contrast to Fletcher's situation ethics, which treats rules and principles alike as always provisional only. See SE 29: "rules and principles"; p. 30: "All laws and rules and principles and ideals and norms"; p. 71: "principles and precepts."

[17] Fletcher mistakes my admiration for "distaste" (SE 14) when I drew Paul Lehmann's attention to the capacity of an "interpersonalistic," and even a "contextual," ethics to reach this particular conclusion about a doctor's truth-telling (see p. 82 above). If there was any irony in that passage it was directed at Lehmann for faltering in his discussion of "special ethics" and for not being thorough enough in probing the question of truth-telling.

or amplified? At the moment, however, the question is whether Fletcher has altogether succeeded in resisting the pressure exerted upon him by the claims of Christian love reaching toward some quite general ethical conclusions. Does he never say "never" or "always" (SE 43)? In Fletcher's characterization of this new "class" of Christian ethicists called "the situationists" (a "class," so far as I can see, with only one member[18]), does the use of this *method* of ethics never permit one to reach a general rule or principle?

Even in *Situation Ethics* one comes upon at least one general rule of behavior, or general principle of ethics, besides love itself; and a single instance of even a mistaken general conclusion in specific ethics is quite sufficient to dissolve the exclusive claims made in behalf of a situational method (as here defined). That rule is: ". . . No unwanted or unintended baby should ever be born" (SE 39). Or, to express this for a *subject* other than the child: no woman should be forced to bear an unwanted child. The fact that she would be permitted to bear an unwanted and unintended child—if on taking thought, she wanted to—is no exception to this.

It is true that, in discussing this case of pregnancy following rape, Fletcher first says that "the situationist . . . would almost certainly, *in this case*, favor abortion . . ." (SE 38). But pregnancy following rape is a *kind* of case; and to state concerning this *kind* of situation that abortion is justifiable is to make a general moral judgment. It is to render a general moral verdict upon a kind of case and not alone upon a particular case. This does not depend on situational variables, such as the fact that in this particular case the young woman was in a mental hospital. Instead, the particulars were covered by the general rule applied to it, namely that the norm of Christian love of neighbor finds quite sufficient warrant for abortion after rape or incest.

Moreover, Fletcher does not limit the situationist's verdict

[18] That is, so far as I can see from an examination of the assemblage of theologians and moralists with whom Fletcher wants to keep company. In this respect at least Fletcher is a consistent *nominalist*. The word "situationalist" is a mere *name* for a number of theologians gathered together here by non-contextual quotation from their works, and who have in common chiefly the fact that Fletcher makes them bear this name.

to this *kind* of case. He includes this within a far more inclusive type of case, within a quite general justification of abortion. He writes that, in judging this particular case, "it is even likely they [the situationists] would favor abortion for the sake of the victim's self-respect or reputation or happiness or simply on the ground that *no unwanted and unintended* baby should ever be born" (SE 39).[19] Clearly this is to "milk" a universal from a universal. The fact that Fletcher does not *prohibit* his situationist from employing any such intervening love-embodying norm, and says instead that this will "even likely" be the criterion, shows a glaring inconsistency. "No direct abortion" is not the only "universal," the only "legalism" there is. It is only the one Fletcher opposes—by his own rules in regard to the life of the fetus and the life of the mother. And he does not trouble to tell the reader that defenders of the position he opposes have also attempted by their arguments in its behalf to trace the movement of charity into actual practice or that both his kind of permissions and the traditional prohibitions depend on *some* view of the *nature* (bad word, that!) of nascent life. The locus of the argument is *between* these general verdicts. The disagreement is not to be settled by appeals to a novel method that selectively eschews some sorts of charitable general norms (the ones wanted to be got rid of) but not all others.

Fletcher's situationist is "likely" to affirm that, in reforming our present abortion law, the rule of law that abortions be performed upon request would be the most love-fulfilling general practice; he *also* affirms that this action would without exception be justified by a penetrating understanding of and care for

19 Fletcher's justifications of abortion are sometimes expressed in a way that connects one of these repeatable ingredients or characteristics of situations with another. In the discussion with Herbert McCabe on "The New Morality" in *Commonweal*, January 14, 1966, he wrote that to terminate pregnancy "would nevertheless be right to do . . . to a conceptus following rape or incest, at least if the victim wanted an abortion" (C 430). In the case of the woman confined in a mental institution, if Fletcher's justification in any way depended on this situational particularity, his view might have been expressed by saying that abortion following rape or incest would be right, at least if the victim falls below some measure of competence for motherhood and if the victim (or someone acting in her behalf) wanted an abortion. I suspect that the insertion of this *limiting* reference to a type of particularity in situations in order to determine what's right would fail to obtain Fletcher's approval. This would not be the general rule to which love should lead us.

the persons involved. Abortion upon request (or abortion for the sake of reputation, health, or happiness, or to save the mother's life, or after rape or incest) would be what love requires for *them* (or for *her*), *and also* what love requires *as a social practice*. The assertions that no child should be required to be born, or no woman should be forced to accept responsibility for a child, following rape or incest, or that no woman should be required to risk sacrificing her life in giving birth, or to undergo serious injury to her health, or that (to be yet more forbidding) no unwanted or unintended child should be deemed rightfully born if this required moral suasions upon the mother, are all quite general (correct or mistaken) judgments which Fletcher's situationist reaches, or may reach, by "love's casuistry." Again, no one has as yet asserted that under these kinds of conditions abortion *should* be thrust upon pregnant women. Therefore, it would be no exception to any of these proposed love-embodying rules for us to say that, even so, a woman *may* bear her child—if, on taking thought, she wanted to or thought she should—even though this endangered her life or health, or seemed likely to make her unhappy, or would require that she alone take responsibility for a life that was the consequence of another's injustice.

There is more. Again and again Fletcher writes that people are to be loved and things are to be used, and that "things" include "principles" as well as material objects. This says a lot about people, things, and principles, on the truth of which the requirements of love will depend. Then it can be objected that the statement that "people are to be loved and things (including principles) used" is itself a sort of intervening principle, and not a self-evident one, or evidently only an analysis of the meaning of love. Still I grant that it may be an effective answer to this to say that the statement is only a pleonasm for *agapé*, an explication of the meaning of the ultimate norm of "C-love"— Christian love (SE 15). Such would probably be Fletcher's reply.

However that may be, what are we to say of the statement that "sex which does not have love as its partner, its *senior* partner, is wrong" (C 492)? This unhesitating verdict about right and wrong in terms of a general principle governing human conduct is certainly not a pleonasm for love. It is not a statement about love alone, or only about its seniority. In the statement something is said about sex which immediately requires further explication to be meaningful at all, or for anyone to tell whether it is true or not. We shall have to ask whether the requirements of love, the "senior partner," can be properly determined without knowing a great deal more about the *nature* (that word again!) of human sexuality. We shall have to ask whether some of the actions Fletcher approves in cases he takes up do not entail the use of people (oneself, or another) through using sex. Any answer to this question must stem from *some view* (Fletcher's, or another) upon the question whether one's sexuality is, in any sense or measure, *the person.*

For the moment, however, we need to begin at the beginning —or rather *before* the beginning, before the situationist's seeming achievement of relativism—with a practice that seems *ab initio* to be ruled out. Discussing the proposition that "only persons are ends," Fletcher "restates" that restatement of love as ultimate norm by saying that "sin is the exploitation or use of persons." But he does not leave it there, nor add only an unbounded variety of situational possibilities for the expression of non-exploitive regard for persons. He immediately writes: "This is precisely what prostitution is" (C 430).[20] This would seem to be another universal moral verdict rendered upon cases (or, in this instance, upon an institution as well as upon certain kinds of actions). It is true, we will have to be vigilant to see whether Fletcher means what he says, and does not elsewhere withdraw this judgment in his desire to be all things to all men (especially contemporaries). True, he promptly opens the way to an apparent mitigation by bringing in *comparative* judgments. The prostitute is "far more sinned against than sinning"; "she is infinitely closer to righteousness than are her customers." One cannot, however, make moral contrasts, even for the effect of reducing the force of one or another of the judgments, without

---

[20] Also: ". . . The classical capitalistic theory of labor . . . is or was a sinful, evil principle." Here we have two principles, or rules, or synthetic moral judgments, intervening between the ultimate norm of love and situational freedom and relativity.

first having clear ground for the validity of at least one (I should think, both) of the decisions concerning agents, acts, or institutions that are then brought into comparison with one another. Therefore, at least the prostitute's customers do wrong; and, no doubt about it, prostitution is precisely exploitation. So Fletcher says.

Next, take the case of sexual promiscuity. Here the identification of Fletcher's quite general verdict is clear enough, even if his language searches for the class to which to belong: "Not all legalists and not all relativists are agreed" about this, he writes; but "the chances are that the Christians among them look upon promiscuity as irresponsible, care-less, insincere, even as indifference [which, rather than hate or malice, is the opposite of love]. They (we) believe that promiscuity ignores and flouts the value and integrity of persons . . ." (C 431).

Again, by launching into comparisons, Fletcher seems, but only seems, to qualify the certainty of the judgment concerning promiscuity to which he has been driven by the searching requirements of a care-full love. "Even a transient sex liaison," he writes, "if it has the elements of caring, of tenderness and selfless concern, of mutual offerings, *is better than* a mechanical, egocentric exercise of conjugal 'rights' . . ." (C 431, italics added). That observation in no way withdraws the judgment already made. It only serves (along with the observation that sexual intercourse is not right solely because it is *legal* nor wrong solely because it is not) as a bridge over which Fletcher goes astray. Common-law marriages, he writes, recognize this.

Common-law marriages precisely do *not* recognize that sexual intercourse is not wrong if, or because, it is outside the law or outside of marriage. Such marriages indicate instead that *marriage* is not wrong because it is outside the written law and that marriage is still marriage even if extra-legal. This simply reveals that it is only against a bourgeois concept of marriage that this series of observations can be directed with any telling effect. Fletcher, however, seems to believe that *marriage* is still where the county clerk says it is, or is not, i.e. only in the legalities; and so he arrives, verbally, at the conclusion that "there is nothing against extra-marital ["extra-*legal*" would not be incorrect]

172

sex as such, in this ethic, and in *some* cases it is good." To do moral reasoning in such fashion is precisely to fail to make use of the realities in the relations of a man and a woman to which common-law marriage points. It is to fail to probe the fact that not only "in this [situational] kind of Christian sex ethic [but in other kinds as well] the essential ingredients are caring and commitment." It all depends on the meaning given to that performative word "commitment"; and only by opening that question do any important moral issues come up for discussion—not by drawing the marriage line where the county clerk says it is and where the common law says it is not. "A couple who cannot marry legally or permanently," Fletcher writes, "but live together faithfully and honorably and responsibly, are living in virtue—in Christian love" (C 431). Before passing judgment on this case, the reader may demand to know in more detail how they can do the latter without being able to do the former. He may wonder whether their faithfulness is not in doubt; or, if this lacks nothing of its performative power, what could possibly obstruct their getting married. But suppose both aspects of this couple's relation to one another is verified. Then it will be discovered that where there is evidence brought before the courts of any state in which the common law prevails that a man and a woman not "legally" married live together honorably and responsibly as Fletcher says his couple do, then they *are* married. Married, moreover, as legally, and as "permanently" as the law enforces among the obligations of marriage in the case of couples who marry one another with a license. It is the evidence and not the marriage that is doubtful in common-law cases. It is impossible for a couple by any written or unwritten contracts they make up to withdraw even in common-law marriage the pledge of permanence from among their responsibilities to and for one another. This the state will presume to guarantee in the case of proven common-law marriages just as much as it still does this in the case of licensed marriages, by means of the various facsimiles, or relics, or minimum embodiments of permanent responsibility, that are (still) within the power of the *written* law of marriage to insure for *any* marriages within the commonwealth. Thus, Fletcher is more hung up by the legalities than was the Christian tradition for most of the centuries of Western history. Otherwise he might have clarified the pre-"legal" meaning of marriage instead of using the very real covenant commitment between the parties, by which they marry one another, to give (only) seeming support to the justification of extra-*marital* sexual intercourse.

Thus, Fletcher is not a little confused about what he means to compare sexual promiscuity with, when he says that it is not worse than something else, or that a transient sex liaison may indeed be better than some sorts of acts of marriage. Who ever doubted this? For all the birdlime of his sexual ethics, St. Augustine kept his "moral-species-terms" clear when he went about making innumerable statements like "a sober married woman is better than a drunken virgin," or "a faithful concubine is better than a lascivious wife." After all, this is the only way to keep in touch with the wisdom in the language of ordinary moral discourse while doing ethics. Still—and this is the point here—there is no doubt that in his ethics Fletcher forbids sexual promiscuity, and not just unloving acts; nor does he rule out only promiscuous acts of sexual intercourse when they *happen* to be unloving. Doubtless promiscuity is not wrong apart from its unlovingness, but then it is never apart from its unlovingness. Promiscuity is wrong because it is a sort of thing that is always unloving and can never be done with sufficient care for the person. The statement of this intervening rule or principle was not a mistake Fletcher made while doing "special ethics." Yet it is plainly inconsistent with the method of ethics Fletcher proclaims.

Again, concerning "temporary trial marriages of limited duration and with parental consent," Fletcher's notation—and the internal parenthesis does not indicate any uncertainty about his own judgment—is: "From a Christian perspective, most situationists (if not all) would hold that the teenagers would simply be practicing on each other, and the mere fact that their using each other would be mutual would only compound the evil, not justify it" (C 431). Still this might be described as "doing good" if the principles of our presently accepted ethics could be pushed aside; and one may wonder what will be the ingredients to sustain this judgment of Fletcher's in the future if, as he says is the case in other "coital adventures," many or most of the emotional reactions such a couple would experience may be "largely guilt feelings." Such guilt feelings the "changing cultural norms are making archaic or even antediluvian. *The guilt is going*" (C 432, italics added). The reader will have to be vigilant to see whether Fletcher in other cases applies the same searching regard for the persons involved as he did in his negative verdict upon trial marriages (which would seem a relatively responsible coital adventure).

The foregoing are enough general principles, or conclusions, to show where love may lead if one relentlessly follows its leading. This leads not only to verdicts based on sensitivity to unique situational factors but to verdicts based on sensitivity to quite general features in moral experience or in the nature of responsible moral relationships and bonds of life with life. It leads to love-embodying principles of conduct, and to prohibitions of a number of things that could not possibly be loving.

Thus merely summary principles or rules, when taken to be the only kinds of principles there are, tend, because of the very nature and meaning of such principles, to disperse into their elements: individual acts of *agapé*. At the same time a Christian love that does not waver in prolonging itself into life can hardly be held back from positing some quite general rules, principles, actions, or abstentions that are necessarily to be observed if human behavior and human institutions are to be most love-fulfilling.

With the breakup of summary rule-agapism, with the breakup of situationism as Fletcher originally defined it, the resulting ethical system resembles remarkably the manner by which Christians and moralists in all ages have found it necessary to reflect upon moral problems: making use of principles of various sorts with their varying prudential applications to concrete situations. If this is the case, perhaps the attempt should be given up to create new schools of Christian ethics. Perhaps we should instead reopen and renew our universe of moral discourse with one another, with Christian moralists of all ages past and with moralists of all denominations in the ecumenical age to come, as together we search all the meaning in Christian faith and love, for deeper meaning in the moral principles to which love leads, for the meaning of the actions and abstentions these principles and precepts require, and the fitting application of them in various situations in actual life to which a charitable prudence will lead us.

2. *Again, the last Puritan*

The observation that insistently came to mind while reading many of Joseph Fletcher's sex cases was a single sentence in a public lecture given a few years ago at Princeton by the distinguished literary critic Leslie Fiedler. "The American people are so puritanical," said Mr. Fiedler, "that they would readily commit fornication if they could be persuaded that it would do them some good." Now, it is a pity to have to yield to the going conception of the meaning and spirit of Puritanism. Our forefathers on this continent are popularly castigated as simple rule-book legalists, or as people who always too solemnly went about "doing good," knowing nothing about the vitalities of life or of spontaneous, uncalculating goodness. That is simply a mistake which many people make, including some Christians, while swapping their birthright for a pot of message. Accepting for the moment this caricature of Puritanism, it can be asserted that in many of its features Fletcher's sex ethics is a reversed Puritanism, but a Puritanism nonetheless. His campaign against anything being good in itself is carried to such an extreme that every act and relationship becomes only good-for "doing some good." An action is to be justified only by what comes from it, largely by goods consequent to and future to the act itself.

Thus the "co-hero" of *Situation Ethics* (13–14) is the Texas rancher in the play *The Rainmaker* who grabbed a pistol away from his outraged son to prevent him from killing the rainmaker for sleeping in the barn with his sister. "Noah, you're so full of what's right," the rancher said, "that you can't see what's good." The good was that a lonely, "spinsterized" girl was restored to a sense of defrigidized womanliness by the rainmaker's lovemaking. Presumably that was the rainmaker's heroism, too. He went about doing good in the barn that night. He pushed principles aside and did the right thing.

This is an ethic of deliberation *uber alles*. Just as a Christian would not give heroin to an addict "because he wants it" but may do so "as part of a cure," so (according to Fletcher) he will act in regard to all "pleas," pleas for sex or anything else (SE 117). Confronted by the plea of some male, presumably a young woman's reason for yielding will not be because sex is to her a creaturely delight, or to him; but she may do this if she sees it as part of some cure, some consequent good to be done. ". . . Nothing is right unless it *helps* somebody" (C 431). So Fletcher repeats the by now tiresome vindication of the prostitute in the Greek movie *Never on Sunday* who picks up a sailor in deep insecurity over his own virility and then "*manages* things *deliberately* (i.e. responsibly) so that he succeeds with her and gains his self-respect" (SE 126–27, italics added). She cured him, and did so deliberately; this made it a loving thing to do. At least, that made it a *responsible* loving thing to do.

It can scarcely be argued that this was what the Lord God meant when he created Eve, or Adam and Eve in their man-womanhood, for the cure of human loneliness. Sexuality has present, immediate meaning *in itself* which a Christian ethicist should undertake to clarify even if this places him in dread danger of "intrinsicalism." This means that sexual love is a good immediately shared by the parties; it is not a good secondary to progeny, or to someone's consequent integration, or to some cure of souls, or to getting effectively married in the eyes of society, or to espionage. In these and other respects, Fletcher's ethics makes human sexuality, along with everything else, a matter to be "managed" and "weighed and weighted" (SE 128) with a view to its future good effects. One cannot imagine a deeper violation of the *humanum* in human sexuality as a power of self-utterance and of present self-communication. In Fletcher's ethics this violation becomes a policy, and the chief warrant to be invoked in offering ethical justifications.

A young unmarried couple making their decisions "Christianly," Fletcher writes (SE 104), might decide to have sexual intercourse with one another in order to get pregnant in order to overcome their selfish parents' opposition to their marriage—but not because they *like* one another! It is true that at this point the author is contrasting *loving* with *liking,* and disposing of *Playboy's* disposable-playmate notion even of *liking.* But *liking* admits of degrees, and if ever Fletcher's penchant for comparative ethical evaluations does more than confuse issues, this is the place to formulate a comparison. I should say that for that unmarried couple to have sexual intercourse because they *like* one another would be "better than," at least it "is not worse than," for them to go to bed together with boldness to overcome overbearing parental opposition. It has already been suggested how differently the moral analysis would proceed if we are to suppose that this couple were only consummating by a potentially life-giving act of love a marriage which was already established pre-legally through the real exchange of performative marriage vows on their own parts, and if we are not to suppose that they were naïvely attempting by means of copulation and by means of the subsequent pregnancy to transform their love or liking for one another, and to transform their mere engagement (i.e. their intention to be married later when their parents and the county clerk say so) into an actual marriage.

Fletcher can *write* that "by love we live in the *present"* (SE 142), but this is said to exclude the past from providing any of the decisive warrants for behavior. It is clear that, in the *kairos* of the present, love is only, or mainly, future-regarding. For everything of present significance one must be persuaded that some good will come of it. One of Fletcher's mistakes—perhaps his fundamental mistake—is his supposition that Christian ethics is always only a "teleological" or *goal*-aspiring ethics. No doubt his situational ethics is (SE 16).

The results are devastating, if anyone is interested in unhurried, orderly, and many-sided reflection upon moral questions. It is Fletcher's reversed Puritanism that account for the sensationalism of so many of his illustrations which pass for proofs. One readily commits anything because the sole question to be asked of every proposed act, or line of action, is whether it can be believed that it will *accomplish* something. Fletcher is simply an old-fashioned *consequentialist,* as McCabe pointed out (C 439).

Thus, "Is adultery wrong?" is a question Fletcher refuses to answer until he is given a case of it (SE 142–43), and giving him a case *means* showing who believed it would do whom some good. ". . . Baby-making can be (and often ought to be) separated from love-making" (SE 140). This is not only supposed to be an argument for A.I.D. (artificial insemination by a non-husband donor) which in *Morals and Medicine* was defended because, among other things, it is a means by which babies can be made *without* the *love-giving* act of life-giving which is ordinary in sexual and in conjugal union. With attention now fixed even more singlemindedly upon the aspired-to goal of baby-making, there is no longer any person-centered reasons for abstention from simple fornication or adultery. Those hoary methods will do as well as A.I.D. "In a particular case, why should not a single woman who could not marry become a 'bachelor mother' *by natural means* or artificial insemination, even though husbandless, as a widow is?" (SE 126, italics added). An instance of this deliberate, teleologically justifiable, management of adultery was proposed by Fletcher in the *Commonweal* discussion of the new morality (C 428). This was the case of a Puerto Rican woman in East Harlem who "made friends" with a married man in order to have a son, and who when told she should repent the act replied: "Repent? I ain't repentin'. I asked the Lord for my boy. He's a gift of God." Fletcher's notation is: "She is *right*"; but he does not signify by this what any theologian knows has always been said—that she is right about the goodness of the gift of her son. He signifies rather that she was right in the act done; indeed, he must say this since he knows no other determination of the rightness or wrongness of actions except the goods forthcoming from them (in this case, the boy). Fletcher qualifies her undifferentiated verdict, and his, only by saying in a parenthesis that this does not mean that the situationist approves in the abstract of the absence of any husband in so many disadvantaged families, which would seem to have been under discussion in the instant case. If he means by not mentioning this detail in the body of the case to hypothecate among its particularities an exception from all those concrete disadvantages that fall upon fatherless children, then his is the most abstract sort of moral reasoning.

The same cannot be said of another morally significant detail that was mentioned, namely, the married man who, from other impulses no doubt, joined the woman in baby-making. This case would seem to show, therefore, that Fletcher believes that the overriding good to be accomplished in getting a baby may justify that woman's degree of complicity in violating the man's faithfulness to the person to whom he was married and the cause that was between them. Unlike the absented disadvantages of fatherlessness, this was a concrete ingredient of the case; only, it was a *present* reality and not the forthcoming supposable good to be accomplished by the adultery.[21]

With this understanding of ethics there is really nothing that can be said and nothing that can be *not* said about the moral life. It looked like a good beginning as well as a good story—that one about the young woman who said Yes, she'd sleep with a man who offered her $100,000, and again replied affirmatively for $10,000, but when the offer dropped to $500 grew indignant and exclaimed, "What do you think I am?"—to be met with the answer, "We have already established *that*, now we're haggling over the price." But if not exactly the price, still "what she accomplishes for herself or others" does have according to Fletcher (SE 17–18) the power to change the characterization of what she'd be doing. Given $100,000 and a couple of additional suppositions, the events that night could be described not as high-priced prostitution but as "a lovely young woman building parks for the children of the poor to play in."

Fletcher's answer to the case of "even *paid* sex," introduced by this story, is in the end (SE 146) to leave open its possible justification. This is to render human sexuality instrumental to even remoter ends than was true of the prostitute in *Never on Sunday* who "managed" herself and the man so as in the act itself to bestow or evoke his confidence in himself as a male; more remote also from the matter of sexuality than the goals of

---

[21] This case of justifiable seduction for the sake of baby-making may be compared with Fletcher's statement that if a girl seduces a man "in order to lure him into marriage, she is committing a far greater sin than simple fornication [which, presumably, people *like*]" (C 430). Below, sec. 3, 2, we shall bring under scrutiny the apparent *arbitrariness* among Fletcher's ethical verdicts as he moves from case to case.

the East Harlem woman who used a man (and his marriage) to get her with child. This brings us to the case of "patriotic prostitution," left for the reader of *Situation Ethics* simply to ponder (SE 163–64), yet answered in the affirmative by a brief assertion and without argument in the catalogue of reasons why "women have done it" which gave (SE 146) the situationist's answer to the $100,000 case of "*paid* sex" (or was it $500?) and by an argument of sorts in *Commonweal*. There Fletcher asks rhetorically the same question beguilingly put to the girl, so said she, by C.I.A. recruitment officers. "Is the girl who gives her chastity for her country's sake any less approvable than the boy who gives his leg or his life?" This question Fletcher answers with an exclamation point: "No!" (C 431). That is clear enough. Yet it is equally clear that whether this is a correct answer to the question depends on *some* view of the nature of sex and the person no less than does the opposite opinion rejected out of hand everywhere in this book as intrinsicalist and legalistic. Fletcher's is simply an intrinsically instrumental view of the meaning of sex, to which he has come from an urgent puritanical impulse to reduce every significance to "doing good." No wonder that for the period in a human life when some other pedagogy may be needed in order for adolescents ever to acquire the maturity which Fletcher thinks his moral outlook both requires and makes possible, the only thing that can be said is: "It may well be, especially with the young, that situationists should advise continence or chastity for practical *expedient* reasons . . ." (SE 80–81). The Puritan ethic of "weighing and weighting" the consequences is getting to be a bourgeois ethic of managing and managing oneself and others; and any firstrate adolescent today can see through the expediency to the lack of present substantive reason for an important feature of the moral life here proposed to be recommended to him.

The upshot of this relentless determination to accomplish something as the sum and substance of all morality is to be seen best of all in two comments Fletcher makes concerning biblical teachings. The first is the story of the woman of Bethany who anointed Jesus and for this "purpose" poured from an alabaster box a very precious ointment. When the disciples saw it they said with indignation, To what *purpose* is this waste? But Jesus commended her admittedly useless action as an immediate expression of love (Matt. 26:6–13). "If we take the story as it stands," Fletcher comments, "Jesus was wrong and the disciples were right" (SE 97). Indeed he must say this. Fletcher's interpretation of the anointing at Bethany indicates a principal meaning "eisegeted" into Scripture by a later resolute statement of his: "Modern Christians ought not to be naïve enough to accept any other view of Jesus' ethic than the situational one" (SE 139).[22]

The second and equally astonishing interpretation attributes situation ethics to Scripture by a reading of the prophet Isaiah's statement that "in that day seven women shall take hold of one man, saying, . . . Let us be called by thy name, to take away our reproach" (4:1). The prophet's words are words of seering judgment upon the *evil* times and the evil *doing* to come upon men with the coming of the Lord. Fletcher asserts they prove that a new and candid morality, declaring anything and everything to be right or wrong according to the situation, is actually as ancient as Isaiah's "foreseeing a day when the sex ratio would be imbalanced," thus requiring a change in the *mores* "to even things up" (SE 124)! If the great Isaiah and Jesus of Nazareth do not rise from the dead to protest this treatment, then any number of modern theologians may remain content whom Fletcher makes "almost situationists" by isolating quotations from the main body and meaning of their ethical writings.

The conclusion to which we have come from an examination of some of Joseph Fletcher's cases concerning the consequentialism and the puritanical "doing good" that are controlling in this account of the moral life is not a matter of the case record alone. This viewpoint is systematically set forth in Chapter Seven concerning ends and means where the narrowness and inadequacy of this ethics is plain to see.

The author contends that while "not any old end will justify

---

22 The author's strange statement (SE 131) that Jesus' prohibition of divorce "poses a problem for Biblical scholarship . . . but it does not confuse Christian ethics, at least of the situationist stamp" is the very opposite of the case. Jesus' prohibition of divorce presents no greater problem for objective biblical scholars than any other *logion*. Instead, it poses a chief and a perplexing problem for Christian ethics, and gravely threatens any ethics of a situational sort that is proposed to be erected upon Christian foundations.

any old means" (SE 121), still it is the end and only the end that justifies the means. What else would there be to justify a means except its usefulness? Obviously, nothing (SE 120)! Fletcher has not noticed that by saying "means" and asking what justifies a "means" he has begged the question and imposed upon human life his one and only answer to all moral issues. A "means" is *by definition* oriented upon some end. Whether it is a good *means* would, of course, be determined by that end. This is the very *mean*ing of a "means." Certainly, then, a *means* "only becomes *meaningful* by virtue of an end beyond itself" (SE 121, italics added). Certainly, a *means* would be "haphazard if it is without an end to serve" (SE 121). Certainly, "it is the end sought that gives the means used their *meaningness*" (SE 122, italics added). A *means*, certainly, cannot justify itself. These are all *analytic* and entirely uninformative statements, as also it would be an informing, Christian, yet still analytic statement to say "nothing can justify *a means* except a loving *purpose*" (cf. SE 125). Still Fletcher begs, he does not demonstrate, nor try to demonstrate, that every relevant ethical warrant falls within the means-end relationship, or that this comprises the entirety of the Christian moral life. Only a late Puritan do-gooder can take this to be obviously the case.

Against all this it has to be affirmed that not every *action* in human life is *menial*, nor every moral relation instrumental. We can let stand all the statements in the previous paragraph as correct statements *about means* and the justification of means; yet deny them every one if it is proposed to make these assertions universally concerning human actions. A moral action, a fitting moral response, a moral relation is not by definition the means to any end. Therefore, not every human *action* becomes *meaningful* by virtue of an end beyond itself, though that is the way a means becomes *means*-ingful. Not every human action becomes haphazard if it is without an end to serve, though such a silly means would indeed be hapless and haphazard. While it is the end sought that gives a means used its meaningness, not every human action or relationship needs such meaningness to be meaningful. While a means cannot justify itself, not every human action needs to find its justification by becoming a means.

Fletcher tries in vain to give depth and humanity to this

unilinear means-end analysis by complicating the picture a little. The means must be "appropriate and faithful" to the end. Means are "proximate ends." They are in fact "ingredients" of the end, not merely neutral tools for accomplishing an end beyond the tools (SE 121). The means ought to be *fitting* to the end (SE 122).[23] We must ask whether a means, which is evil (*sic!*), may not *nullify* a good end, to which it is ingredient (SE 126). Finally, there is a "contributory hierarchy," or reciprocity of means to ends and ends to means, in which *"in their turn* all ends eventually become means to some end higher than themselves" (SE 129). Fletcher comes closest to breaking out from the limits of cause-effect, means-end thinking when he writes that the righteousness of an act does not reside in the act itself (and presumably not in its consequences either) but "holistically *in its* Gestalt, *in the loving configuration"*; and perhaps when he speaks of situation ethics as "an ecological ethics" concerned with "the shape of the action as a whole" (SE 141–42). Still, the model confining analysis of the moral life to the means-end relationship remains intact. This is evident not least of all in the assertion that in their turn ends become means to some end higher than themselves. Even where "good" is equated with "loving-kindness" this is said to mean what we *do*, not what we *are* (SE 61). Thus the moral life is comprised of no finalities, no immediate goods, no present fitness, no responsibilities, and no appropriate responses that are just what they are and which do not need to run off into deliberation about what may be accomplished by means of them. This is the Puritan managerial spirit restlessly weighing and weighting all the immediate and remote consequences, to which in the present age man and his spiritual, aesthetic, and moral life have become wholly *menial*. This has to be denied and rejected by anyone concerned for the full humanity of man.

What is at stake here has in the past too often been set forth in terms of another doctrine of "means." There is an autonomous ethics of means, it is asserted, or at least free play

---

23 It is hard to see how *"paid* sex" can be compatible with these criteria. But then Fletcher disavows any pretense of being a systematic thinker, and on the first page of this book he even suggests that this is a non-book.

between the rightness of means and the goodness of ends so that the righteousness of the means can be defined in some measure apart from estimating their usefulness. The means must be right and *also* useful. In some way or degree right and wrong *means* can be determined apart from the ends of action. There are, one proposal says, means that conform to "natural" right or "natural" justice; and the means that do not (e.g. cruel forms of punishment) are never to be used for the sake of any end however good. This is the usual understanding of the maxim, the end does not justify the means. Fletcher opposes this doctrine of means, charging it with "intrinsicalism." There are, he believes, no inherently right or wrong means; it all depends on the ends, and of course the circumstances under which goods or ends are sought. He rejects a doctrine of inherently right or wrong means limiting the human pursuit of good consequences.

It must be granted, as above we have granted, that Fletcher proposes a more logical and defensible understanding of *means* as deeds set within a line of action toward the production of some good. The primary meaning of a means is that it be useful. But the price paid for this insight is, so long as consequentialism is still said to be the exclusive form of human action, the reduction of the moral life and the very *humanum* of man to a purely menial position and opening every human relation and all the covenants among men to the possibility of being used as instruments only. This is the genesis of Fletcher's ethics. The price is too great to pay for a clarification of the doctrine of means; yet it is the price that will be exacted by a consistent consequentialism.

Moreover, the price need not be paid. One need not simply riposte the old doctrine of inherent right and wrong means, though it must be said that this afforded more protections for the human spirit and for man's moral life, preventing their total reduction to tests of utility, than are to be observed in Fletcher's ethics. One has only to deny that man and morals are wholly devoted to goal-reaching. One has only to deny that the category of means embraces all human actions and relations. One has only to affirm that means are simply one department of human behavior having moral significance. One has only to affirm that the analysis of human action, the proper characterization of actions, and the evaluation of human behavior includes a great deal more than the estimation of means and ends. The business of ethics is the reflective clarification of the significance of all human actions, not of means only. There is an independent ethics of human *conduct*, even if there is not an independent ethics of *means*. There is human conduct and human moral activity that is *independent on* ends or consequences, even if there is no action independent of ends altogether. It may be the case, for example, that there are some kinds of essentially non-menial human actions that have a moral order of their own which does not need and does not find positive warrant in ends, but which would be voided if bad consequences regularly flowed from such behavior. The business of Christian ethics is to articulate what this may mean, and not always to talk of means only or of conduct that *is* dependent on ends. Unless this is admitted as possibly a large part of what we reflect upon in doing Christian ethics, then sooner or later ethics will become a matter of self-violation and the violation of others for the sake of the results. How soon will depend on how many pages one allows himself to write and how many cases he takes up.

One may say that nothing makes a thing good except *agapé*, but not that "nothing makes a thing good except agapeic *expedience*" (SE 125). One may say that nothing can justify *a means* except a loving *purpose*. Still what justifies *an action* that is of present significance may not be this at all, nor need all the actions of life have a purpose beyond themselves. The appropriateness of many actions may be simply the love unfolded, expressed, spoken in and through them. By them we dwell together. By them we are men with other men, men for other men. We enjoy one another, often with little thought of producing joy, not even of giving joy. In the covenants of life with life there is coinherence, and so some inherent presence of one to another. There is a speech in actions and lines of action and in steadfast relationships that have no ends beyond themselves. The business of Christian ethics embraces the living in rational reflection of these aspects of the Christian moral life and of human life, good in themselves, having no purpose, certainly no expediency, beyond themselves. Fletcher's error is not his *agapism*, but his conse-quentialism, his incessant "doing good." In this he is, once more, "the last Puritan."

With one of Fletcher's positions the present writer wishes to be completely associated. At the end of his chapter in the preparatory study volume for the World Council of Churches Conference on Church and Society, Geneva, 1966, among the "issues for ecumenical study," Professor Fletcher asks: "Is it true . . . that there are tragic situations in which the best that we can do is evil? Is it possible to say that the *best* we can do . . . is wrong?"[24] He takes this to be the question whether we can divorce right from good. I take it to be better expressed as the question whether the "lesser evil" is not the same as the "greatest good" possible, and therefore better characterized as the good or the right thing to do. Well do I remember D. C. Macintosh making this same logically compelling point at the onset of Niebuhrian Christian realism. This is still the mood: going about responsibly doing the greatest good possible, and gaining a general sense of guiltiness by calling it the lesser evil. One may say this out of a sense of tragedy, but not in penitence embracing the good or lesser evil to be done even while doing it. A long review of *Situation Ethics* published in one of our leading church periodicals has only this to object to in the entire book; this is ethics in cold blood, the ethics seems all right, but the author is pretty cool about the evil of the good that must be done.[25] This review and the general reception given *Situation Ethics* makes nothing more evident than the parlous state of Christian ethics in church thought today. The reverse has to be said: if the author has instructed us about the nature of the Christian life and a Christian's actions, the contention will hold that this is the right or the good thing to do. It can only confuse ethics if in order to aggravate our sense of sinfulness we *insist on* calling the greatest possible good the lesser evil (which, of course, it is tragically, but not immorally). Once or twice in this volume

24 "Anglican Theology and the Ethics of Natural Law," in John Bennett, ed., *Christian Social Ethics in a Changing World* (New York, 1966), p. 328.
25 "Ethics in Cold Blood," by Norman F. Langford. *Presbyterian Life*, April 15, 1966, pp. 10–11.

Fletcher adopts as a tactic Luther's language *pecca fortiter* in regard to some decision he believes to be situationally right (SE 152), but in one of these instances he immediately says that we must "change 'guilt' to *sorrow*, since such tragic situations are a cause for regret, but not for remorse" (SE 124). Everywhere else he emphasizes the doing of the good or the right in particular situations, at the risk of making a mistake, no doubt, but not, even so, fashionably self-censuring oneself as sinful. It may be objected that Fletcher displays a deficient sense of the tragedy of all human decisions and actions, but not that his greatest possible good (if this has been properly identified, and if it can be proved that this is an apt and sufficient summary of the Christian life) is still somehow morally evil.

The focus of attention must not be taken off the situational cause-and-effect understanding of right and wrong doing. Here lies the flaw, not elsewhere. The accusation of consequentialism that has been brought against Fletcher's ethics, and in objection to his reduction of every expression or exercise of the Christian life to a menial status, can now be brought to a head. Fletcher's war against intrinsicalism is carried to such an extreme that not only can a moral agent not know the good prior to particular situations but also he can never get to know the right and the good in any way. This is not only because his knowledge and experience are limited or because situations vary. It is primarily because his future-facing right-doing itself never comes to rest in a good done. The good was done, perhaps; but, since conscience is prospective, one cannot look back on that or learn from it concerning the meaning of the right and the good. One is always about to do the good. Better said, one is always about to *have done* the good, in an infinite regress reaching ahead.

This follows from combining what Fletcher says about "happening to be good" with what he says about the relativity of all ends and means to one another in an onreaching "contributory hierarchy" by which not only means but also all ends contribute to some good other than themselves. *"Not only means but ends too* are . . . extrinsically justifiable. They are good only if they happen to contribute to some good other than themselves" (SE 129). The word "good" in that last sentence, on which depends the goodness of everything that went before in the series, can only be given the same meaning: this will depend on something to come after, or if not chronologically after it on something extrinsic to it, on something beyond and other than its present goodness, and so on *ad infinitum*. Thus, every finality, every means, every activity is always about to be good or always about to have been good, in chronological or in logical outreach toward ends that are, of course, not good when they are not yet realized—and toward ends that when realized are not good (because this depends on something else that is not yet).

This is the fate that necessarily overtakes an exhaustive *ex*trinsicalism. Fletcher may try to stop loving actions in their flight. He may say that actions "are only right *when* or while or as long as they are loving!" (SE 141). But what does that mean, except that every action in the meanwhile which constitutes its dying life is always about to have been loving, or to have happened to have been loving? The point here is not to argue directly against Fletcher that good and evil are properties and not predicates, but to show the meaning of this life of restless predication if good and evil never become properties, qualities, or attributes of anything any time anywhere except in God. It sounds all right to say that "value is what *happens to* something when it happens to be useful to love working for the sake of persons" (SE 50), and it sounds all right to say that everything "gains or acquires its value only because it happens to help persons (thus being good) or to hurt persons (thus being bad)" (SE 59). But when these insights are set within the thought-forms of consequentialism or within the thought-forms of an exhaustive *ex*trinsicalism or nominalism, their meaning can only be expressed by saying that everything is always about to have been valuable.[26]

It is not that there must be certain pieces of behavior that antecedently count for loving or unloving. It is rather that there must be certain pieces of behavior that come to count for loving or unloving out of the experience of love itself or (how can this

---

[26] I can think of no alternative to using this temporal or chronological expression to exhibit the meaning of both the consequentialist order and the logical regress entailed in an exhaustive extrinsicalism.

possibility be ruled out?) by some analysis of the persons *in situ* whose good love seeks to serve. Restless Puritan that he is, Fletcher seems not to need to know in any way the meaning of love even by getting to know what actions or pieces of behavior mean or count for loving or unloving. He only needs to "know" that anything and everything may be about to have been *used* for loving or unloving. There is greater wisdom, by contrast, in the line in *The Gondoliers*, "When everyone is somebodee, then no one's anybody." Where everything may count for loving, then nothing can significantly count for loving. There can be no Christian life, nor Christian ethics reflecting on the nature of this Christian life, but only an attitude of loving compressed and imprisoned in the innermost recesses of human hearts amid a world of doings—hearts that are questing for the good-for-the-neighbor that is never to be found in an infinite logical or chronological regress of happenings.

There is one exit—one not taken by Fletcher until the end, as it were, of an infinite series of doings good, and not expressly then. Under the heading of "all ethics are happiness ethics," Fletcher writes that for the pragmatist this is *satisfaction* but for the Christian situationist "happiness is in doing God's will as it is expressed in Jesus' Summary" (SE 96). He promptly limits this definition of happiness, as elsewhere he limits the *summum bonum*,[27] to an understanding of the happiness of *the moral agent* alone: "his utility method sets him to seeking his happiness (pleasure, too, and self-satisfaction!) by seeking his neighbor's good on the widest possible scale." That internal reference to the neighbor's "good" has the power to set us off in directions we have already traversed *to no end* and *to no immediate good*.

Surely, however, we can say that what's happiness for the agent is happiness for the patient of Christian love, for we know in advance that the primary good for the neighbor—simply that he be loving—is the same as the agent's good, satisfaction, right-

---

[27] ". . . the *summum bonum*, the end or purpose of all ends. . . . We cannot say that anything we do *is* good, only that it is a means to an end and therefore *happens* in that cause-and-effect relation to have value" (SE 129). This is to bring the *summum bonum* to bear only upon determining an agent's cause-and-effect actions, not upon determining the immediate good of self and neighbor *independent on* such agency.

eousness, happiness. Fletcher indeed says this, in qualification of the assertion that "situation ethics is closer to teleology, of course" than to deontology (which is an assertion that can be questioned if made of Christian ethics as such). ". . . One's 'duty,'" he writes, "is to seek the goal of the most love possible in every situation, and one's goal is to obey the command to do just that!" Here in the words "duty" and "goal" the models of deontology and teleology are still intact; but Fletcher aims at this point to overcome them. Is his meaning not better expressed by saying that Christian ethics sees so far into the heart of man as to be able to say that the immediate good for him is "the most love possible," and to say that as the happiness of the moral agent is to be loving so the happiness and greatest good of persons who are the objects of this love is that they too be loving? This would be to say more and something other than that love is the ultimate norm of the good that happens to actions in a long line of doings (even reciprocated doings) the last of which cannot be the last but must in its turn become menial to something else. This would avoid saying that everything is only about to have been good. It would be to say more and something other than that love as the property of God is the extrinsic reference of all things else which are only nominally good. We would say that *to be loving* is the intrinsic immediate good or happiness, if you will, of self and neighbor alike, apart from their doings (i.e. apart from their use of means, or of ends in their turn as means to anything). Simply to express and to dwell in love is, here and now, the good for man, the good of selves, and the defining quality of covenants among men that are to be called right. Being loving is better than doing things (which is not, however, to be neglected), even as doing is better than having things (which nobody neglects).

This would be to open the way to the amplification of a Christian ethics of human actions, behavior, activities, relations, moral bonds, covenants of life with life, the good in law and institutions, the good life in community and in daily communication. These moral realities do not, or do not always, or do not to the whole extent of their being, fall under any means-end way of apprehending the structures of human action. They point, rather, to the good-*of* selves, not to the good-*for*. Professor John Hallowell says this about the fundamental nature of political community (using Aristotle's distinction between *making* and *doing*): "We do not build the state to live in (as we live in a house)—*we live the state*. Our living state is an integral part of our lives. Here the builders are what they build."[28] So with the life of Christian love, for the better part of it. The business of Christian ethics is to say what this may mean, and what in this sense counts for love, situationally or generally. If we ethicists took this approach in all our works, we might come to a better understanding of moral questions case by case, and possibly also contribute something to the philosophy of law and of man's communities so greatly needed in the present age.

3. On properly describing human acts

One way for Protestant Christian ethics to bring some order and solidity into what we have to say on moral questions would be for us to enlarge our community of discourse to include all of the analysis, characterization, and reflective evaluation of human actions that has gone on in the past or in the present within Christian communities. This would mean, for one thing, that we Protestants should wrestle with our Roman Catholic brethren over the verdict upon moral issues to which we have not given much thought heretofore. This would mean that attention must be paid in a wider community of discourse to the description of the human behavior we are talking about; and we would necessarily place ourselves in the position of having to learn from all past and present Christian moral analysis, without distinction as to denomination. In such a bracing context we would have to defend our descriptions of actions and demonstrate before all Christian consciences the worth of our verdicts. This must begin to be done if there is any prospect of an ecumenical ethics—I would add, if there is any prospect of Christian ethics in the present age. For it can scarcely be argued that we can get to know all that we Christians mean when we speak of man and of

---

[28] "The Nature of Government in a Free Society," in Z. K. Mathews, ed., *Responsible Government in a Revolutionary Age* (New York, 1966), p. 185 (italics added).

the Christian life by beginning *de novo* with minds already acculturated in one degree or another by the thought-forms and the moral premises and conclusions of the present age. The meaning of situational ethics today is that this attempt has been made. Far from this being a radical form of Christian ethics, it is the most palpable victimization by contemporaneity.

Another way for Protestant Christian ethics to discipline itself to the sound discussion of moral questions would be for us to enlarge our community of discourse to include all the analysis, characterization, and reflective evaluation of human actions that is going on *today*. Specifically, this means that we would take with utmost seriousness the ethics being done by contemporary philosophers; and in particular, the considerable body of literature upon the subject of moral discourse and the nature and characterization of human action.

I propose now to illustrate some of the benefits that might be forthcoming from a "coalition" of Christian ethics with the *best* of philosophical ethics today, by introducing some remarks based on Eric D'Arcy's excellent book entitled *Human Acts: An Essay on their Moral Evaluation*.[29] Then we will ask whether what this author has to say about properly describing human acts may not enable us to tell better what has gone wrong in Fletcher's ethics.

In regard to many human actions the answer to the question, "What is he doing now?" may be properly re-described as, or elided into a description of, the doing of the intended consequences. Instead of "flicking on a switch," we can say "turning on the lights." Instead of "singing a song," we can say "entertaining a group of people," or in the case of a USO artist at some military encampment, "helping the war effort." Instead of "omitting to eat," we can say "dieting" or "observing Lent." Instead of "flying over the Nevada desert," we can say "testing a new jet."

There are some human actions, however, whose description cannot be elided into or re-described as the doing of the intended consequences. Not, at least, without proposing to abandon the moral discourse in which people have customarily said more exactly what they are doing. We can say "Macbeth killed Duncan"

[29] (Oxford, Eng., 1963).

instead of "Macbeth stabbed Duncan, and so killed him," but not *in that act* that "Macbeth succeeded Duncan on the throne." We cannot (*contra* Fletcher) re-describe euthanasia as "a particular case of loving-kindness" (SE 130), or *apartheid* as "good-neighborliness" (which was Dr. Verwoerd's characterization of what South Africa is doing). We cannot re-describe killing imperious Caesar as "stopping a hole to keep the wind away," though that might be one service of his death. We cannot properly characterize "telling a lie" as "loving" or "promoting the glory of God." A Nero cannot properly say that in his action in "burning Rome" he was "illuminating the imperial palace," even though this was what he did *by means of* that action. A Judith cannot re-describe her seduction and killing of the king as "saving Israel." Sexual intercourse is properly termed fornication, adultery, rape, incest, or an act of marriage; but not as maximizing pleasure or administering therapy or curing souls or not frightening the horses. We may not characterize "killing nascent life" as "saving a mother's life," not at least if we do not want to confuse our own subsequent moral reasoning about the question of abortion (no matter what the verdict is). The gassing of a number of babies of Jewish women in medical research is properly called genocide, not promoting the advancement of science or the future health of mankind.

Thus, as Eric D'Arcy says in one of his theses, "certain kinds of act are of such significance that the terms which denote them may not . . . be elided into terms which (a) denote their consequences, and (b) conceal, or even fail to reveal, the nature of the act itself."[30] In the structure of moral language there are case-terms or moral-species-terms and genera-terms, act-terms and end-terms; and if we violate this usage by allowing every species-term to elide into an end-term the result will be a considerable lessening in our ability to grasp by the intellect the nature and the meaning of human action.

There needs to be, of course, a reflective inquiry into the logic of moral discourse in these respects, not simply an acceptance of it, or a blunt use of act-terms or moral-species-terms in making ethical judgments. It is the case, for example, that "very few species-terms are available to denote acts that are thought to

[30] p. 18.

be good, or commendable; but there are many genus-terms which apply to good behavior."[31] The latter commonly have opposites (honesty and dishonesty, justice and injustice) while species-terms often do not: e.g. there are no opposite case-terms to theft, rape, calumny, genocide. We need to reflect upon what may be the meaning of this. It may be that situation ethics is a penchant for replacing moral-species-terms (which are often condemnatory and have no opposites) by genus-terms which have opposites imply-ing good behavior *in the description of the action in question,* if not indeed by the single genera "loving." Thus there could be an "honest" or "candid" adultery, or a "loving" case of it; and if it is allowable to *describe the action* and characterize what was done as honesty, candidness, or loving, then one may not have justified the action itself, properly termed. He may have only replaced one term needing justification by another that does not in the description of the action.

In any case D'Arcy's contention is that there are moral-species-terms where sound usage founded upon the significance of the kinds of actions denoted by these words forbid us from sim-ply describing, "doing X with the consequence Y" as "doing Y." There is need, then, for moral science to inquire into the elida-bility and non-elidability of species-terms. Only then can we identify with confidence the act-, case-, or species-terms that de-note the sorts of actions that are of such particular and immedi-ate human significance that they cannot be elided into terms denoting the end (motives, intention) of the agent or the con-sequence of the act.[32] This may be illustrated from a case formu-lated by J. J. C. Smart. Suppose that during a racial crisis in the United States, a lynch mob furious over a particularly heinous crime is about to hang four Negro men chosen at random. Sup-pose the local sheriff, an honorable man, can prevent this only by "framing" one man he knows to be not guilty to slack the bloodthirsty mob. Is this action to be described as "committing judicial murder" or "saving four men"?

Obviously there are any number of ways to describe the action of the sheriff in executing the innocent man.

"1. He tensed his forefinger.

31 p. 25.
32 p. 32.

2. He pressed a piece of metal.
3. He released a spring.
4. He pulled the trigger of a gun.
5. He fired the gun.
6. He fired a bullet.
7. He shot a bullet at a man.
8. He shot a bullet toward a man.
9. He shot a man.
10. He killed a man.
11. He committed judicial murder.
12. He saved four lives."[33]

"He committed judicial murder" *completes* the description of his action. After that, we can ask only, "What *happened* then as a consequence of what he *did*?" After steps 1. through 10., we can ask "What did he *do* then?" but not after step 11. "He saved four lives" is a description of the consequence of his action, not of the action itself. For the sake of brevity, we may elide 1. or 2., etc. into 11., but not into "saving four lives." *That* was *not* what the sheriff *did*, even if it is said by subsequent moral reasoning that "saving four lives" justified the action properly described. D'Arcy's view is that for some significant sorts of action, for which our moral language has developed species-terms, there is a cut-off point between the physiological description of the action and the consequentialist (or intentional) description of the action, which must be observed if we want to characterize correctly the actions we are talking about. "The point is not," D'Arcy observes, "that these actions are so wicked that sound moral judgment must always condemn them, but that they are so *significant* for human existence and welfare and happiness that they must always be taken into account before sound moral judgment can be passed on them."[34]

D'Arcy does not offer any explanation of the fact that our moral discourse thus signalizes the *significance* and *importance* of some actions, and not others. His book is simply an analysis of the language of morals in regard to the description of human actions. The most likely explanation of the fact that *moral talk*

[33] p. 3.
[34] p. 38 (italics added).

thus registers the importance of some sorts of actions, and not others, must be that men have recognized concerning the actions in question that there are features *other than consequences* affecting the ethical evaluation of some actions and not of others. Philosophers speak of these as considerations of *fairness* and *justice* which (in addition to utility) must be taken into account in appraising conduct. Theological ethicists have good reason not to neglect these considerations—in probing what we may know concerning the *present* righteousness or unrighteousness of behavior, and concerning existing bonds and covenants among men.

As with the intentions of the agent and the consequences of the act, so not all of the modifying circumstances are *constitutive* of the meaning of moral-species-terms; nor for that matter of offense-terms used in evaluating actions described by these species-terms. Some circumstances are constitutive of what was done, some are not. Situation ethics fails to order its moral reasoning by taking account of the very many questions arising in connection with describing the action in question, even situationally; it speaks as if any circumstance may be constitutive of what was actually done, and as if there are not circumstances that serve simply as a possibly warranting or extenuating circumstance. "Killing a man" may or may not be murder, depending on the constitutive circumstances, i.e. those constituting murder. One may speak of justifiable homicide, but not of justifiable life-saving which needs no justification even by an agapeic calculus. An act of sexual intercourse is, by reason of the constitutive circumstances, describable as marital love or fornication or adultery or rape; or adultery would be, by reason of the woman's unwillingness, rendered rape. Cutting off a man's leg may be mayhem or surgery. Because of constitutive circumstances, it is not a lie to tell a verbal untruth, as many a Wagnerian opera singer makes evident when at the top of her lungs she sings, "I die, I die." One cannot say, "I know from consulting a physiologist what the act was; now tell me the circumstances." But neither should we elide the act-term altogether into a circumstance-term. As with intention and consequence, there is a cut-off point between constitutive and non-constitutive circumstances in regard to many

human actions having weighty and immediate human significance.[35]

There are, in short, specifying circumstances and non-specify-
ing circumstances. Some circumstances may *constitute* the act,
some may *change* the proper description of an act from one
species to another (both right or both wrong in offense-terms, as
Aristotle's man who commits adultery for gain and thus is guilty
of injustice as well as profligacy; or from good to bad, as when an
act of charity is accomplished by injustice to one's creditors; or
from bad to good, e.g. from mayhem to surgery), and some circumstances may cause an action to belong also to another moral
species, as when a lie is also perjury, and finally there are some
circumstances that are extenuating, aggravating, enhancing, or
disentitling in the matter of attributing moral worth.[36]

This is enough to show that there is some hard thinking
ahead if we Protestants want seriously to do ethics, whether in
discourse with the Christian moralists of all the ages or in discourse with the better among our contemporary ethicists. Fletcher
may be able to gain a certain following when he exclaims: "Every
little book and manual on 'problems of conscience' is legalistic.
'Is it right to . . .' have premarital intercourse, gamble, steal,
euthanase, abort, lie, defraud, break contracts, *et cetera, ad
nauseum?* This kind of intrinsicalist morass must be left behind
as irrelevant, incompetent and immaterial" (SE 124). But then
there are better books to pick up. These almost without exception call for careful distinctions to be made in the analysis of
human behavior, and for unhurried deliberation in the probing
of moral questions. One who first sees that not just anything may
properly describe human actions is not likely to conclude that
anything that is done may happen to be good.

It was suggested in the $100,000 case of justified prostitu-
tion that, given one or two additional suppositions, *what was
done* that night might be re-described in terms of its consequences
as "building parks for the children of the poor to play in." This
introduces another cardinal failure in the case of Joseph Fletcher's ethics, namely, his failure to deal adequately with the ques-

[35] pp. 61–71.
[36] pp. 88–92.

tion of how properly to *characterize* a human action. Prior to either criminating or exculpating an action we must know its proper *description*. This is only to say that we must know what action we are talking about. Are there some sort (but not all sorts) of circumstances that are *constitutive* of the action and constitutive of the characterization of the actions that are under discussion in ethical discourse? Is the action itself to be re-described in terms of its ultimate and intended consequences, or do these consequences only justify actions that can be aptly and fully characterized without reference to them? Are there also act-terms or only end-terms in ethics? Are moral-species-terms important in orderly moral reasoning, or are all the different kinds of actions spoken of in ordinary human discourse elidable in ethics into *genera* such as "malevolent" or "loving-kindness" or "doing good"?

A reader can hardly grasp what is going on in Fletcher's ethics unless he realizes that (1) he is carrying through a pro-gram of re-describing human actions in terms of all their circum-stances and all their consequences in the course of justifying what was done, and also that (2) the *arbitrariness* of Fletcher's solution of cases stems from the fact that he has an insufficient grasp of how to describe human actions—in a given case and from case to similar case. This is why, within a single situation and abruptly from situation to similar situation, anything can count for love and usually does.

Let us examine Fletcher's ethics under both these heads, to see whether his justifications are not first of all vast and ques-tionable re-descriptions and to see whether the gratuitous way in which he declares first one behavior and then another to be the loving thing to do does not evidence insufficient attention to the description of human actions, even situationally.

1. The first point is a strangely paradoxical one, for it is essential to Fletcher's case that the actions in question be re-characterized and, at the same time, that they not be re-character-ized.

On the one hand, the seeming *success* of Fletcher's program of ethical justification depends on his eliding every *specific* description of human actions into end-terms. He re-describes the actions he brings under scrutiny in terms of all their circumstances and consequences. Or he contends that actions may properly be thus re-characterized in moral discourse and in making decisions. This is the way to know and to speak of what people do in their actions. Then he warrants the actions as thus described. He permits the possible elision of any and every *kind* of actions people do, indeed, into a single *genera* characterizable in terms of intentions (love) and consequences (good). Whether this is the way properly to characterize human actions is a question prior to taking issue with any of Fletcher's ethical verdicts upon particular deeds.

On the other hand, the seeming *sensationalism* of many of his ethical conclusions depends on holding firm the moral-species-terms ordinarily used to characterize the actions he justifies. It must be "murder" and "adultery" that are warranted situationally, and not particular actions specifically or generically re-characterized in terms of their accomplishments.

Thus, Fletcher rejects the argument against euthanasia which holds that such acts "if raised to a general line of conduct would injure humanity," and therefore would be wrong in the individual case. He does not attempt to *answer* the contention that to raise *euthanasia* to a general line of action would be harmful (which may be true or false so far as our present point is concerned). Instead, he *re-describes* the action proposed to be raised to a general line of action in the course of ridiculing the contention: "A particular case of loving-kindness, *if everybody did it*, would mean chaos and cruelty" (SE 130). The argument never was that "loving-kindness" but that "euthanasia," if raised to a general line of action, would make for cruelty. Whether an act of euthanasia is to be characterized as "a particular case of direct killing" or "a particular case of loving-kindness," whether the act-term also and not only the end-term have significance in moral discourse: these are questions concerning how we are to do ethics that are prior to all our justifications and prohibitions. In this instance, Fletcher has re-described the action under scrutiny so extensively that the justification of it becomes superfluous. Indeed, his re-characterization of this particular action is so far inclusive of and indistinguishable from the intention and doing of certain consequences that nothing is left in terms of which to justify the action except the action, i.e. what was *done* or proposed to be done, *as thus re-described*. This is one way to succeed in ethics without really trying!

The fact that Fletcher's method is ethical justification by moral re-characterization seems to me to be evident in other less explicit instances. In Chapter Five, "justice" is simply re-described as "love." Thus as an ethicist he avoids the problem of saying how love and justice may be related, and at the same time rejects the wisdom there may have been in the fact that people in almost all times and places have used both terms in moral discourse in order to say more precisely what they mean. It follows from this re-description of justice as love, of course, that there remains no problem concerning whether an unjust action should ever be done if one finds such an action to be serviceable. That conclusion would seem to be the reason for the re-characterization, and what was sought to be established by it. Whether there is justice in the affairs of men *in*-dependent *on* consequences if not wholly independent *of* them is decided by a questionable re-description of just human actions. Having abolished "justice" as a generic or moral-species-term, there is no more need to inquire into it; and of both a justifiable "injustice" (formerly so-called) and a justifiable "justice" we can say: "He did *right*, he did the loving thing." Indeed, the justification of anything lately called an "injustice" consists in re-describing the action in question as "loving" in motive and consequence. Justice may be what love does when confronted by two or more neighbors (SE 94); but that is to *locate* justice in relation to basic Christian love, not to re-describe the justice to be done as loving, or as "figuring the angles" (SE 90).[37]

Again, what is behind the assertion that "on a vast 'agapeic calculus' President Truman made his decision about the A-bombs on Hiroshima and Nagasaki" (SE 98)? Does this not entail that the President (or our existing moral ethos) simply re-described the action before ordering the dropping of the bombs? He may

---

[37] These references of Fletcher's to my *Basic Christian Ethics* (New York, 1950) are a bit puzzling, since one is to a page (347) on which I introduced Rousseau's concept of "objective generality" as a valid moment in the meaning or definition of justice.

have said, "I am saving lives on the beaches of Japan," or, "I am doing the agapeic thing," which characterization contained in itself its own justification because there was nothing beyond the action to invoke for a warrant except the action itself, i.e. what was *done* or proposed to be done, *as thus described.* He did not say, "I am ordering the bombing of primarily civilian targets," which description would have required further thought. In fact, the persons in government who helped to make this decision gave thought to a greater range of relevant moral considerations because the moral-species-terms, "legitimate military target" or "justice in the conduct of war," had *not* been displaced from their minds as much as they are replaced, simply as apt characterizations of actions, by Fletcher's "vast agapeic calculus."

Still, while this ethical justification by moral re-description is going on, the sensationalism of the outcome depends on keeping intact the act-descriptions that have been the precipitate of centuries of moral decision-making. Indeed, Fletcher often purchases a reputation for radicalness by insisting on using moral-species-terms in a very unrefined fashion, or with a meaning that he should know (and his readers may not know) few, if any, moralists would accept.

Thus, Bonhoeffer was "a modern Christian ethicist who was himself executed for trying to kill, even *murder*, Adolf Hitler— so far did he go as a situationist" (SE 33, Fletcher's italics). If that is the way a situationist goes, it is in the direction of stripping act-terms such as "murder" of the meaning they ever had in moderately sophisticated moral discourse. Yet it somehow must be "murder" that was situationally justified, and not some other sort of killing (or an action better describable by another term). To describe the action more properly might let in justifications other than "love" and "consequences."

Keeping intact the ancient moral-species-terms rather than examining their meaning is a part of the program here proposed for Christian ethics. Bonhoeffer is a man who did not quite make it as a situationist because he decided Hitler was *not inno-cent* and therefore should be assassinated. To make this distinction and "to denounce 'murder' is a very question-begging universal negative" (SE 74–75). This seems to mean that even to attempt closer *specification* of an action in the course of evaluating the morality or immorality of human behavior amounts to the futile exercise of saying "immoral killing is immoral." To the contrary, a careful characterization of actions is the minimum requirement of saying what in ethics we are talking about; and it is Fletcher who is open to the charge that while holding on to the blanket act-term "murder" he has defined this simply as *"unlawful* killing," i.e. unlawful under the Nazi system.

Next, consider cases of "lying." "What if you have to tell a lie to keep a promised secret?" Fletcher asks. His answer is: "Maybe you lie, and if so, good for you if you follow love's lead" (SE 65). At this point Fletcher is discussing Kant. Nevertheless, he himself has about as much interest as Kant had in keeping the meaning of "lying" to "veraciousness" or *verbal* integrity only. He wants the person in this case to be able at one and the same time to re-describe his action as "I followed love's lead" and to describe it very crudely (if in Kantian terms) as "I lied." Therefore he does not open the question whether in this case promise-keeping does not enter into the meaning of truth-telling, and of the act-term "lying." If it is to the credit of "the ethics of the civil law" that failure to tell the necessary lie [*sic!*] might very possibly make one an accessory before the fact to murder" (SE 128), is it not to the greater credit of most moralists of the past that they knew this not to be the meaning of "lying"? Nor can human acts of truth-telling be properly described without reference to the special moral office of speaker, promiser, etc., even if verbal veracity is ordinarily also a part of the description of such acts. Fletcher creates in great part the sensationalism of his own position, his justification of "lying," by not telling the reader that a great many, perhaps most, moralists would *not* say that verbal dissimulation or inaccuracy in order to reserve a promised secret to the one to whom it is due constitutes the meaning of lying. A better case can be made for saying that withholding *this* information from the reader, if known to the author, comes close to culpable deceit.[38]

---

38 "In the name of a 'natural law' of secrecy," Fletcher writes, "they have been known to admonish a doctor to withhold from an innocent girl the fact that she is about to marry a syphilitic man" (SE 80). That is certainly a rare

Fletcher must keep in place the ancient landmarks in order to destroy them even if the ones he places under attack are often not the ones that marked the boundaries of the actions described for approval or disapproval in any people's moral ethos, certainly not by their most reputable and influential moralists or jurists. "Surgeons *mutilate* bodies to remove cancers, . . . nurses *lie* to schizophrenics to keep them calm for treatment," Fletcher calmly says (SE 123, italics added), with never an effort to demonstrate that this is the meaning ascribable to actions falling under the terms "mutilation" and "lying." Perhaps the demonstration was not undertaken because to begin to do so is to see that such a careless use of language can never be the fruit of saying what sorts of actions we are talking about under the act-terms we use.

Thus was his fate prepared for another "almost situationist," William Temple. "Speaking more timidly than a situationist would" is Fletcher's notation concerning the following effort of Temple's (internal to a longer quotation which Fletcher approves) to characterize *specifically what are the actions* under discussion: "It cannot be said that it is wrong to take away a man's possessions against his will, for that would condemn all taxation —or the removal of a revolver from a homicidal maniac; neither of which is stealing—which is always wrong . . ." (SE 59). Fletcher's case, it is evident, depends on the validity of *both* characterizations, both the description few have held: "That is 'stealing,'" *and* the re-description of these actions as "That is following love's lead." It is Fletcher who insists on describing an action he is discussing as *"stealing* a man's gun to keep him from shooting somebody in anger" (SE 125, italics added). He only wants, without withdrawing or examining that preposterous characterization, to call it also a "loving deed" (which undoubtedly

and quite questionable opinion about the obligation to tell the truth in "perplexity" with the obligations of privileged communication. Fletcher's *words* "been known to" allow for this, and so that sentence is strictly speaking correct. How many readers, however, could the author reasonably expect rightly to read this qualification and to take hold of the truth behind this nuance? How close is this sentence to dissimulation, not for the purpose of preserving verbal veracity, but for the purpose of creating in the mind of the reader, to whom was due all the truth known, a sensational opposition between situational ethics and the efforts of moralists in the past carefully to describe in meaningful act-terms the actions they are discussing?

it is). He mistakenly supposes that his argument with "intrinsicalists" at this point is that they only want to say this "stealing" was a "lesser *evil*." The fact is that most moralists, when they go about making moral judgments or rationally reflecting upon judgments to be made, know better how to characterize actions than to call this "stealing"; and so the question whether this is a lesser evil or the greatest good love can do is not at issue.

Or take the case of "Mother Maria's *suicide*" (says Fletcher without batting an eyelash, SE 74, italics added). Mother Maria chose to die in the gas chambers of Belsen in the stead of a young ex-Jewish girl Communist—who survived and later became a Christian. Fletcher characterizes her action as "suicide" and then as "sacrificing her life on the 'model' of Christ." This justifies, he must insist, *suicide*—and then, rapidly in the same paragraph, *euthanasia* (one form of suicide), which proves again that Bonhoeffer fell short of the mark because, while undoubtedly he would have approved of Mother Maria's action, he did not approve of euthanasia. Confusedly, Fletcher asserts that "absurdly" Bonhoeffer "had to invoke a rival law [in the case of euthanasia] that says her [Mother Maria's!] love cannot follow her Master's example *too closely*!" Undoubtedly euthanasia is a species of suicide, in the sense that morally to forbid the latter is to forbid the former. But courageous self-sacrifice has rarely been taken to be a case or a species of the forbidden suicide—or never as lightly and without argument as Fletcher takes this to be obvious. The point here, however, is not to argue these points, but to indicate the degree to which Fletcher's ethics depends on a failure to deal with the prior question of how we are to speak of actions in the doing of ethics, how human actions are to be specifically described; and to indicate the dependence of his ethics on both describing actions by certain act-terms and *at the same time* re-describing them in end-terms. One cannot have it both ways.

Similarly, the woman whose action in *Never on Sunday* might be aptly described as "administering love's therapy" is describable also as not simply a "prostitute" but a "whore," and presumably she was in that act a-whoring, which was up for justification in this particular case. While, of course, the two words for her profession strictly convey no different denotations, still I judge that the word "whore" has connotative weight in the fabricated sensationalism of Fletcher's "proofs" from cases. This is shown by his needless and inexact use of a cognate of this five-letter word ("seductively" would have been correct) in analyzing the case of Judith, in the Apocryphal story, who was praised for *"lying"* to Holofernes and "using her sex . . . *whoringly* in order to *murder* him"* (SE 66, italics added). Here is a whole set of moral-species-terms that must be kept intact in characterizing her actions ("whoringly" most inexactly, the other two without going into the moral discourse relevant to specifying correctly what she did) while at the same time re-describing her action as "saving the people Israel." What was it that she actually *did*, and what were the *consequences* of her action? Is what she did elidable in characterizing her action into the doing of those consequences? These questions are not raised. Here again an "almost situationalist," Bishop James Pike who says many "very promising" things "stoutly," "never really comes off" (SE 66). The issue may be simply that Pike wants still to use the moral-species-term, "homicide," even when he is talking about "justifiable homicide" to save Israel. That is, the act-term "homicide" forestalls the complete elision of the description of what she did into "saving Israel." Why continuing to use the more technical term "homicide" in discussing her case is any worse than using such act-terms as "lying" "using her sex whoringly" and "murder," it would be hard to say. It all depends, I can only suppose, upon what one hopes to justify by subsequently allowing the acts thus described to elide into another description of what she did.

Finally, most of these ancient boundaries in man's moral discourse descriptive of actions are gathered together and thrown at Fletcher's *bete noire,* "legalism." "This pilpul," he writes "has been ground out of the legalistic mills to rationalize war's ruthless methods of forcing, killing, subverting, violating; it has strained to find moral reasons for capital or corporal punishment, diplomatic subterfuge, surgical mutilations, and a whole host of things" (SE 123). Prescending from some of the exaggeration in that list of charges, are not many of these things precisely Fletcher's own descriptions of actions that he wishes to justify as not only not evils or even lesser evils but outright good? One can only stare in amazement at that sentence if he holds together with it in his mind the case of Hiroshima and Nagasaki justified by a vast agapeic calculus (SE 98), various of the cases of justified prostitution, including not only paid sex but, nobler yet, the case of patriotic espionage by means of sex (SE 163–64, 146; C 431), and a number of cases we have not yet mentioned; such as, T. E. Lawrence's killing by his own hands, since he was a "responsible decision maker," the Moor who killed another in a quarrel and thus produced a situation ripe for the outbreak of "endless feud and bloodletting" (SE 98), or the British intelligence officers in World War II who let a number of women agents return to Germany to certain arrest and death in order to keep secret the fact that the British had broken the German code (SE 98: Fletcher's notation is: "situational casuistry could easily approve their decision"), or the case of the Negro woman on the Wilderness Road going West who killed her crying baby with her own hands to keep it silent so that the whole party could be saved from Indian attack (SE 125), or even the case of the God Moloch who offered the ruler of one of the "developing" countries a modern highway system in exchange for 45,000 lives annually, which is the *predictable* number of U.S. deaths in highway accidents each year (SE 118: Fletcher refrains from noting his judgment upon this case but surely the rightfulness of the exchange can be encompassed by a vast agapeic calculus, certainly unless one has first distinguished in the description of actions between direct killing and allowing to die, etc.). One cannot even tell who is the greater rationalizer of monstrous evil —Fletcher or his opponents—until a way is found to clear up this monstrous confusion in the use of language in doing ethics.

The upshot of all this is precisely *not* to disagree with Fletcher or even to join with him in substantive moral argument about these cases. It is rather to assert that there can be no expectation of orderly ethical discussion or hope even for fruitful disagreement unless ethicists have come to some decision concerning how they ought properly to describe the human actions they propose to talk about with a view to evaluating them. This is a question of the language and the logic of moral discourse. It is perhaps a meta-ethical or even a pre-ethical question; certainly it is pre-decisional. And it is the thing most lacking in Fletcher's ethics. For anyone to open this question about our moral discourse and how human actions should or should not be described will expose him immediately to the dread danger of "intrinsicalism." This may be or it may not be the viewpoint in ethics to which one will be driven from having clarified what he means to say about actions, what are the actions of which he is speaking, whether the consequences and all the circumstances are or are not constitutive of the action or the description of the action, etc. The fact that Fletcher will immediately charge that "intrinsicalism" has again reared its ugly head even in my very raising of these questions shows nothing so much as that he has paid no attention to them.

2. Lack of firmness in characterizing human actions is surely the explanation—or one of the explanations—of the gratuitous deeds that from time to time may count as loving. Reading a number of Fletcher's cases one is struck by an unexpected *arbitrariness* of the judgment or decision the author regards as valid. From what he says about a given case one expects him to lean in the same direction in another case that is not too different from the first; yet, unpredictably, in the second case he recommends the option (or one like it) that was refused in the first instance where it seems that this would have been equally appropriate. This may simply be the result of the fact that, as announced in the Foreword, "the reader will find *a method* here, but no system" (SE 11, italics added). Perhaps, Fletcher's method is intended to be applied by men who believe in different substantive value systems or hierarchies of value. Then the method would admit of a certain sort of decision in one instance (when it is applied to a choice of the best from among temporal values) and, in a not dissimilar situation, the same method might lead to another sort of decision (when it is applied to a choice of the best from among eternal along with temporal values).

Yet Fletcher insists that the method of determining absolute love's relative course must "form a coalition with utilitarianism"

(SE 95) in adopting the strategy of doing the greatest good for the greatest number. This might still admit the method's reference to supposable eternal values, entailed in some of his cases, in determining one's situational choice of the greatest good. However, in Chapter Two the author elaborates four "presuppositions" that have to be accepted along with the ultimate norm of Christian love. The coalition is made, then, with these four presuppositions: pragmatism, relativism, positivism, and personalism.[39] Now it may be that none of these gives substance to the ethics or eliminates arbitrariness from the decisions that may be reached. Perhaps they are all, and all together with *agapé*, formal or methodological approaches to making moral decisions. There is evidence for this interpretation of Fletcher's position. Then, in order to account for some of the arbitrariness in Fletcher's consideration of cases, we would have to say that *sometimes* he remembers that his is a complex *method* only and on these occasions he admits it to be a possibly quite proper situational decision for someone to take account of the decisiveness of certain substantive *immediate* or *eternal* values he believes in; while on other occasions Fletcher forgets that his is only a formal method and on these occasions he is inclined to take into decisive account only future, this-worldly consequences—"utilitari-

---

[39] Christian theological ethics is, of course, the Christian *life* lived in rational reflection, as Christian dogmatic theology is the Christian *faith* lived in rational reflection. This means that Christian ethics is a secondary "science" presupposing life's activity and conduct upon the basis of Christian *faith*. In this sense, *agapé* need not be demonstrated to be the norm of the Christian life. But in addition to this Fletcher demands four other "acts of faith"; or rather he reports to the reader that he himself has performed these acts of faith in accepting pragmatism, relativism, positivism, and personalism. These are announced as additional presuppositions that are "at work" in this volume, and not Christian determinants alone, so that the reader "can correct for any bias he thinks they are imposing" (SE 40). This is a genial approach. But it is everywhere evident that the author calls the reader to respond to the same quadruple altar-calls in addition to the first and fundamental Miracle he accepted as a Christian. These four philosophies are "presuppositions" requiring acceptance, however persuasive because they are widespread contemporary opinions. The effect of this is that the author nowhere takes responsibility for demonstrating the reasonableness, or even the necessity, of these decisions. The author simply calls upon the reader not only to accept the fundamental anchorage of the Christian life in the *agapé* of Christ, but to accept the amplifications and articulations of the meaning of this that would prove acceptable to someone who is by faith a utilitarian also, and a pragmatist, a relativist, a positivist, and a personalist. Hence, this volume becomes accumulatively hortatory, persuasive, assertive throughout.

anism," "pragmatism," "positivism" as ordinarily understood to be substantive value systems, in coalition with Christian love and its casuistry.

Finally, a provisional explanation may be to relate the arbitrariness and vacillation of the decisions Fletcher makes from case to case to his failure, previously alluded to, to set his mind in order in regard to how human actions are to be characterized or described in the course of evaluating them. If he is uncertain whether, in order for our minds to "grasp" what we are talking about in moral discourse, an action should or should not be described as the doing of its consequences, then no wonder he seems to be uncertain whether an action under discussion is to be described as the doing of a certain kind of thing or the doing of *these* consequences or *those* consequences, as doing the greatest immediate or some future good, as doing the greatest eternal good or serving positive material values. Sometimes he inclines one way and sometimes another in the cases about to be brought under review; and the way he inclines can mainly be told by looking to see who is being berated as a legalist, etc., for making a judgment in an instant case that, it turns out, is very like Fletcher's in another not wholly dissimilar situation.

This must be enough to show that, as Herbert McCabe pointed out in *Commonweal*, there must be "pieces of human behavior" that count for love, which could or could not be expressions of love, or are or are not expressions of love in certain sorts of situations, or even simply in *this* situation, in order for there to be a Christian life or Christian ethics at all (C 433). Just as there can be no thinking at all unless there are pieces of behavior that count as muddled thinking, so "if 'love' is to have any meaning at all, there must be pieces of behavior which count as unloving" or loving (C 435). Fletcher found this point to be incomprehensible, and treated it (C 438) as requiring that, antecedent to love, there must be pieces of behavior that count as right or wrong, or of use proper to love. This smacked of intrinsicalism, and of *prefabricated* morality. It was nothing of the sort. It was only the requirement that in order to live at all or to do ethics at all we must know what we mean by love, situationally or not. The requirement was only a minimum one, comparable I suppose to the possibility of falsification in distinguishing clear thinking from muddled thinking. Something must count as clear and something must count as muddled thinking; and some piece of behavior must count as love and another as unloving. This may be to say that a given piece of behavior is loving *because of the love that is in it*, not because of something else antecedently intrinsic in it (say "justice"), and that another thing would be unloving because it could not be, or is not in this situation, possibly an expression of love. If generally or situationally any number of behaviors can pass for love, then the love in question has no meaning, no possible pertinent characterization. If as we move from case to case what counts for love in one instance is quite arbitrarily and for no apparent reason not allowed to count for love in another and similar situation, then the love in question has no meaning, no possible pertinent characterization.

Of course, in a *given* case Fletcher says clearly enough what he thinks would be love's leading in that situation; but it is apparent as we move from case to case that he might have said otherwise. The following cases have to be cleared up by eliminating the arbitrariness of the decisions apparently recommended: this would require the introduction of a greater wealth of characterization of the actions in question, a better "grasp" and understanding of them, and bringing to bear upon them a more disciplined moral reflection informed by all the wisdom of our Christian ethical tradition. This would mean that Christian ethical discourse would be about what pieces of behavior count or do not count as loving. Or else this ethic, by holding on to the notion that anything may *happen* to be the good and the loving thing to do, will be forced to become not only *at root* an ethics of subjective intention, a *Gesinnungs-ethik*, an attitudinal ethic (SE 79), but will become this for its entire length and breadth. In that case no books can henceforth be written on ethics. The only volume needed would be one containing the single statement that love is this inner attitude having no significant expression because it has every expression since anything and everything can count as its expression and a great variety of things can count for love in the same situation. This would be to reduce ethics not only to a non-system, but to a non-book; and a non-book on non-ethics (cf. SE 11). More importantly, there could be no such thing as the Christian life since no one could tell, generally or situationally, what counts for love. He could not know what his own love means or should mean. He could only attitudinize, he could not know what to do, since the given piece of behavior that proposes itself as counting for or exhibiting love always might have been otherwise—indeed, might not have been at all and something else might have been instead.

During World War II a priest in the underground resistance in a daring raid bombed a Nazi freight train. In retaliation for this sabotage, the occupying authorities began killing twenty hostages a day and announced they intended to continue to do so until the saboteur surrendered. After three days and sixty lives, a fellow member of the resistance movement, himself a Communist, betrayed the priest to stop the carnage. Now, I submit, by the time he gets to this case the reader of *Situation Ethics* has some reason to expect Fletcher to approve of the betrayal of the priest because of the cost in lives otherwise entailed, or else censure the betrayal because of the importance of general immunity from betrayal by one's comrades to the underground cause with its more remote reference to a greater number of lives. One has just read a calculus, which indeed can scarcely be improved upon, which states that while "we do not prefer one neighbor to another," or self or neighbor over one another, "we prefer to serve more neighbors rather than fewer" (SE 113) and that "it is right to deal lovingly with the enemy *unless to do so hurts too many friends*" (SE 115).[40] To apply these principles amplifying the requirements of love, a member of the resistance would be in enough of a quandary in telling what he should do; and the two options just mentioned would seem to exhaust the possibly responsible choices facing the Communist, or a Christian situationalist member of the resistance who had effected a coalition of *agapé* and its calculus with utilitarianism, pragmatism, positiv-

[40] Does this mean that it is right to deal lovingly with one's friends unless to do so hurts too many enemies? This is enough to show that Christian ethics cannot consist of a vast agapeic calculus alone, but must include the specific covenants and responsibilities peculiar to political community, society, family, friendship, etc.

ism, relativism, and personalism. Perhaps these options do correctly state the alternatives for a member of the resistance other than the priest himself.

Nevertheless, I submit that it will come as something of a shock that Fletcher does *not* say that the priest should have turned himself in to stop the carnage. Moreover, he did not refuse to do so because he was needed for more heroic deeds of sabotage in the future or because his life or death could count for more for the cause, in a calculus of neighbor-good, than the lives that were being sacrificed. That might well have been a predictable situational solution. Instead, the priest said, "There is no other priest available and our people's souls need my absolution for their eternal salvation." Fletcher's somewhat surprising verdict upon the priest's refusal to turn himself in is: "One may accept the priest's assumptions about salvation or not . . . but no situationist could quarrel with his *method* of ethical analysis and decision" (SE 115–16).

If it was situationally proper for the priest to refuse to turn himself in, then what are we to make of Fletcher's unqualified approval of decisions made that give priority to this-worldly values in the case of pretended apostasy (SE 72) and in the case of the seal of confession (SE 132). In the first case, the life of an illegal underground church and the lives of dependents justify pretending to have no faith in God; and in the second, love for an innocent man about to die for a penitent's crime warrants violating the secrecy of the latter's confession. Of course! But the point is that the opposite verdict might equally well be reached according to anyone's greater esteem for eternal values; and there be no justice in Fletcher's excoriation that neighbor-love comes last after the sacrosanctities. He might as well have told different stories, and said that one may not accept these assumptions about salvation, apostasy, or the confessional, yet no situationist could quarrel with the method by which these opposite verdicts were reached.

The issue this raises is *not* whether there is anything outside the situation which by going into it can prejudge it (cf. SE 74). The issue is rather what counts for responsible loving action in contrast to irresponsible unloving action *within* a particular situation. The priest and the Communist each thought he knew; but Fletcher does not know because in actual fact neither of the protagonists really knew which piece of behavior counts for love. There are two possibilities for situation ethics, therefore, disclosed within the boundaries of this case: (1) Either situation ethics must clearly admit the position to be subjectivism or an ethics entirely of inner attitude, which would amount to much the same thing as the existential ethics of the moment rejected at the outset. This, indeed, seems to be Fletcher's position in many of his extreme statements on sexual ethics: ". . . if people do not believe it is wrong to have sex relations outside marriage," Fletcher writes, "it isn't, unless they hurt themselves, their partners, or others" (SE 140). The latter stipulation obviously requires that there be sorts of behavior that do or do not count for love; but this is rather clearly for Fletcher a self-fulfilling non-prophecy, since he immediately states that *all situationists would agree* with Mrs. Patrick Campbell's remark that they can do as they want 'as long as they don't do it in the street and frighten the horses'." (2) Or, on the other hand, situation ethics might take a turn in the other direction, and responsibly undertake the description and characterization of behavior upon the basis of which some account might then be given of the loving and the unloving thing to do. In the instant case this would mean for Christian ethics some attempt to determine the importance of the priest's assumptions about salvation, and a substantive choice for or against the course of action that Fletcher does not methodologically deny might be most loving. This would open up questions about the relationship and the hierarchy of values between pieces of behavior devoted to eternal values and pieces of behavior directed toward the integrity of the underground resistance or determined by a calculus of the most lives likely to be saved. Finally one would have to pay attention to the view of moralists of the past that no matter how important eternal values may be, this never gives warrant for a direct action violating goods of the natural order. By contrast Fletcher lumps the goods anyone happens to believe in into a vast calculus which permits the heavenly completely to overwhelm the earthly. It can be said without any hesitation that traditional Christian ethics has been far more humane and humanistic than to allow any such procedure to be possible for a care-ful love.

There would seem to be enough arbitrariness of decision within the confines of the situation of the priest-saboteur. There is more when one places this case beside other cases that Fletcher considers. On the same page, immediately above, he rendered two decisions with the certainty of an Olympian that no one could have any doubt about them. Confronted by a choice between "your own father and a medical genius who has discovered a cure for a common fatal disease," only one of whom can be saved from a burning building, "you carry out the genius if you understand *agapé*" (SE 115). This is because of a quantitative agapeic calculus in coalition with utilitarianism: "we choose what is most 'useful' for the most people." But what if the choice is between saving a baby or Da Vinci's *Mona Lisa* from the burning building? "You take the baby," Fletcher says, "if you are a personalist."

The point is not to disagree with any of this, but to know how to agree or disagree. Nor again is the point to seek for something outside the situation which by going into it can determine the works of love. The point is rather how we are to determine the responsible thing to do, apart from Fletcher's own whimsy as an alternative, unless something in the situation can be identified, properly described, and judged to count for love. The case of the *Mona Lisa* brings in values of a different order from material ones; it adds to the quantitative calculus considerations of quality, and the vast numbers of people who in the future may or may not be able to enjoy the original masterpiece depending on the decision taken in that instance. This may be compared in its different order to the priest's "salvation." Why does not Fletcher allow that "one may accept the art-lover's assumptions about aesthetic values or not, but no situationist could quarrel with his *method* of ethical analysis and decision," if he saves the picture and lets the baby perish? How can he be so sure that a personalist would save the baby in this case, and yet not say the same concerning saving one's comrades in the underground resistance? The statement that there are copies and reprints of the painting is a weak excuse. The priest might with greater reason have had resort to a comparable factor, namely, that according to his own faith the priest's absolution is, as it were, an effective copy of the mercies of God which alone his people's souls absolutely require for salvation.

Three additional cases may profitably be placed back to back. The first is the case of the longboat of the *William Brown*. The first mate and highest-ranking officer aboard, named Holmes, ordered most of the males aboard to be thrown into the sea lest the overcrowded lifeboat founder in the storm and all the lives be lost. He was subsequently *judged* guilty of manslaughter and given a *suspended* sentence because of the extenuating circumstances. Fletcher's notation on this case is directed mainly at the judge: "Regardless of the *kairos*, says legalism, Holmes did an evil thing not a good thing. Situation ethics says it was bravely sinful, it was a good thing" (SE 136. Almost everywhere else in this book the solemn sorrowfulness entailed by the expression "bravely sinful" is removed: it was a *good* thing).

Yet immediately below on the same page is the case of Captain Scott's expedition to the South Pole. One of his men was injured and had to be carried. Without him, they all but one might have made it to the coast. Scott decided to stick with the man, not abandon him, and they all perished. Fletcher's notation on this case is: ". . . It was an authentic *kairos*, and assuming that Scott was not simply legalistic in his decision, it does him as much honor as Holmes's" (SE 136). He chose what love *immediately* required; Holmes chose to exhibit a more calculating love. Yet I seriously suggest that Fletcher's notations could be reversed in these two cases with no more puzzlement to the reader. Holmes might have been honored for perishing with all the lives aboard since not all could be saved (and in some sense censured for not doing so, out of regard for what Edmond Cahn called in discussing this same case the "congeneric" demands of "the morals of the last days"), and Captain Scott might have been praised for doing the brave, good deed of getting his party safely to the coast in the only way this could possibly be done (by abandoning the injured man). It all depends—as is Fletcher's wont to say—on whose legalism is being gored. Fletcher could have readily "judged Holmes' judge" as Edmond Cahn also did, while saying that love's immediate requirements might have been judged to be as paramount as Captain Scott apparently believed them to be.[41]

There is no way to give stability to the discussion of Christian ethics and to introduce some order into our search for an understanding of love's requirements, even when these are only situational requirements, except by learning better how to characterize the actions we have placed under scrutiny. Situation ethics is revealed as an arbitrary subjectivism and existentialism, or *Gesinnungs-ethik,* or by any other name a non-ethics, unless it takes the other turn and joins a community of ethical discourse that is seeking to determine what pieces of behavior count or do not count as loving—upon the basis of a prior proper and exhaustive description of what was done or proposed to be done. It is worth repeating that this would not (necessarily) be a quest for something that entering into the situation from outside would determine the rightness or wrongness of actions. It is not *pre*-judgment, but any moral judgment at all that is at stake. There may be a way, without going outside the longboat situation, to indicate the behavior that would have harmonized love's immediate and love's future-regarding requirements better than either of the alternatives between which (putting the two cases together) Fletcher vacillates, namely, all dying together or throwing people overboard.[42] Casting lots to determine who should go overboard would, though a crude device, have the virtue of being a way love for each and everyone could provide for all *equal* opportunity to survive while saving all that can be saved. This is only what Holmes's judge said, and it is not to be identified with "legalism"—or with "intrinsicalism"—unless by this is meant the love for persons of equal dignity and ultimate sacred-

---

[41] See 26 Federal Case 360 (C.C.E.D. Pa. 1842); and Edmond Cahn, *The Moral Decision: Right and Wrong in the Light of American Law* (Bloomington, Ind., 1955), pp. 61–71.

[42] See my *Nine Modern Moralists* (Englewood Cliffs, N.J., 1962, pp. 245–51. Captain Scott's action can be compared with the more responsible pattern of behavior that developed among groups of Englishmen on the desperate trek out of Burma to India during World War II: whoever found himself too ill to go farther, silently dropped behind so that the company would not be tempted to endanger the many by a vain attempt to save him. *Basic Christian Ethics,* p. 337.

ness that is intrinsic in extending equality of treatment to them. Besides all this there remain important distinctions to be made in our characterizations of behavior with a view to moral judgment upon it, between what love requires in one's own case and in the "official" action of Captain Scott or first mate Holmes, and between direct killing and allowing to die, which must be brought into view if anyone wants to reflect in orderly fashion upon ethical questions and to eliminate the arbitrariness endemic to any mere agapeic calculus.

The third case, to be put back to back with these two, is brought into view by Fletcher's statement that Captain Scott's action "did him as much honor as Holmes's or the Arizona lady's" (SE 136). This is the case of Mrs. Sherri Finkbine who in 1962 went to Sweden to secure an abortion of her thalidomide baby, denied her in Arizona. Strictly speaking, an analogy can be found to our first two cases only in the situation of a mother in a birth-room emergency in which both she and her child will die unless to save hers the fetus is aborted or killed. This would place Fletcher in the strange position of saying that provided only the woman is not simply a legalist, a decision on her part that *both* should die might do her as much honor as Scott's or Holmes's. The only way to avoid this possible situational conclusion is to abandon the notion that love can mean anything, or be meant by everything, because love may happen to be meant by any piece of behavior as well as by any other.

No one could know that Sherri Finkbine's baby was hideously deformed. Fletcher's notation is: "It was a brave and responsible and right decision, even if the embryo had been all right" (SE 136). The doctor who aborted Mrs. Finkbine told her afterward, "It was not a baby. You must think of it as an abnormal growth within you." But some there may be who will think that her husband, still within the decision they had risked making, found better words to say to Sherri Finkbine. "When she came out of anesthesia, Bob was standing by her bed. 'Did you hear what the doctor said?' he asked. 'The baby was deformed.' *He repeated it over and over again* to make sure that she understood."[43]

Now, these various statements, some coldly compassionate,

[43] Lawrence Lader, *Abortion* (New York, 1966), p. 16 (italics added).

others warmly compassionate, are not introduced here in order to settle one way or another the ethical question of abortion. They are introduced in order to show again that there can be no ethics flowing from "love's casuistry," but only intolerable vacillation and arbitrariness in decision-making, without first a proper characterization of what was done or proposed to be done, this time depending on statements of fact or philosophy about nascent life. They are introduced to remind the reader of the several different characterizations of abortion that Fletcher himself has used from case to case in the course of justifying this procedure, and of the many different descriptions Fletcher can produce for any single case.

These range all the way from "*no unwanted and unintended* baby should ever be born," the "likely" situational judgment, to "the situationists . . . would almost certainly, *in this case*, favor abortion," another likely judgment, the case being abortion following rape by a fellow mental patient. In support of the general rule that *no unwanted and unintended* baby should ever be born, Fletcher interjects the way he presumably believes it is correct to describe an act of abortion (operative in his verdict concerning the Finkbine case): "They [situationists] would, one hopes, reason that it is *not* killing because there is no person or human life in an embryo at an early stage of pregnancy [*sic!*]" (SE 39). Then, lest anyone still believes that nascent life is human life, he avails himself of another characterization of, at least, abortion following rape (no doubt also the criterion that may be used when the nascent life is in late stages of pregnancy in fatal competition with that of the mother): "Even if it *were* killing, it would not be murder because it is self-defense against, in this case, not one but *two* aggressors" (SE 39), both "innocent" (the insane and therefore innocent rapist and the resulting embryo). This latter description and verdict is to take up a minority opinion among moralists of the past, who held that it is *material* aggression and not culpable aggression that justifies the taking of a human life. Finally, Fletcher brings it as an additional accusation against biblicist literalism if women who conscientiously refuse blood transfusions are "carrying a quickened fetus that will be lost too" (SE 26). Yet despite all this Fletcher fashions one of his strangest comparative ethical judgments: "*In most situations* birth control by prevention, for example, is better than abortion" (SE 122). Even someone who accepts abortion as a means of birth control will demand a description of the act of abortion that is better than *conception* control.

These are all many different ways to determine what pieces of behavior count for love and what actions *mean* love in abortion situations. It is sheer prejudice to suppose that Fletcher has established that there can be an ethics flowing from an agapeic calculus without such descriptions of behavior proved to be proper to the action in question, many or most of which in these cases depend on some finding of fact or philosophy about the intrinsic nature of nascent life; or that he is any less an "intrinsicalist" than proponents of the view he opposes. Anyone, for example, who like Fletcher proposes the argument that the fetus following rape should be removed because it is a material though innocent aggressor, thereby makes himself responsible for meeting (and not simply dismissing) the contention of reputable moralists who say the fetus in this instance is only trying to grow and to be born, not aggressing at all, and that at most it is a mislaid trespasser on whom one should not execute capital punishment. Nascent life, in any case, is not something coming into the situation prejudging it; such life is ingredient to the situation, and to determining what is done or proposed to be done, which then is pertinent to the evaluation to be placed upon such action. For a situationist to have a Christian life at all he must be, in the matter of abortion at least, some sort of an "intrinsicalist." Else one simply moves about from one intrinsicalism to another on the excuse that this is the meaning of Christian liberty. This only means that he is a poor Christian ethicist who does not take responsibility for what he says by first taking responsibility for a firm and a proper description of the behavior under scrutiny.

Fletcher needs to place far higher premium on "knowing what's what when we act" (SE 84).

To sum up: Fletcher's announced program in ethics is to attach an *exception-making criterion* to every summary rule or principle. His proposal is that "guidelines" have a force or moral authority in the Christian life which can best be expressed by saying, for example, "Tell the truth (or lying is wrong) except when in a given case to lie has a generalized agapeic utility that is positive (or not negative)." Or: "Preserve nascent life (or abortion is wrong) except when in a given case the destruction of nascent life has a generalized agapeic utility that is positive (or not negative)." Or: "Killing is wrong, except when the effects of killing would be better than the effects of not killing, all things considered."

Of course, a theologian ordinarily does not express himself by using this formulation. It is enough for a theological ethicist who is a situationalist simply to talk all the time about the exception *without saying anything about it.* Less rhetorically, the philosopher will formulate an exception-making criterion: "unless it would be better on the whole to do so or not to do so" limiting every maxim that experience seems to suggest. This is to recommend the same mode of ethical reasoning—that of singular deed decision-making.

Ostensibly it would not be enough simply to attach a *ceteris paribus* qualification to rules or principles that serve to guide or direct or illuminate moral decisions. It would not be enough simply to say that "other things being equal" we ought not to tell a lie and should preserve nascent life or not kill a human being. Instead the criterion that *generates* exceptions can and may and should be stated precisely in terms of a direct appeal to *agapé* determining in each action whether the rule should be observed or broken.

It is obvious, as we have pointed out, that such summary rules or principles are logically quite dispensable. Such summaries of moral wisdom drawn from experience, or from past acts of obedience to love's requirements, do not oblige. They merely recommend a way of deliberating and effectively solving problems of conduct that will ordinarily ensure conformity to *agapé.* Each cautionary maxim, therefore, includes an exception-making criterion that guarantees the agent's present, untrammelled choice. Therefore, summary principle or summary rule-agapism is always on the way to becoming single act-agapism. It already is only that. The *exception-making* criterion is designed to ensure that this will be so. This is the case even if it can be argued that with regard to *some* basic moral guidelines one will probably most often do the most loving thing in one's singular decisions *if he does not think as an act-agapist should,* but instead acts *as if* there are rules or principles of behavior that to some degree are binding. On this view, given an exception-making condition, it is always *as if* one has learned something; it is always *as if* human civilization has accumulated certain worthwhile discriminations between right and wrong.

On the other hand, Fletcher cannot avoid giving utterance to certain quite general judgments concerning love's requirements. His inadvertent statement of these general moral verdicts, it is important to note, can be correlated with descriptions of actions that are in effect made complete, or relatively complete. Thus it is possible for a situationist to *say so much about the exception* that he marks off a class or species of acts to be done or not done. While Fletcher rejects such a sweeping verdict as "Lying is wrong," he obviously thinks better of the judgment, "Lying is wrong, except to save life." This is to state an *exempting condition* which can and must be expressed in general terms. This is radically different from an exception-making criterion. It states the class or species of falsehoods that are right to tell; and it does not matter that "lying to save life" is only the beginning of a disjunctive list of exempting conditions that cannot be completed any more than one can complete the situational agapeic calculus which act-agapism (and summation ethics) proposes as the preferred method of moral deliberation.

Parenthetically, it is interesting to note what happens when one attaches an *exception-making criterion* after the statement of an *exempting condition.* Suppose, for example, we say that "Lying is wrong, except to save life, unless in a given case not to lie to save life would have a generalized agapeic utility." This obviously abolishes the injunction to "lie" to save life. One was all along only acting *as if* that were right, *as if* human beings had gathered a worthwhile discrimination between right and wrong and expressed this in an exempting condition which more completely describes the kind of actions that are praiseworthy. It does not matter how rare are the cases when not to lie to save

222

life would be the most loving thing to do, or how frequent the cases in which the rule holds that to lie to save life best serves love. One has already referred this to the exception-making criterion. The *incidence* of truth-telling or the *incidence* of dissimulation to save life is not enough to show that these moral-species-terms have any weight or bearing. Only agapeic acts count.

Obviously Fletcher's penchant for exception-making inhibits the development of exempting conditions in his ethics. This impedes the elaboration of moral-species-terms qualifying genus-terms, or act-terms qualifying end-terms. Notably, the exception-making criterion impedes the elaboration of general judgments in Fletcher's ethics *to the degree that* it directs attention away from the proper description or characterization of the human actions that are placed under scrutiny. Perhaps it is in abortion cases that Fletcher is driven to say most adequately the *kind* of action he means to talk about. This is the case despite the fact that the reader never quite knows which general verdict he means to espouse. This may be the most general one: no unwanted or unintended baby should ever be born. Such a statement of the conditions warranting the destruction of nascent life is vastly different from the exception-making rule that one should preserve nascent life (i.e. abortion is wrong) except when the effects of destroying it would be better than the effects of not killing it, all things considered—since there may be good agapeic reasons put forward for killing many more than unwanted or unintended babies, and moreover reasons which may be so grave as to cast some shadow of a doubt upon whether "unwantedness" alone is a sufficient condition justifying abortion.

It may be that Fletcher means to settle for some one of the alternative general moral verdicts he gave expression to in the course of completing the description of the actions in question. He may mean to espouse one or another or all of the following *exempting conditions*: one should preserve nascent life (abortion is wrong)—except following rape or incest if the woman wants an abortion, *or* if she is mentally deficient, *or* following rape if the fetus is properly regarded as only a material though innocent aggressor, and is not to be termed a trespasser merely, *or* to save the mother's life and health, *or* if there is sufficient 'socio-medical' indication that this would be best for the mother and her other children, *or* if there is probability of serious fetal damage or defect, *or* certainty of this. It is evident, in any case, that anyone who proposes in this manner that there are good reasons for abortion is proceeding to specify in quite general terms, or in moral-species-terms, the meaning of respect for life, the protection of life, and the sanctity of life in Christian ethics. He is not simply attaching an exception-making criterion to the general injunction to save rather than kill life.

To undertake a careful and complete description of the specific human actions we are talking about in doing Christian ethics is to move in the direction of general rule-agapism. Indeed, a recent book on the *Forms and Limits of Utilitarianism*[44] mounts a formidable argument for the proposition that pure rule-utilitarianism and act-utilitarianism are "extensively equivalent" systems of ethics, provided a proponent of the latter view *completes the proper description* of the single act whose simple utility he proposes to estimate in determining right action. That is to say, the two questions posed at the beginning of the present volume— Which *action* will be most love-fulfilling? and Which *rules of action* are most love-fulfilling?—lead in every case to the same conclusion concerning the deed to be done or not done. Provided only that the action is adequately characterized, or described, whose simple agapeic consequences are directly appraised, this will be the same action that falls under the most love-embodying general rule or principle and is to be justified only by direct appeal to such a rule or principle.

I do not know whether in all cases this is a correct conclusion or not. In any case this argument is strikingly similar to my two concepts of general rules, or two ways in, to the elaboration of general principles in Christian social ethics. It is not unreasonable to suppose that, at least in some cases or realms of moral behavior, the person-centered approach and the practice-oriented way of being compassionate to persons lead to the same deter-

---

[44] By David Lyons (Oxford, Eng., 1965). The terms "exception-making criteria" and "exempting conditions," used in the text above, are taken from this volume, pp. 125, 127.

mination of the action to be done or not done. This was the case, for example, in Fletcher's treatment of the patient's right to know the truth: his verdict followed from a searching concern for the patient who is the subject of his own dying and also from asking what would be the most love-embodying rule of medical practice. Nevertheless, it seems not unreasonable to suppose that this congruence may not be true in every case. This question need not be settled here. It is sufficient to point out the tendency of apt and adequate descriptions of actions in terms of their general and specific characteristics to lead us in the direction of general and not merely situational decisions.

In any case, also, anyone who proposes to effect a coalition between Christian ethics and utilitarianism in propounding situation ethics should make it abundantly clear that he is making common cause with a beleaguered sect among contemporary utilitarians, namely, the act-utilitarians. It is difficult to tell whence comes the resulting rule-less and un-principled version of Christian ethics—whether from the mistaken belief that the freedom of *agapé* is unbinding or from the act-pragmatism that is begged. The one feeds the other, with the consequence that we Christians and church-social-action people, set up as we are to do Christian social ethics contextually, come to the not surprising conclusion that Christian social ethics is altogether contextual and can only make particular pronouncements. A stream can rise no higher than its source; the substance of our ethics can be no better than its method.

Nor do I know whether a promise is the same as a rule of practice, or whether fairness and justice and other considerations that are important in determining the rightness in covenants among men, are strictly to be compared with rule-utilitarian rules. Still this much seems evident: anyone who attaches an *exception-making* criterion to his promises does not know the meaning of promising anyone anything. If he means to say "Promises should be kept, except when on the whole it would be better not to" he had better say so, since the one whom he promises (unless he is a like-minded consequentialist who has been briefed) will not take it that way.

VIII

A Letter to John of Patmos from a Proponent of "the New Morality"[1]

Venerable John, Greetings in the name of our Lord Jesus Christ:

Just how that article I wrote years ago for the *Caesar's Household Christian* on "The New Morality" came to your attention at this late date I cannot imagine. Was it, too, shipwrecked there on the island? Anyway, I thank you for your letter. There is time if there is the strength for me to put down some of my thoughts in answer to you. Things *have* turned out as neither of us expected, haven't they?

Strange, but I do still have here among my cluttered old papers a copy of your *Revelation*. Why ever did I keep it? Was it because that pamphlet of yours, for all its bombast and your copious imagination, contained something I unbelieving believed, even while in believing unbelief I wrote that series of articles on "Christ or Rome: A Misplaced Debate"? (Perhaps you never saw the other articles.)

Well do I remember how utterly misguided I thought you were when first your pamphlet began to circulate among a cer-

[1] Reprinted from Religion in Life, Spring 1966. Copyright © 1966 by Abingdon Press.

tain class of people here in our city! It wasn't that about the "seven hills." Of course, it hardly required "a mind with wisdom" to see through to the subversion you were up to. No, it wasn't that you thought our Roman "world come of age" was going to perish—or be destroyed by bolts of lightning or whatever else your imagination conjured up.

It was rather that you did not *value* the city, and you didn't realize what a wonderful opportunity we Christians had to make the gospel *relevant* to modern times. You named it "the great city which is allegorically called Sodom or Egypt"; and so far as I could tell you never obeyed that "voice from heaven saying, 'Seal up what the seven thunders have said, and do not write it down.'" Thunderation, that was all you ever wrote down! It was easy to attribute your jaundiced views to a stomach naturally bitter and not from any "little scroll" you ate. Even now this seems a plausible explanation, since you didn't turn out to be right either. All of us in Caesar's household could agree with your benedictions ("Blessing and glory and wisdom and thanksgiving and honor and power and might be to our God for ever and ever! Amen!"); but then we weren't sure we meant the same thing you did by such words, and the main trouble was that they didn't seem to bring your fulminations to an end as an "Amen!" should.

Looking back now I can see that it does take a lot of "patient endurance" even to go on living here at the Jupiter Home for the Aged (to which I was fortunately admitted some years ago because of my long years in Domitian's service). But your "tribulations," and all those horses and seals, your first and second deaths, and I know not what else were the thing you said "is and is to take place hereafter": this was not so much fantastically incredible as it seemed to require us who are Christians to miss a great opportunity to speak a meaningful word to the modern world by showing people how Christian they already are. We were among those upon whom you delivered the verdict, "Alas, alas for the great city." Your words were, as you said ("quoting," it is true, the angel of the church in Pergamum), "the words of him who has the sharp two-edged sword." "Come out of her, my people" was your only proposal.

227

Back in Secular City we did have a different view of things. And I have no doubt that my words in that old article which has somehow reached you must seem to you as bland as a butter knife. We were Christ's people in the world, and "dialogue" seemed the only thing helpful to be done. But, cheer up, we were both wrong; and when next you write tell me where are *you* now living?

Now that great age is upon us we can afford to be more honest, don't you think? Also, we are only writing letters and not articles or tracts for public circulation. Let us begin with something I thought you always kept coming back to and circling around, though a word count of your *Revelation* gives no evidence of this, namely, sexual immorality. In fairness I have to acknowledge, upon reading my article again after many years, that *I* kept coming back to and circling around that point too, even while I was protesting against "the narrowing down of the concept of sin to place an exaggerated emphasis on sexual sin." Perhaps you wanted one judgment upon that subject to be enforced by crying against "the woman arrayed in purple and scarlet, bedecked with gold and jewels and pearls, holding in her hand a golden cup full of abominations and the impurities of her fornication." Perhaps I, in contrast, had another judgment upon that subject already in mind which I proceeded to enforce by a somewhat more refined campaign (at least I didn't give my imagination such free reign as you did) to "clean up" the church's attitude toward sex. The reason for this, though I do not offer this as an excuse for any flaws in my argument, was that I wanted desperately to find nothing in the gospel that might prove offensive to the cultivated, freedom-loving Romans of our advanced and mature age.

Before taking up some of the questions you asked me or the objections you raised, we might get off on a good footing by admitting that maybe it wasn't alone the fact that we were younger then that led us to be so fascinated by this subject. Perhaps sex *is* a fascinating subject. Maybe, also, because sex is such a fascinating good, and one that in its nature is so deeply and intimately personal, it is a matter appropriately surrounded by protections, prohibitions, and moral recommendations of a specific character.

Anyway, I have to confess that the more we cleaned up sex, the more unwanted babies there were to expose. When chaplains to the Student Christian Movement at the Eternal City University sponsored conferences on how to be sexually mature, and invited me and the editor of *Banquet Boy* to represent our respective philosophies in a panel discussion, the participants concluded that there was "something in" both points of view and said they'd think about it. As it turned out "the guidelines which experience throws up to us" weren't "the costly demands of a mature love." So the more we enjoined our young people to "follow the way of love right into the heart of the situation" and told them "to experience in personal relations the exploration of another personality and the greater understanding of oneself" (come to think about it, sex being what it is, there was some phallic suggestiveness in those expressions!), the more Christian young people grew "mature" like the Romans around them. The more we said sex is a matter of personal passion, the more mechanical and languid it became in practice.

I'm not conceding anything to your crass talk about those who "*defiled* themselves with women." You must admit that I proved *that* to be the wrong thing to say, by my analysis of *sarx*. Nor do I withdraw what I said about "the law" judging "the external act" only, while Christ's message is "constantly addressed to persons." Still, that latter way of stressing freedom *apart* from entailments as to acts may have been wrong too. Anyway, if history proves anything, it has proved that neither of us had a very good cause in religion.

Therefore, looking back over the years I have to admit that our campaign to clean up sex came to nothing. Not at least to anything we meant to come to. This was not because you can't remove the fascination from it no matter how antiseptic your manner of discussion. It was rather, I now think, because you can't remove sinners from it or sex from sinners (which means all men and women, of course). Certainly, I still believe that the church ought not to narrow the concept of "sins" (note the plural) to sexual sins only. But this does not mean that "sin" is not among the concepts the church should use whenever it comments on anything human, including sex. The body cannot be so pure a God-given good that this concept should be left out of a discussion of the problems of sexual behavior. *That* would be "dualism." I'm saying, I guess, that the only thing wrong with sex is that there are so many people connected with it; and sin, of course, is in people and not in their bodies first of all. Still it gets there too, and as universally as sin is. I am astonished to note that not once in that article did I use the word "sin" except to say what I thought the church should *no longer say.* I guess I was a little too eager to talk about maturity and explore the meaning of this with my fellow Romans.

There was no excuse for this, since a traveler from Britain had recently brought me a book by C. S. Lewis, *Christian Behaviour.* A donish enough person he seemed to be but, nevertheless, somewhat barbaric and conservative in his views in comparison with the emancipated people around me to whom I wanted to preach the gospel (by making it clearly preachable to them). I had read, and dismissed as not liberal enough, his paragraphs:

> You can get a large audience together for a striptease act—that is, to watch a girl undress on the stage: now suppose you came to a country where you could fill a theatre by simply bringing a covered plate on the stage and then slowly lifting the cover so as to let everyone see, just before the lights went out, that it contained a mutton chop or a bit of bacon, wouldn't you think that in that country something had gone wrong with the appetite for food? And wouldn't anyone who had grown up in a different world think there was something equally queer about the state of the sex instinct among us? . . .
>
> They'll tell you sex has become a mess because it was hushed up. But in the last twenty years it has *not* been hushed up. It has been chatted about all day long. Yet it is still in a mess. If hushing it up had been the cause of the trouble, ventilation would have set it right. But it hasn't. I think it is the other way round. I think the human race originally hushed it up because it had become such a mess.[2]

But neither these words nor, of course, your excoriations were sufficient to awaken me from my dogmatic slumbers. To tell the

[2] C. S. Lewis, *Christian Behaviour* (New York, 1944), pp. 26–27.

truth, *you* saw the trends of our times better than I did for all my vaunted "situationalism"; and you saw some facets of the Christian truth that I was blind to. Only your answer was no better than mine.

Now to your specific objections. I'll try to say something about the main ones, although maybe now only God knows what I meant then! I see that you don't reject what I said about *sarx* as man in his wholeness, nor even do you object to my use of the *word* "maturity" as a crucial Christian term. You say rather that the whole man, *sarx* and all, is set within *another* context than the given *secular* situation; and that this decides what he should do in and with his body and defines the meaning of maturity for a Christian. You deny that "the full maturity of man as a responding, deciding, acting human being within a given situation" is exactly "in accord with *the whole* teaching of Christ on the wholeness of man."

Evidently you are ready to call up one of your angels to pour his bowl upon me for saying that "the perfection of wholeness" is quite the same as "being perfect as our Father in heaven is perfect." And on the positive side (which I take as proof you too have somewhat mellowed with the passage of time) you say that the whole man, *sarx* and all, should find the meaning of his maturity and of true wholeness from what we know of God in Jesus Christ and of the end toward which man is destined, and not from what otherwise he might be and do as a responding, deciding, acting human being within a given situation.

You quote Scripture rather effectively, and in a way which (unlike your *Revelation*, which you made up out of your own fancies) I cannot now dismiss as a "fruitless game of bandying one text against another." Your point does seem founded upon the "overall picture of a way of living set forth by one who claimed to be the Way." In extenuation I can only say that when I read those same texts while I was active among the cultivated despisers of our religion and was myself excited by the advancement of modern knowledge and the opportunity this opened up for Christians to speak a relevant word, those verses did seem to me to mean the "wholeness" *they* meant.

You assert also that I ought to have gone to the blessed St. Paul and not to the Bishop of Woolwich to find my source for understanding Christian morality, and Christian marriage in particular. Not of course, you say, those excessive and time-bound views of St. Paul on sex and women (which, since time went on for you, you have now thought better about); but to the basic ingredient of Christian marriage which the apostle set forth in *Ephesians* 5. I admit that some of those expressions about "fixity rather than freedom" and "relativism within the situation" came from the Bishop and not from the Apostle; but they seemed to me to be simply more congenial modern ways of saying "love not law."

The one I coined about "Christ calling people to a relationship rather than to rules" seems to provoke you most. You say that "relationship" is a neutral word like "wholeness" or "maturity" until it is filled with adequate Christian meaning— or meaning drawn from somewhere else. And you assert that the marriage *relationship* to which we are called was better exhibited in its Christian meaning by St. Paul's "husbands, love your wives as Christ loved the church and gave himself up for her, that he might sanctify her; . . . that the church might be presented before him in splendor, without spot or wrinkle or any such thing, that she might be holy and without blemish," than by Woolwich when he stressed the "personal" in the context of bread and board. The requirements of the latter, or for that matter of the quest for maturity, are not apt to provide enough light to show up for what it is our current practice of wives and husbands giving one another up because they have many a wrinkle and blemish! There you have a point, John.

Then there was my contention that "the church's ethic on most matters of public morality is situational." Why should we only speak of "an absolute ethics in all realms of private morality"? Why not have a situational ethic both private and on questions of public policy? Why should not a young man simply seek to discover what "makes sense" in his relationships with his girl friend, even as that is what we advise the emperor and our senators to do on complex public questions?

Some of your most telling points in reply to that just seem to me to be a debater's points. You say that a young man can get married in our society long before he is expected to have the maturity to be a senator; and he can certainly perform sexual intercourse before he is legally allowed, for example, to vote or own property or is presumed to be responsible enough to make decisions entirely on his own in many other of the realms of human activity. Perhaps, you say, there is (from the human point of view) a *pedagogical* need for rules of behavior in sexual conduct that are not just guidelines experience throws up and that have the purpose of helping a boy and a girl to "make sense"; and if God knows our human condition and the importance of sexual communication in human lives and in our attainment of maturity, you ask, why exclude this from the Divine pedagogy, or from God's will for his human families?

You go on to say that actually the situation is not such as I describe it. You assert that "the church in the world" is year by year becoming ever more certain it knows the meaning of what is justly due in questions of public policy (race relations, for example, and world peace), while year by year it becomes ever more uncertain it knows anything about what is justly due in sexual behavior and in marriage. So it is the situationalism in sex ethics combined with an ethic of principles on a number of public questions to which you object; and you want to assert (just like a debater) that the private and the public realms are equally complex, and equally intractable and equally corrigible by Christian moral insights.

But, I take it, you mainly mean to say that I beg the question about the wholly situational character of social ethics. If you are correct in this, I would have to grant that my argument falls to the ground. My argument was not a logical demonstration anyway; rather, it was an appeal for persuasion from analogy—and as you say, one has to establish the analogy first (and next I in particular would have to establish that there are no general principles governing in social ethics).

We were not, however, as unconcerned about personal sexual morality as you charge. We rather put in place of appeals for personal conduct of a certain order our hope for a radical revolution in how our whole culture regards sex and uses it commercially. Our "real concern for chastity" was exhibited in our effort to devise ways of "exercising restraint as a community

233

on the mass of commercial incentive to unchastity." That was the meaning of my quotation from Harvey Cox. We hoped to take hold of the grave immorality of the whole age by grasping it "structurally," and effecting some structural reform, a utopian one at that, which would rebound to the glory of personal chastity.

As it turned out your fanciful expectation of how Christ would assume his reign over the kingdoms of this world was no more brash than our more sober vision of effecting a radical structural change in the Roman banquet system. Sexual immorality remained a badge of social distinction, in fact human sexual behavior became more and more immature, and this spread to the lower classes because of the incorrigible social image of it. You awaited one great change; we awaited another. While waiting we neglected the small things that might have been done. Not only so, but we condemned the attempt to save even one of the little ones from the burning by appeals to the personal adoption of rules of moral behavior. At the same time we condemned all attempts to preserve the virtues of Cato's times that were still left in the ethos, as we condemned less sweeping ways of taking hold of commercialized sex and controlling this less radically than by a revolution in the economic order. Back in Secular City all such efforts were called the defense of "town" virtues. Scorn was heaped on all this, even as you lumped everything together for judgment.

Thinking about our enthusiasm now, I rather imagine a good bit of it was attributable to the fact that most of us had so lately come from the provinces. Therefore we thought that the city was evidence of man's triumph which God's action must surely intend in our day. Therefore we thought the city could be subdued and rationalized by principles inherent in it. We had not lived here long enough.

No events, however untoward, could disturb our optimism. Nothing shocked us into a realistic awareness that city man can provide only "proximate solutions to insoluble problems" (Niebuhr). Not even the ordinarily distraught face of traffic commissioner Barnes. Not even the great sewer failure, when our experts talked after the event of a "systems failure" and of how one sewer which man had contrived got to "quarreling" with another, awakened us to the fact that city man is still the man of whom the psalmist spoke. Our affirmation of a negative (there is no *special* Christian ethics) may be compared to the affirmation of the negative (God is dead) by some of our way-out theologians. It is hard to tell now why this should not have been regarded as simply a mark of incompetence in a Christian ethicist or a theologian. As it was, the spirit of the times told us that the facility with which we reached these conclusions was rather a measure of distinction. That was especially impressive on those of us who had only lately come to Rome from the towns.

Now I have given way to you enough for you to know that I too have grown charitable! Are your eyes so dim that you cannot read? Don't you see those places where I said much the same thing as you are saying? I too said that "the norms by which we make our decisions in all realms of life will be by bringing to bear upon the situation the insights revealed in the Bible." I too spoke of "knowing as Christ did more clearly what is in man." He "long ago showed us the way." And I said that it is in the public forum that we need to seek "common moral ground" with non-believers; there we should not "confront contemporary man with an ethic which is only possible for a Christian who believes in supranatural grace and all the spiritual strength which comes from the life of sacrament and prayer." Is this not enough of a christocentric ethic and a christocentric doctrine of man to satisfy any Patmosite (except that once you believed this could be expressed only in eschatological terms)?

But you say that it is precisely these statements in my article that you don't understand at all, that they are inconsistent with many other statements, and that I take back in another sentence everything each of these sentences establishes. There, where I spoke of the need not to confront modern man with the full substance of Christian ethics and of the need rather to enter into "dialogue" with him to discover "an ethic by which all may live," you point out that in the very same paragraph I denied there is any such thing as a Christian ethic after all and wrote that "the *essential difference* between the Christian and the non-Christian does not lie so much in the manner by which moral decisions in life are made but rather in the spiritual *strength* available to the Christian in living." Thus, there are no ethical entailments that the nonbeliever would need supranatural grace to live up to but only power for the Christian in living up to the ethic he and the humanist discover they have in common when they walk hand in hand. The Christian has grace for "living," not for any particular requirement Christ places upon his disciples. Thereupon I brought in a nonbiblical, non-Christian notion of "maturity" to be filled like a basket by "the values which are perceptible to both Christian and humanist" (quoting, again quite inconsistently you assert, from what *Ephesians* tells us about our attaining "to mature manhood, to the measure of the stature of the fullness of Christ").

And you demand to know why, in explaining the changes that have come about in Christian teachings over the years on such matters as women, usury, war, slavery, hanging, etc., I simply equated "a better understanding of the situation and of people" with "knowing as Christ did more clearly what is man." These, you say, are not necessarily the same source of changes in morality. Then at the end of my article I affirmed the same common ethic to come from two sources: "Christ long ago showed us the way, and modern psychological thinking only confirms the approach which was already his." You protest that this makes Christ (the one foundation that was laid) a disappearing historical moment in mankind's moral progress, while it is modern learning that alone affords sure knowledge into moral truth. Christ is recommended because he already knew this.

Hell, John (for a man of your former opinions this would be an explicative; for me it is only a manner of speaking), this is what we here in Rome call "apologetics." There were among us some apologists who believed that was a rigorous discipline requiring manifold intellectual labor. But the need was too urgent for that. Our age needed "new forms of the ministry," and opportunity called to the church if it could find the relevant word to say. What you call inconsistency I call subtlety in persuasion. What you call identifying Christ with our highest cultural achievements I call spreading his Lordship. There was so much at stake in showing that Christ teaches all men what they should be most interested in attaining that to do this seemed worth constructing a series of statements that passed from the secular to the religious even if they did not logically quite hold together. Since our fathers' ways of believing were acceptable no longer, we had to find some way to get the hooks of the gospel message into our contemporaries. This was an altogether laudable intention, I think you'll agree. I wanted to set going "a dialogue between Christians and non-Christians." Since non-Christians are the most closed-minded people you can imagine (not having lived much among them), I had, on the one hand, to make it very clear that this was to be a study of "the common factors of maturity for which we may all work together in the same work or neighborhood or situation" and, on the other hand, to affirm that this would be indistinguishably a study of "what Christian insights mean in terms of contemporary situations."

It was necessary, I thought, to "take into account the ways in which people are thinking." "No one will be heeded today who ignores or flies flat contrary to the kind of thinking that is going on." Your *Revelation*, to say the least, "invited lack of attention to what one is saying." It was "put aside as irrelevant" by everyone who rejected authority in every field of endeavor and who took the empirical approach to the solution of problems. Putting those two premises together, it was evident that "the only kind of authority recognized today is the authority of what is scientifically knowable." So I began with that, and got to Christ later. You wanted to begin with Christ and get relevant later. (That's what provoked in you such a disturbed imagination, when you tried to assume that he had begun to reign in the real world we can know empirically.)

There was nothing wrong with my approach except that as apologetics it didn't work. Just why it didn't I still don't know, but the fact is that it was no more effective than your way. Of this I am certain, and I think with a certain sadness of my three sons and their generation that I was so concerned about. One of my sons works in Caesar's financial office, another is an architect, and another established the emperor's new public relations office. I am proud of their worldly success; and beyond that each is, I know, a fine, fine man. Yet somehow they did not take from

237

me the faith in our Lord Jesus that I derived from my father (who was rather like you, only less extreme).

I always tried to teach them that morality was a matter of "relevant action for an individual in order that he might live his life in its wholeness and secure the maximum welfare of all concerned in the situation," and that Jesus Christ leads and guides us in this endeavor. They say they do exactly that—and I'm sure they do, for they are fine, upstanding men—but that they don't find any guidance in Christ or need any guidance from him that is not there in the situation. All my life I tried "to educate them in situational moral awareness," and I succeeded beyond my own expectations. But today my sons say that they have a realistic grasp of the environment. They have a sense of their own identity. They are able to cope with practical tasks. They have deep personal relationships with other people. They are not hampered by rules, yet they are men of integrity (wholeness). None of this can I deny. In fact, my own situational moral awareness means that I must affirm that all this is true, and as a father I am quite proud of my sons. Yet I cannot say that they are Christian men. In fact, quite expressly, they are not. They say there is no need to learn of that from Christ. The connection seems obvious to me but not at all obvious to them. Over this connection I thought to bring more and more people to Christ; but they went on to whatever it was I said recommended him. Without him. It's disturbing to think about this now and still not know why it turned out the way it did.

You and I tried in utterly different ways to testify to the lordship of Christ. Each of us thought ours was His way. Maybe we tried too hard to bring this to pass. I for one cannot fathom, as much as once I thought I did, how to set him forward in this our age. Just the other day I read some words that once would have seemed to me to cut athwart every reasonable expectation, yet which today I cannot deny.

> Cultural Christianity [that is, what I proposed as the way!] is not, evidently, more effective in gaining disciples for Christ than Christian radicalism [that's you, John!] is. In so far as part of its purpose is always that of recommending the gospel to an unbelieving society, or to some

special group, such as the intelligentsia, or political liberals or conservatives, or workingmen, it often fails to achieve its end because it does not go far enough, or because it is suspected of introducing an element that will weaken the cultural movement. It seems impossible to remove the offense of Christ and his cross even by means of these accommodations; and cultural Christians share in the general limitation all Christianity encounters when it fights or allies itself with "the world."[3]

Those seem to me to be words well worth pondering—by you on your island and me here in an "old folks" home nominally dedicated to a Roman god.

When, too, I think of my three sons, with a mixture of sadness and admiration for them, I am reminded of some other words that once I thought very foolish indeed. You'll like the martial imagery in this.

> Imagine a fortress, absolutely impregnable, provisioned for eternity.
>
> There comes a new commandant. He conceives that it might be a good idea to build bridges over the moats—so as to be able to attack the besiegers. *Charmant!* He transforms the fortress into a country-seat—and naturally the enemy takes it.
>
> So it is with Christianity. They changed the method —and naturally the world conquered.[4]

You'd have to drop the martial imagery in order to make that an apt representation for the procedure we adopted in our "world come of age" in the Roman Secular City. We undertook to build a king's highway into the castle in order to increase the ease of access to it—and naturally my sons and their generation went out from there to dwell in a land that has no memory of the meaning of Jesus Christ, nor seems to need any.

So you and I discerned the signs of our times. Neither of us discerned quite correctly what the trends were leading to. Since you discerned the trends a little better than I did, perhaps it

[3] H. Richard Niebuhr, *Christ and Culture* (New York, 1951), p. 108.
[4] Søren Kierkegaard, quoted by Walter Lowrie, *A Short Life of Kierkegaard* (Princeton, N.J., 1942), p. 234.

would be better to say that neither of us knew what the world was coming to, or what our faith should be about what was coming into the world.

At least I can say, "Come, Lord Jesus! The Grace of the Lord Jesus be with all the saints wherever inscrutably they are. Amen."

Index